Artificial Intelligence

for
dummies
A Wiley Brand

Artificial Intelligence

2nd Edition

by John Paul Mueller and Luca Massaron

A Wiley Brand

Artificial Intelligence For Dummies®, 2nd Edition

Published by: **John Wiley & Sons, Inc.**, 111 River Street, Hoboken, NJ 07030-5774, www.wiley.com

Copyright © 2022 by John Wiley & Sons, Inc., Hoboken, New Jersey

Published simultaneously in Canada

For general information on our other products and services, please contact our Customer Care Department within the U.S. at 877-762-2974, outside the U.S. at 317-572-3993, or fax 317-572-4002. For technical support, please visit https://hub.wiley.com/community/support/dummies.

Wiley publishes in a variety of print and electronic formats and by print-on-demand. Some material included with standard print versions of this book may not be included in e-books or in print-on-demand. If this book refers to media such as a CD or DVD that is not included in the version you purchased, you may download this material at http://booksupport.wiley.com. For more information about Wiley products, visit www.wiley.com.

Library of Congress Control Number: 2021948054

ISBN: 978-1-119-79676-3

ISBN 978-1-119-79677-0 (ebk); ISBN ePDF 978-1-119-79678-7 (ebk)

SKY10071172_032724

Contents at a Glance

Table of Contents

Introduction

You can hardly avoid hearing about AI today. You see AI in the movies, in books, in the news, and online. AI is part of robots, self-driving (SD) cars, drones, medical systems, online shopping sites, and all sorts of other technologies that affect your daily life in so many ways. Some people have come to trust AIs so much, that they fall asleep while their SD cars take them to their destination — illegally, of course (see "Tesla driver found asleep at wheel of self-driving car doing 150km/h" at The Guardian.com.)

Many pundits are burying you in information (and disinformation) about AI, too. Some see AI as cute and fuzzy; others see it as a potential mass murderer of the human race. The problem with being so loaded down with information in so many ways is that you struggle to separate what's real from what is simply the product of an overactive imagination. Just how far can you trust your AI, anyway? Much of the hype about AI originates from the excessive and unrealistic expectations of scientists, entrepreneurs, and businesspersons. *Artificial Intelligence For Dummies,* 2nd Edition is the book you need if you feel as if you really don't know anything about a technology that purports to be an essential element of your life.

Using various media as a starting point, you might notice that most of the useful technologies are almost boring. Certainly, no one gushes over them. AI is like that: so ubiquitous as to be humdrum. You're using AI in some way today; in fact, you probably rely on AI in many different ways — you just don't notice it because it's so mundane. This book makes you aware of these very real and essential uses of AI. A smart thermostat for your home may not sound very exciting, but it's an incredibly practical use for a technology that has some people running for the hills in terror.

This book also covers the really cool uses for AI. For example, you may not know there is a medical monitoring device that can actually predict when you might have a heart problem, but such a device exists. AI powers drones, drives cars, and makes all sorts of robots possible. You see AI used today in all sorts of space applications, and AI figures prominently in all the space adventures humans will have tomorrow.

In contrast to many books on the topic, *Artificial Intelligence For Dummies,* 2nd Edition also tells you the truth about where and how AI can't work. In fact, AI will never be able to engage in certain essential activities and tasks, and won't be able to do other ones until far into the future. Some people try to tell you that these activities are possible for AI, but this book tells you why they can't work, clearing away all the hype that has kept you in the dark about AI. You also discover potential security issues in using AI and the kinds of hardware that work best for implementing it. One takeaway from this book is that humans will always be important. In fact, if anything, AI makes humans even more important because AI helps humans excel in ways that you frankly might not be able to imagine.

About This Book

Artificial Intelligence For Dummies, 2nd Edition starts by helping you understand AI, especially what AI needs to work and why it has failed in the past. You also discover the basis for some of the issues with AI today and how those issues might prove to be nearly impossible to solve in some cases. Of course, along with the issues, you also discover the fixes for some problems and consider where scientists are taking AI in search of answers. Most important, you discover where AI is falling short and where it excels. You likely won't have an SD car anytime soon, and that vacation in space will have to wait. On the other hand, you find that telepresence can help people stay in their homes when they might otherwise need to go to a hospital or nursing home.

For a technology to survive, it must have a group of solid applications that actually work. It also must provide a payback to investors with the foresight to invest in the technology. In the past, AI failed to achieve critical success because it lacked some of these features. AI also suffered from being ahead of its time: True AI needed to wait for the current hardware to actually succeed. Today, you can find AI used in various computer applications and to automate processes. It's also relied on heavily in the medical field and to help improve human interaction. AI is also related to data analysis, machine learning, and deep learning. Sometimes these terms can prove confusing, so one of the reasons to read this book is to discover how these technologies interconnect.

This book also contains an extraordinary number of links to external information (hundreds, in fact) because AI has become such a huge and complex topic. These links provide you with additional information that just won't fit in the book but that you really do need to know to gain a full appreciation of just how astounding the impact of AI is on your daily life. Many of the links are embedded in the name of the article, and print readers can search for them using your favorite search engine; e-book readers can simply click the links. Many other links use what is called a TinyURL (https://tinyurl.com/). The reason for using a TinyURL is that the original link is too long and confusing to type into a search engine without the risk of errors. If you want to check a TinyURL to make sure it's real, you can use the preview feature by adding the word *preview* as part of the link, like this: `https://preview.tinyurl.com/pd88943u`.

AI has a truly bright future today because it has become an essential technology. This book also shows you the paths that AI is likely to follow in the future. The various trends discussed in this book are based on what people are actually trying to do now. The new technology hasn't succeeded yet, but because people are working on it, it does have a good chance of success at some point.

To make absorbing the concepts even easier, this book uses the following conventions:

» Web addresses appear in monofont. If you're reading a digital version of this book on a device connected to the Internet, note that you can click the web address to visit that website, like this: `www.dummies.com`. Many article titles of additional resources also appear as clickable links.

» Words in *italics* are defined inline as special terms that you should remember. You see these words used (and sometimes misused) in many different ways in the press and other media, such as movies. Knowing the meaning of these terms can help you clear away some of the hype surrounding AI.

Icons Used in This Book

As you read this book, you see icons in the margins that indicate material of interest (or not, as the case may be). This section briefly describes each icon in this book.

TIP

Tips are nice because they help you save time or perform some task without a lot of extra work. The tips in this book are time-saving techniques or pointers to resources that you should try in order to get the maximum benefit from learning about AI. Just think of them as extras that we're paying to reward you for reading our book.

WARNING

We don't want to sound like angry parents or some kind of maniacs, but you should avoid doing anything marked with a Warning icon. Otherwise, you could find that you engage in the sort of disinformation that has people terrified of AI today.

Whenever you see this icon, think advanced tip or technique. You could fall asleep reading this material, and we don't want to be responsible for that. However, you might find that these tidbits of useful information contain the solution you need to create or use an AI solution. Skip these bits of information whenever you like.

If you don't get anything else out of a particular chapter or section, remember the material marked by this icon. This text usually contains an essential process or a bit of information that you must know to interact with AI successfully.

Beyond the Book

This book isn't the end of your AI discovery experience; it's really just the beginning. We provide online content to make this book more flexible and better able to meet your needs. That way, as John receives email from you, we can address questions and tell you how updates to AI or its associated technologies affect book content. In fact, you gain access to all these cool additions:

>> **Cheat sheet:** You remember using crib notes in school to make a better mark on a test, don't you? You do? Well, a cheat sheet is sort of like that. It provides you with some special notes about tasks that you can do with AI that not everyone else knows. You can find the cheat sheet for this book by going to www.dummies.com and searching for *Artificial Intelligence For Dummies.* Under the title, click Cheat Sheet and look for the one for this book. The cheat sheet contains really neat information, such as the meaning of all those strange acronyms and abbreviations associated with AI, machine learning, and deep learning.

>> **Updates:** Sometimes changes happen. For example, we might not have seen an upcoming change when we looked into our crystal balls during the writing of this book. In the past, that simply meant that the book would become outdated and less useful, but you can now find updates to the book by going to www.dummies.com and searching this book's title.

In addition to these updates, check out the blog posts with answers to readers' questions and for demonstrations of useful book-related techniques at http://blog.johnmuellerbooks.com/. In addition, you will find blog posts providing information updates as we become aware of them.

Where to Go from Here

It's time to start discovering AI and see what it can do for you. If you don't know anything about AI, start with Chapter 1. You may not want to read every chapter in the book, but starting with Chapter 1 helps you understand AI basics that you need when working through other places in the book.

If your main goal in reading this book is to build knowledge of where AI is used today, start with Chapter 5. The materials in Part 2 help you see where AI is used today.

Readers who have a bit more advanced knowledge of AI can start with Chapter 9. Part 3 of this book contains the most advanced material that you'll encounter. If you don't want to know how AI works at a low level (not as a developer, but simply as someone interested in AI), you might decide to skip this part of the book.

Okay, so you want to know the super fantastic ways in which people are either using AI today or will use AI in the future. If that's the case, start with Chapter 12. All of Parts 4 and 5 show you the incredible ways in which AI is used without forcing you to deal with piles of hype as a result. The information in Part 4 focuses on hardware that relies on AI, and the material in Part 5 focuses more on futuristic uses of AI.

1

Introducing AI

Chapter **1**

Introducing AI

A rtificial Intelligence (AI) has had several false starts and stops over the years, partly because people don't really understand what AI is all about, or even what it should accomplish. A major part of the problem is that movies, television shows, and books have all conspired to give false hopes as to what AI will accomplish. In addition, the human tendency to *anthropomorphize* (give human characteristics to) technology makes it seem as if AI must do more than it can hope to accomplish. So, the best way to start this book is to define what AI actually is, what it isn't, and how it connects to computers today.

REMEMBER

Of course, the basis for what you expect from AI is a combination of how you define AI, the technology you have for implementing AI, and the goals you have for AI. Consequently, everyone sees AI differently. This book takes a middle-of-the-road approach by viewing AI from as many different perspectives as possible. It doesn't buy into the hype offered by proponents, nor does it indulge in the negativity espoused by detractors. Instead, it strives to give you the best possible view of AI as a technology. As a result, you may find that you have somewhat different expectations than those you encounter in this book, which is fine, but it's essential to consider what the technology can actually do for you, rather than expect something it can't.

Defining the Term AI

Before you can use a term in any meaningful and useful way, you must have a definition for it. After all, if nobody agrees on a meaning, the term has none; it's just a collection of characters. Defining the idiom (a term whose meaning isn't clear from the meanings of its constituent elements) is especially important with technical terms that have received more than a little press coverage at various times and in various ways.

REMEMBER

Saying that AI is an artificial intelligence doesn't really tell you anything meaningful, which is why there are so many discussions and disagreements over this term. Yes, you can argue that what occurs is artificial, not having come from a natural source. However, the intelligence part is, at best, ambiguous. Even if you don't necessarily agree with the definition of AI as it appears in the sections that follow, this book uses AI according to that definition, and knowing it will help you follow the rest of the text more easily.

Discerning intelligence

People define intelligence in many different ways. However, you can say that intelligence involves certain mental activities composed of the following activities:

>> **Learning:** Having the ability to obtain and process new information

>> **Reasoning:** Being able to manipulate information in various ways

>> **Understanding:** Considering the result of information manipulation

>> **Grasping truths:** Determining the validity of the manipulated information

>> **Seeing relationships:** Divining how validated data interacts with other data

>> **Considering meanings:** Applying truths to particular situations in a manner consistent with their relationship

>> **Separating fact from belief:** Determining whether the data is adequately supported by provable sources that can be demonstrated to be consistently valid

The list could easily get quite long, but even this list is relatively prone to interpretation by anyone who accepts it as viable. As you can see from the list, however, intelligence often follows a process that a computer system can mimic as part of a simulation:

1. Set a goal based on needs or wants.

2. Assess the value of any currently known information in support of the goal.

3. Gather additional information that could support the goal. The emphasis here is on information that could support the goal, rather than information that you know will support the goal.

4. Manipulate the data such that it achieves a form consistent with existing information.

5. Define the relationships and truth values between existing and new information.

6. Determine whether the goal is achieved.

7. Modify the goal in light of the new data and its effect on the probability of success.

8. Repeat Steps 2 through 7 as needed until the goal is achieved (found true) or the possibilities for achieving it are exhausted (found false).

REMEMBER

Even though you can create algorithms and provide access to data in support of this process within a computer, a computer's capability to achieve intelligence is severely limited. For example, a computer is incapable of understanding anything because it relies on machine processes to manipulate data using pure math in a strictly mechanical fashion. Likewise, computers can't easily separate truth from mistruth (as described in Chapter 2). In fact, no computer can fully implement any of the mental activities described in the list that describes intelligence.

As part of deciding what intelligence actually involves, categorizing intelligence is also helpful. Humans don't use just one type of intelligence, but rather rely on multiple intelligences to perform tasks. Howard Gardner of Harvard has defined a number of these types of intelligence (see the article "Multiple Intelligences" from Project Zero at Harvard University for details), and knowing them helps you to relate them to the kinds of tasks that a computer can simulate as intelligence (see Table 1-1 for a modified version of these intelligences with additional description).

Discovering four ways to define AI

As described in the previous section, the first concept that's important to understand is that AI doesn't really have anything to do with human intelligence. Yes, some AI is modeled to simulate human intelligence, but that's what it is: a simulation. When thinking about AI, notice an interplay between goal seeking, data

TABLE 1-1 The Kinds of Human Intelligence and How AIs Simulate Them

Type	Simulation Potential	Human Tools	Description
Visual-spatial	Moderate	Models, graphics, charts, photographs, drawings, 3-D modeling, video, television, and multimedia	Physical-environment intelligence used by people like sailors and architects (among many others). To move at all, humans need to understand their physical environment — that is, its dimensions and characteristics. Every robot or portable computer intelligence requires this capability, but the capability is often difficult to simulate (as with self-driving cars) or less than accurate (as with vacuums that rely as much on bumping as they do on moving intelligently).
Bodily-kinesthetic	Moderate to High	Specialized equipment and real objects	Body movements, such as those used by a surgeon or a dancer, require precision and body awareness. Robots commonly use this kind of intelligence to perform repetitive tasks, often with higher precision than humans, but sometimes with less grace. It's essential to differentiate between human augmentation, such as a surgical device that provides a surgeon with enhanced physical ability, and true independent movement. The former is simply a demonstration of mathematical ability in that it depends on the surgeon for input.
Creative	None	Artistic output, new patterns of thought, inventions, new kinds of musical composition	Creativity is the act of developing a new pattern of thought that results in unique output in the form of art, music, and writing. A truly new kind of product is the result of creativity. An AI can simulate existing patterns of thought and even combine them to create what appears to be a unique presentation but is really just a mathematically based version of an existing pattern. In order to create, an AI would need to possess self-awareness, which would require intrapersonal intelligence.
Interpersonal	Low to Moderate	Telephone, audio conferencing, video conferencing, writing, computer conferencing, email	Interacting with others occurs at several levels. The goal of this form of intelligence is to obtain, exchange, give, and manipulate information based on the experiences of others. Computers can answer basic questions because of keyword input, not because they understand the question. The intelligence occurs while obtaining information, locating suitable keywords, and then giving information based on those keywords. Cross-referencing terms in a lookup table and then acting on the instructions provided by the table demonstrates logical intelligence, not interpersonal intelligence.

Type	Simulation Potential	Human Tools	Description
Intrapersonal	None	Books, creative materials, diaries, privacy, and time	Looking inward to understand one's own interests and then setting goals based on those interests is currently a human-only kind of intelligence. As machines, computers have no desires, interests, wants, or creative abilities. An AI processes numeric input using a set of algorithms and provides an output; it isn't aware of anything that it does, nor does it understand anything that it does.
Linguistic (often divided into oral, aural, and written)	Low for oral and aural None for written	Games, multimedia, books, voice recorders, and spoken words	Working with words is an essential tool for communication because spoken and written information exchange is far faster than any other form. This form of intelligence includes understanding oral, aural, and written input, managing the input to develop an answer, and providing an understandable answer as output. In many cases, computers can barely parse input into keywords, can't actually understand the request at all, and output responses that may not be understandable at all. In humans, oral, aural, and written linguistic intelligence come from different areas of the brain (see **"Say What? How the Brain Separates Our Ability to Talk and Write"** from John Hopkins University), which means that even with humans, someone who has high written linguistic intelligence may not have similarly high oral linguistic intelligence. Computers don't currently separate aural and oral linguistic ability — one is simply input and the other output. A computer can't simulate written linguistic capability because this ability requires creativity.
Logical-mathematical	High (potentially higher than humans)	Logic games, investigations, mysteries, and brain teasers	Calculating a result, performing comparisons, exploring patterns, and considering relationships are all areas in which computers currently excel. When you see a computer beat a human on a game show, this is the only form of intelligence that you're actually seeing, out of seven kinds of intelligence. Yes, you might see small bits of other kinds of intelligence, but this is the focus. Basing an assessment of human-versus-computer intelligence on just one area isn't a good idea.

processing used to achieve that goal, and data acquisition used to better understand the goal. AI relies on algorithms to achieve a result that may or may not have anything to do with human goals or methods of achieving those goals. With this in mind, you can categorize AI in four ways:

>> **Acting humanly:** When a computer acts like a human, it best reflects the Turing Test, in which the computer succeeds when differentiation between the computer and a human isn't possible (see "The Turing Test" at the Alan Turing Internet Scrapbook for details). This category also reflects what the media would have you believe AI is all about. You see it employed for technologies such as natural language processing, knowledge representation, automated reasoning, and machine learning (all four of which must be present to pass the test). To pass the Turing test, an AI should have all four previous technologies and possibly integrate other solutions (such as expert systems). Mitsuku (found at https://chat.kuki.ai/ and http://www.square-bear.co.uk/mitsuku/home.htm), a chatbot that won the Loebner Prize five times for the most human-like artificial intelligence, is an example of such integration.

TECHNICAL STUFF

The original Turing Test didn't include any physical contact. Harnad's Total Turing Test does include physical contact, in the form of perceptual ability interrogation, which means that the computer must also employ both computer vision and robotics to succeed. Here's a quick overview of other Turing Test alternatives:

- **Reverse Turing Test:** A human tries to convince a computer that that the human is not a computer (for example, the Completely Automatic Public Turing Test to Tell Computers and Humans Apart, or CAPTCHA).

- **Minimum Intelligent Signal Test:** Only true/false and yes/no questions are given.

- **Marcus Test:** A computer program simulates watching a television show, and the program is tested with meaningful questions about the show's content.

- **Lovelace Test 2.0:** A test detects AI through examining its ability to create art.

- **Winograd Schema Challenge:** This test asks multiple-choice questions in a specific format.

Modern techniques include the idea of achieving the goal rather than mimicking humans completely. For example, the Wright Brothers didn't succeed in creating an airplane by precisely copying the flight of birds; rather, the birds provided ideas that led to aerodynamics, which eventually led to human flight. The goal is to fly. Both birds and humans achieve this goal, but they use different approaches.

>> **Thinking humanly:** When a computer thinks like a human, it performs tasks that require intelligence (as contrasted with rote procedures) from a human to succeed, such as driving a car. To determine whether a program thinks like a human, you must have some method of determining how humans think, which the cognitive modeling approach defines. This model relies on three techniques:

- **Introspection:** Detecting and documenting the techniques used to achieve goals by monitoring one's own thought processes.

- **Psychological testing:** Observing a person's behavior and adding it to a database of similar behaviors from other persons given a similar set of circumstances, goals, resources, and environmental conditions (among other things).

- **Brain imaging:** Monitoring brain activity directly through various mechanical means, such as Computerized Axial Tomography (CAT), Positron Emission Tomography (PET), Magnetic Resonance Imaging (MRI), and Magnetoencephalography (MEG).

After creating a model, you can write a program that simulates the model. Given the amount of variability among human thought processes and the difficulty of accurately representing these thought processes as part of a program, the results are experimental at best. This category of thinking humanly is often used in psychology and other fields in which modeling the human thought process to create realistic simulations is essential.

>> **Thinking rationally:** Studying how humans think using some standard enables the creation of guidelines that describe typical human behaviors. A person is considered rational when following these behaviors within certain levels of deviation. A computer that thinks rationally relies on the recorded behaviors to create a guide as to how to interact with an environment based on the data at hand. The goal of this approach is to solve problems logically, when possible. In many cases, this approach would enable the creation of a baseline technique for solving a problem, which would then be modified to actually solve the problem. In other words, the solving of a problem in principle is often different from solving it in practice, but you still need a starting point.

>> **Acting rationally:** Studying how humans act in given situations under specific constraints enables you to determine which techniques are both efficient and effective. A computer that acts rationally relies on the recorded actions to interact with an environment based on conditions, environmental factors, and existing data. As with rational thought, rational acts depend on a solution in principle, which may not prove useful in practice. However, rational acts do provide a baseline upon which a computer can begin negotiating the successful completion of a goal.

HUMAN VERSUS RATIONAL PROCESSES

Human processes differ from rational processes in their outcome. A process is *rational* if it always does the right thing based on the current information, given an ideal performance measure. In short, rational processes go by the book and assume that the book is actually correct. Human processes involve instinct, intuition, and other variables that don't necessarily reflect the book and may not even consider the existing data. As an example, the rational way to drive a car is to always follow the laws. However, traffic isn't rational. If you follow the laws precisely, you end up stuck somewhere because other drivers aren't following the laws precisely. To be successful, a self-driving car must therefore act humanly, rather than rationally.

The categories used to define AI offer a way to consider various uses for or ways to apply AI. Some of the systems used to classify AI by type are arbitrary and not distinct. For example, some groups view AI as either strong (generalized intelligence that can adapt to a variety of situations) or weak (specific intelligence designed to perform a particular task well). The problem with strong AI is that it doesn't perform any task well, while weak AI is too specific to perform tasks independently. Even so, just two type classifications won't do the job even in a general sense. The four classification types promoted by Arend Hintze (see "Understanding the four types of AI, from reactive robots to self-aware beings" at Conversation.com for details) form a better basis for understanding AI:

>> **Reactive machines:** The machines you see beating humans at chess or playing on game shows are examples of reactive machines. A reactive machine has no memory or experience upon which to base a decision. Instead, it relies on pure computational power and smart algorithms to re-create every decision every time. This is an example of a weak AI used for a specific purpose. (The "Considering the Chinese Room argument" section of Chapter 5 explains the meaning of a weak AI.)

>> **Limited memory:** An SD car or autonomous robot can't afford the time to make every decision from scratch. These machines rely on a small amount of memory to provide experiential knowledge of various situations. When the machine sees the same situation, it can rely on experience to reduce reaction time and to provide more resources for making new decisions that haven't yet been made. This is an example of the current level of strong AI.

>> **Theory of mind:** A machine that can assess both its required goals and the potential goals of other entities in the same environment has a kind of understanding that is feasible to some extent today, but not in any commercial form. However, for SD cars to become truly autonomous, this level of AI

must be fully developed. An SD car would not only need to know that it must go from one point to another, but also intuit the potentially conflicting goals of drivers around it and react accordingly. (Robot soccer, `http://www.cs.cmu.edu/~robosoccer/main/` and `https://www.robocup.org/`, is another example of this kind of understanding, but at a simple level.)

>> **Self-awareness:** This is the sort of AI that you see in movies. However, it requires technologies that aren't even remotely possible now because such a machine would have a sense of both self and consciousness. In addition, instead of merely intuiting the goals of others based on environment and other entity reactions, this type of machine would be able to infer the intent of others based on experiential knowledge.

Understanding the History of AI

The previous sections of this chapter help you understand intelligence from the human perspective and see how modern computers are woefully inadequate for simulating such intelligence, much less actually becoming intelligent themselves. However, the desire to create intelligent machines (or, in ancient times, idols) is as old as humans. The desire not to be alone in the universe, to have something with which to communicate without the inconsistencies of other humans, is a strong one. Of course, a single book can't contemplate all of human history, so the following sections provide a brief, pertinent overview of the history of modern AI attempts.

Starting with symbolic logic at Dartmouth

The earliest computers were just that: computing devices. They mimicked the human ability to manipulate symbols in order to perform basic math tasks, such as addition. Logical reasoning later added the capability to perform mathematical reasoning through comparisons (such as determining whether one value is greater than another value). However, humans still needed to define the algorithm used to perform the computation, provide the required data in the right format, and then interpret the result. During the summer of 1956, various scientists attended a workshop held on the Dartmouth College campus to do something more. They predicted that machines that could reason as effectively as humans would require, at most, a generation to come about. They were wrong. Only now have we realized machines that can perform mathematical and logical reasoning as effectively as a human (which means that computers must master at least six more intelligences before reaching anything even close to human intelligence).

The stated problem with the Dartmouth College and other endeavors of the time relates to hardware — the processing capability to perform calculations quickly enough to create a simulation. However, that's not really the whole problem. Yes, hardware does figure in to the picture, but you can't simulate processes that you don't understand. Even so, the reason that AI is somewhat effective today is that the hardware has finally become powerful enough to support the required number of calculations.

WARNING

The biggest problem with these early attempts (and still a considerable problem today) is that we don't understand how humans reason well enough to create any sort of simulation — assuming that a direct simulation is even possible. Consider again the issues surrounding manned flight described earlier in the chapter. The Wright brothers succeeded not by simulating birds but rather by understanding the processes that birds use, thereby creating the field of aerodynamics. Consequently, when someone says that the next big AI innovation is right around the corner and yet no concrete dissertation exists of the processes involved, the innovation is anything but right around the corner.

Continuing with expert systems

Expert systems first appeared in the 1970s and again in the 1980s as an attempt to reduce the computational requirements posed by AI using the knowledge of experts. A number of expert system representations appeared, including rule based (which use if...then statements to base decisions on rules of thumb), frame based (which use databases organized into related hierarchies of generic information called frames), and logic based (which rely on set theory to establish relationships). The advent of expert systems is important because they present the first truly useful and successful implementations of AI.

TIP

You still see expert systems in use today (even though they aren't called that any longer). For example, the spelling and grammar checkers in your application are kinds of expert systems. The grammar checker, especially, is strongly rule based. It pays to look around to see other places where expert systems may still see practical use in everyday applications.

A problem with expert systems is that they can be hard to create and maintain. Early users had to learn specialized programming languages such as List Processing (Lisp) or Prolog. Some vendors saw an opportunity to put expert systems in the hands of less experienced or novice programmers by using products such as VP-Expert (see *The Illustrated VP-Expert* at Amazon.com), which rely on the rule-based approach. However, these products generally provided extremely limited functionality in using smallish knowledge bases.

In the 1990s, the phrase *expert system* began to disappear. The idea that expert systems were a failure did appear, but the reality is that expert systems were simply so successful that they became ingrained in the applications that they were designed to support. Using the example of a word processor, at one time you needed to buy a separate grammar checking application such as RightWriter. However, word processors now have grammar checkers built in because they proved so useful (if not always accurate; see the *Washington Post* article "Hello, Mr. Chips PCS Learn English" for details).

Overcoming the AI winters

The term *AI winter* refers to a period of reduced funding in the development of AI. In general, AI has followed a path on which proponents overstate what is possible, inducing people with no technology knowledge at all, but lots of money, to make investments. A period of criticism then follows when AI fails to meet expectations, and, finally, the reduction in funding occurs. A number of these cycles have occurred over the years — all of them devastating to true progress.

AI is currently in a new hype phase because of *machine learning*, a technology that helps computers learn from data. Having a computer learn from data means not depending on a human programmer to set operations (tasks), but rather deriving them directly from examples that show how the computer should behave. It's like educating a baby by showing it how to behave through example. Machine learning has pitfalls because the computer can learn how to do things incorrectly through careless teaching.

Five tribes of scientists are working on machine learning algorithms, each one from a different point of view (see the "Avoiding AI Hype and Overestimation" section, later in this chapter, for details). At this time, the most successful solution is *deep learning*, which is a technology that strives to imitate the human brain. Deep learning is possible because of the availability of powerful computers, smarter algorithms, large datasets produced by the digitalization of our society, and huge investments from businesses such as Google, Facebook, Amazon, and others that take advantage of this AI renaissance for their own businesses.

People are saying that the AI winter is over because of deep learning, and that's true for now. However, when you look around at the ways in which people are viewing AI, you can easily figure out that another criticism phase will eventually occur unless proponents tone the rhetoric down. AI can do amazing things, but they're a mundane sort of amazing (such as doing the repetitive work for finding a Covid-19 vaccine; see "How AI is being used for COVID-19 vaccine creation and distribution" at TechRepublic.com). The next section describes how AI is being used now.

Considering AI Uses

You find AI used in a great many applications today. The only problem is that the technology works so well that you don't know it even exists. In fact, you might be surprised to find that many home devices already make use of AI. For example, some smart thermostats automatically create schedules for you based on how you manually control the temperature. Likewise, voice input that is used to control some devices learns how you speak so that it can better interact with you. AI definitely appears in your car and most especially in the workplace. In fact, the uses for AI number in the millions — all safely out of sight even when they're quite dramatic in nature. Here are just a few of the ways in which you might see AI used:

>> **Fraud detection:** You get a call from your credit card company asking whether you made a particular purchase. The credit card company isn't being nosy; it's simply alerting you to the fact that someone else could be making a purchase using your card. The AI embedded within the credit card company's code detected an unfamiliar spending pattern and alerted someone to it.

>> **Resource scheduling:** Many organizations need to schedule the use of resources efficiently. For example, a hospital may have to determine where to put a patient based on the patient's needs, availability of skilled experts, and the amount of time the doctor expects the patient to be in the hospital.

>> **Complex analysis:** Humans often need help with complex analysis because there are literally too many factors to consider. For example, the same set of symptoms could indicate more than one problem. A doctor or other expert might need help making a diagnosis in a timely manner to save a patient's life.

>> **Automation:** Any form of automation can benefit from the addition of AI to handle unexpected changes or events. A problem with some types of automation today is that an unexpected event, such as an object in the wrong place, can actually cause the automation to stop. Adding AI to the automation can allow the automation to handle unexpected events and continue as if nothing happened.

>> **Customer service:** The customer service line you call today may not even have a human behind it. The automation is good enough to follow scripts and use various resources to handle the vast majority of your questions. With good voice inflection (provided by AI as well), you may not even be able to tell that you're talking with a computer.

>> **Safety systems:** Many of the safety systems found in machines of various sorts today rely on AI to take over the vehicle in a time of crisis. For example, many automatic braking systems (ABS) rely on AI to stop the car based on all the inputs that a vehicle can provide, such as the direction of a skid.

Computerized ABS is actually relatively old at 40 years from a technology perspective (see "ABS (Anti-Lock Braking System) — A Brief History Of A 40-Year-Old Life-Saver" at DriveSpark.com for details).

>> **Machine efficiency:** AI can help control a machine in such a manner as to obtain maximum efficiency. The AI controls the use of resources so that the system doesn't overshoot speed or other goals. Every ounce of power is used precisely as needed to provide the desired services.

Avoiding AI Hype and Overestimation

This chapter mentions AI hype quite a lot. Unfortunately, the chapter doesn't even scratch the surface of all the hype out there. If you watch movies such as *Her* and *Ex Machina*, you might be led to believe that AI is further along than it is. The problem is that AI is actually in its infancy, and any sort of application such as those shown in the movies is the creative output of an overactive imagination. The following sections help you understand how hype and overestimation are skewing the goals you can actually achieve using AI today.

Defining the five tribes and the master algorithm

You may have heard of something called the singularity, which is responsible for the potential claims presented in the media and movies. The *singularity* is essentially a master algorithm that encompasses all five tribes of learning used within machine learning. To achieve what these sources are telling you, the machine must be able to learn as a human would — as specified by the seven kinds of intelligence discussed in the "Discerning intelligence" section, early in the chapter. Here are the five tribes of learning:

>> **Symbologists:** The origin of this tribe is in logic and philosophy. This group relies on inverse deduction to solve problems.

>> **Connectionists:** This tribe's origin is in neuroscience, and the group relies on backpropagation to solve problems.

>> **Evolutionaries:** The evolutionaries tribe originates in evolutionary biology, relying on genetic programming to solve problems.

>> **Bayesians:** This tribe's origin is in statistics and relies on probabilistic inference to solve problems.

>> **Analogizers:** The origin of this tribe is in psychology. The group relies on kernel machines to solve problems.

The ultimate goal of machine learning is to combine the technologies and strategies embraced by the five tribes to create a single algorithm (the *master algorithm*) that can learn anything. Of course, achieving that goal is a long way off. Even so, scientists such as Pedro Domingos at the University of Washington are currently working toward that goal.

To make things even less clear, the five tribes may not be able to provide enough information to actually solve the problem of human intelligence, so creating master algorithms for all five tribes may still not yield the singularity. At this point, you should be amazed at just how much people don't know about how they think or why they think in a certain manner. Any rumors you hear about AI taking over the world or becoming superior to people are just plain false.

Considering sources of hype

There are many sources of AI hype out there. Quite a bit of the hype comes from the media and is presented by persons who have no idea of what AI is all about, except perhaps from a sci-fi novel they read once. So, it's not just movies or television that cause problems with AI hype; it's all sorts of other media sources as well. You can often find news reports presenting AI as being able to do something that it can't possibly do because the reporter doesn't understand the technology. Oddly enough, many news services now use AI to at least start articles for reporters (see "Did A Robot Write This? How AI Is Impacting Journalism" at Forbes.com for details).

Some products should be tested a lot more before being placed on the market. The "2020 in Review: 10 AI Failures" article at SyncedReview.com discusses ten products hyped by their developer but which fell flat on their faces. Some of these failures are huge and reflect badly on the ability of AI to perform tasks as a whole. However, something to consider with a few of these failures is that people may have interfered with the device using the AI. Obviously, testing procedures need to start considering the possibility of people purposely tampering with the AI as a potential source of errors. Until that happens, the AI will fail to perform as expected because people will continue to fiddle with the software in an attempt to cause it to fail in a humorous manner.

Another cause of problems comes from asking the wrong person about AI. Not every scientist, no matter how smart, knows enough about AI to provide a competent opinion about the technology and the direction it will take in the future. Asking a biologist about the future of AI in general is akin to asking your dentist to perform brain surgery — it simply isn't a good idea. Yet, many stories appear with people like these as the information source. To discover the future direction of AI, it's best to ask a computer scientist or data scientist with a strong background in AI research.

Understanding user overestimation

Because of hype (and sometimes laziness or fatigue), users continually overestimate the ability of AI to perform tasks. For example, a Tesla owner was recently found sleeping in his car while the car zoomed along the highway at 90 mph (see "Tesla owner in Canada charged with 'sleeping' while driving over 90 mph"). However, even with the user significantly overestimating the ability of the technology to drive a car, it does apparently work well enough (at least, for this driver) to avoid a complete failure.

However, you need not be speeding down a highway at 90 mph to encounter user overestimation. Robot vacuums can also fail to meet expectations, usually because users believe they can just plug in the device and then never think about vacuuming again. After all, movies portray the devices working precisely in this manner. The article "How to Solve the Most Annoying Robot Vacuum Cleaner Problems" at RobotsInMyHome.com discusses troubleshooting techniques for various robotic vacuums for a good reason — the robots still need human intervention. The point is that most robots need human intervention at some point because they simply lack the knowledge to go it alone.

Connecting AI to the Underlying Computer

To see AI at work, you need to have some sort of computing system, an application that contains the required software, and a knowledge base. The computing system could be anything with a chip inside; in fact, a smartphone does just as well as a desktop computer for some applications. Of course, if you're Amazon and you want to provide advice on a particular person's next buying decision, the smartphone won't do — you need a really big computing system for that application. The size of the computing system is directly proportional to the amount of work you expect the AI to perform.

The application can also vary in size, complexity, and even location. For example, if you're a business and want to analyze client data to determine how best to make a sales pitch, you might rely on a server-based application to perform the task. On the other hand, if you're a customer and want to find products on Amazon to go with your current purchase items, the application doesn't even reside on your computer; you access it through a web-based application located on Amazon's servers.

The knowledge base varies in location and size as well. The more complex the data, the more you can obtain from it, but the more you need to manipulate it as well. You get no free lunch when it comes to knowledge management. The interplay between location and time is also important. A network connection affords you access to a large knowledge base online but costs you in time because of the latency of network connections. However, localized databases, while fast, tend to lack details in many cases.

IN THIS CHAPTER

» **Seeing data as a universal resource**

» **Obtaining and manipulating data**

» **Looking for mistruths in data**

» **Defining data-acquisitions limits**

» **Considering data security**

Chapter **2**

Defining the Role of Data

There is nothing new about data. Every interesting application ever written for a computer has data associated with it. Data comes in many forms — some organized, some not. What has changed is the amount of data. Some people find it almost terrifying that we now have access to so much data that details nearly every aspect of most people's lives, sometimes to a level that even the person doesn't realize. In addition, the use of advanced hardware and improvements in algorithms make data the universal resource for AI today.

To work with data, you must first obtain it. Today, applications collect data manually, as done in the past, and also automatically, using new methods. However, it's not a matter of just one to two data collection techniques; collection methods take place on a continuum from fully manual to fully automatic. You also find a focus today on collecting this data ethically — for example, not collecting data that a person hasn't granted permission for. This chapter explores issues surrounding data collection.

Raw data doesn't usually work well for analysis purposes. This chapter also helps you understand the need for manipulating and shaping the data so that it meets specific requirements. You also discover the need to define the truth value of the data to ensure that analysis outcomes match the goals set for applications in the first place.

Interestingly, you also have data-acquisition limits to deal with. No technology currently exists for grabbing thoughts from someone's mind through telepathic means. Of course, other limits exist, too — most of which you probably already know about but may not have considered. It also doesn't pay to collect data in a manner that isn't secure. The data must be free of bias, uncorrupted, and from a source you know. You find out more about acquisition limits and data security in this chapter.

Finding Data Ubiquitous in This Age

Big data is more than a just a buzz phrase used by vendors to propose new ways to store data and analyze it. The big data revolution is an everyday reality and a driving force of our times. You may have heard big data mentioned in many specialized scientific and business publications, and you may have even wondered what the term really means. From a technical perspective, *big data* refers to large and complex amounts of computer data, so large and intricate that applications can't deal with the data simply by using additional storage or increasing computer power.

Big data implies a revolution in data storage and manipulation. It affects what you can achieve with data in more qualitative terms (meaning that in addition to doing more, you can perform tasks better). From a human perspective, computers store big data in different data formats (such as database files and .csv files), but regardless of storage type, the computer still sees data as a stream of ones and zeros (the core language of computers). You can view data as being one of two types, structured and unstructured, depending on how you produce and consume it. Some data has a clear structure (you know exactly what it contains and where to find every piece of data), whereas other data is unstructured (you have an idea of what it contains, but you don't know exactly how it is arranged).

Typical examples of structured data are database tables, in which information is arranged into columns, and each column contains a specific type of information. Data is often structured by design. You gather it selectively and record it in its correct place. For example, you might want to place a count of the number of people buying a certain product in a specific column, in a specific table, in a specific database. As with a library, if you know what data you need, you can find it immediately.

Unstructured data consists of images, videos, and sound recordings. You may use an unstructured form for text so that you can tag it with characteristics, such as size, date, or content type. Usually you don't know exactly where data appears in an unstructured dataset because the data appears as sequences of ones and zeros that an application must interpret or visualize.

REMEMBER

Transforming unstructured data into a structured form can cost lots of time and effort and can involve the work of many people. Most of the data of the big data revolution is unstructured and stored as it is, unless someone renders it structured.

This copious and sophisticated data store didn't appear suddenly overnight. It took time to develop the technology to store this amount of data. In addition, it took time to spread the technology that generates and delivers data, namely computers, sensors, smart mobile phones, and the Internet and its World Wide Web services. The following sections help you understand what makes data a universal resource today.

Understanding Moore's implications

In 1965, Gordon Moore, cofounder of Intel and Fairchild Semiconductor, wrote in an article entitled "Cramming More Components Onto Integrated Circuits," at IEEE.org, that the number of components found in integrated circuits would double every year for the next decade. At that time, transistors dominated electronics. Being able to stuff more transistors into an Integrated Circuit (IC) meant being able to make electronic devices more capable and useful. This process is called *integration* and implies a strong process of electronics miniaturization (making the same circuit much smaller). Today's computers aren't all that much smaller than computers of a decade ago, yet they are decisively more powerful. The same goes for mobile phones. Even though they're the same size as their predecessors (and sometimes even smaller), they have become able to perform more tasks.

What Moore stated in that article has actually been true for many years. The semiconductor industry calls it Moore's Law (see http://www.mooreslaw.org/ for details). Doubling did occur for the first ten years, as predicted. In 1975, Moore corrected his statement, forecasting a doubling every two years. Figure 2-1 shows the effects of this doubling.

TECHNICAL STUFF

Starting in 2012, a mismatch began to occur between expected speed increases and what semiconductor companies could achieve with regard to miniaturization. Many engineers are now saying that Moore's Law is dead. However, a few, such as Jim Keller, Intel's head of semiconductor engineering, say that there is still ample room for chip improvement. Charles Leiserson and Neil Thompson are of a different mindset, saying that improvements will come from better software, algorithms, and specialized chip architecture.

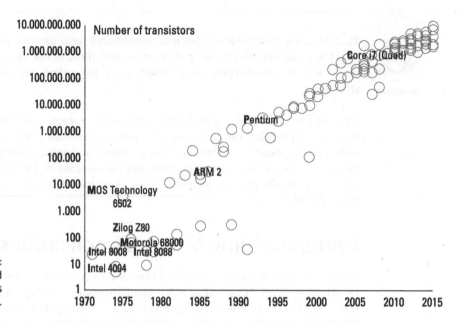

FIGURE 2-1:
Stuffing more and
more transistors
into a CPU.

In the future, Moore's Law may not apply because industry will switch to a new technology, such as making components by using optical lasers instead of transistors (see the "Optical Computing: Solving Problems at the Speed of Light" article at BBVAOpenMind.com for details about optical computing). Another solution relies on quantum computers, such as those under development by Google and IBM (you can read more about this technology in "Google confirms 'quantum supremacy' breakthrough" at The Verge.com). What matters is that since 1965, the doubling of components every two years has ushered in great advancements in digital electronics that has had far-reaching consequences in the acquisition, storage, manipulation, and management of data.

Moore's Law has a direct effect on data. It begins with smarter devices. The smarter the devices, the more diffusion (as evidenced by electronics being everywhere today). The greater the diffusion, the lower the price becomes, creating an endless loop that drives the use of powerful computing machines and small sensors everywhere. With large amounts of computer memory available and larger storage disks for data, the consequences are an expansion of data availability, such as websites, transaction records, measurements, digital images, and other sorts of data.

Using data everywhere

Scientists need more powerful computers than the average person because of their scientific experiments. They began dealing with impressive amounts of data years before anyone coined the term *big data*. At that point, the Internet wasn't producing the vast sums of data that it does today. Remember that big data isn't a fad created by software and hardware vendors but has a basis in many scientific fields, such as astronomy (space missions), satellite (surveillance and monitoring), meteorology, physics (particle accelerators) and genomics (DNA sequences).

Although an AI application can specialize in a scientific field, such as IBM's Watson, which boasts an impressive medical diagnosis capability because it can learn information from millions of scientific papers on diseases and medicine, the actual AI application driver often has more mundane facets. Actual AI applications are mostly prized for being able to recognize objects, move along paths, or understand what people say and speak to them. Data contribution to the actual AI renaissance that molded it in such a fashion didn't derive from the classical sources of scientific data.

The Internet now generates and distributes new data in large amounts. Our current daily data production is estimated to amount to about 2.5 quintillion (a number with 18 zeros) bytes, with the lion's share going to unstructured data like videos and audios. All this data is related to common human activities, feelings, experiences, and relations. Roaming through this data, an AI can easily learn how reasoning and acting more human-like works. Here are some examples of the more interesting data you can find:

>> Large repositories of faces and expressions from photos and videos posted on social media websites like Facebook, YouTube, and Google provide information about gender, age, feelings, and possibly sexual preferences, political orientations, or IQ (see "Face-reading AI will be able to detect your politics and IQ, professor says" at The Guardian.com).

>> Privately held medical information and biometric data from smart watches, which measure body data such as temperature and heart rate during both illness and good health. Interestingly enough, data from smartwatches is seen as a method to detect serious diseases, such as Covid-19, early (check out "Using Smartwatch Data to Detect COVID-19 Cases Early" at JAMA Network.com for details).

>> Datasets of how people relate to each other and what drives their interest from sources such as social media and search engines. For instance, a study from Cambridge University's Psychometrics Centre claims that Facebook interactions contain a lot of data about intimate relationships (see "Your computer knows you better than your friends do, say researchers" at The Guardian.com).

>> Information on how we speak is recorded by mobile phones. For instance, OK Google, a function found on Android mobile phones, routinely records questions and sometimes even more, as explained in "Google's been quietly recording your voice; here's how to listen to—and delete—the archive" at Quartz.com.

Every day, users connect even more devices to the Internet that start storing new personal data. There are now personal assistants that sit in houses, such as Amazon Echo and other integrated smart home devices that offer ways to regulate and facilitate the domestic environment. These are just the tip of the iceberg because many other common tools of everyday life are becoming interconnected (from the refrigerator to the toothbrush) and able to process, record, and transmit data. The Internet of Things (IoT) is becoming a reality. In 2015, the installed base of IoT devices was 3.6 billion. Experts estimate that by 2025, the installed base of IoT devices will reach 30.9 billion, an increase of 858 percent (see "How Many IoT Devices Are There in 2021?" at TechJury.net and "Internet of Things (IoT) and non-IoT active device connections worldwide from 2010 to 2025 (in billions)" at Statista.com.

Putting algorithms into action

The human race is now at an incredible intersection of unprecedented volumes of data, generated by increasingly smaller and powerful hardware. The data is also increasingly processed and analyzed by the same computers that the process helped spread and develop. This statement may seem obvious, but data has become so ubiquitous that its value no longer resides only in the information it contains (such as the case of data stored in a firm's database that allows its daily operations), but rather in its use as a means to create new values. Some people call such data the "new oil." These new values mostly exist in how applications manicure, store, and retrieve data, and in how you actually use it by means of smart algorithms.

Algorithms and AI changed the data game. As mentioned in the previous chapter, AI algorithms have tried different approaches along the way in the following order:

1. Simple algorithms

2. Symbolic reasoning based on logic

3. Expert systems

In recent years, AI algorithms have moved to neural networks and, in their most mature form, deep learning. As this methodological passage happened, data turned from being the information processed by predetermined algorithms to becoming what molded the algorithm into something useful for the task. Data turned from being just the raw material that fueled the solution to the artisan of the solution itself, as shown in Figure 2-2.

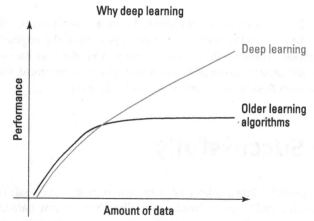

Why deep learning

Performance

Deep learning

Older learning
algorithms

Amount of data

FIGURE 2-2:
With the present
AI solutions,
more data
equates to more
intelligence.

Thus, a photo of some of your kittens has become increasingly useful not simply because of its affective value — depicting your cute little cats — but because it could become part of the learning process of an AI discovering more general concepts, such as what characteristics denote a cat, or understanding what defines cute.

On a larger scale, a company like Google feeds its algorithms from freely available data, such as the content of websites or the text found in publicly available texts and books. Google spider software crawls the web, jumping from website to website, retrieving web pages with their content of text and images. Even if Google gives back part of the data to users as search results, it extracts other kinds of information from the data using its AI algorithms, which learn from it how to achieve other objectives.

Algorithms that process words can help Google AI systems understand and anticipate your needs even when you are not expressing them in a set of keywords but in plain, unclear natural language, the language we speak every day (and yes, everyday language is often unclear). If you currently try to pose questions, not just chains of keywords, to the Google search engine, you'll notice that it tends to answer correctly. Since 2012, with the introduction of the Hummingbird update (read the details in "FAQ: All About The New Google 'Hummingbird' Algorithm" at Search Engine Land.com), Google has steadily become better able to understand synonyms and concepts, something that goes beyond the initial data that it acquired, and this is the result of an AI process.

A few years after Hummingbird, Google deployed an even more advanced algorithm named RankBrain ("FAQ: All about the Google RankBrain algorithm" at Search Engine Land.com), which learns directly from millions of queries every day and can answer ambiguous or unclear search queries, even expressed in slang or colloquial terms or simply riddled with errors. RankBrain doesn't service all the queries, but it learns from data how to better answer queries. After its introduction in 2015, it quickly began to handle 15 percent of the engine's queries, but it won't replace Hummingbird (see "7 Things You May Not Know About Google's RankBrain" at Act On.com and "The Rankbrain, Hummingbird, and Search Engine Optimization Fusion" at Connectica.com for details).

Using Data Successfully

Having plentiful data available isn't enough to create a successful AI. Presently, an AI algorithm can't extract information directly from raw data. Most algorithms rely on external collection and manipulation prior to analysis. When an algorithm collects useful information, it may not represent the right information. The following sections help you understand how to collect, manipulate, and automate data collection from an overview perspective.

Considering the data sources

The data you use comes from a number of sources. The most common data source is from information entered by humans at some point. Even when a system collects shopping-site data automatically, humans initially enter the information. A human clicks various items, adds them to a shopping cart, specifies characteristics (such as size and quantity), and then checks out. Later, after the sale, the human gives the shopping experience, product, and delivery method a rating and makes comments. In short, every shopping experience becomes a data collection exercise as well.

Many data sources today rely on input gathered from human sources. Humans also provide manual input. You call or go into an office somewhere to make an appointment with a professional. A receptionist then gathers information from you that's needed for the appointment. This manually collected data eventually ends up in a dataset somewhere for analysis purposes.

Data is also collected from sensors, and these sensors can take almost any form. For example, many organizations base physical data collection, such as the number of people viewing an object in a window, on cellphone detection. Facial recognition software could potentially detect repeat customers.

However, sensors can create datasets from almost anything. The weather service relies on datasets created by sensors that monitor environmental conditions such as rain, temperature, humidity, cloud cover, and so on. Robotic monitoring systems help correct small flaws in robotic operation by constantly analyzing data collected by monitoring sensors. A sensor, combined with a small AI application, could tell you when your dinner is cooked to perfection tonight. The sensor collects data, but the AI application uses rules to help define when the food is properly cooked.

Obtaining reliable data

The word *reliable* seems so easy to define, yet so hard to implement. Something is reliable when the results it produces are both expected and consistent. A reliable data source produces mundane data that contains no surprises; no one is shocked in the least by the outcome. Depending on your perspective, it could actually be a good thing that most people aren't yawning and then falling asleep when reviewing data. The surprises make the data worth analyzing and reviewing. Consequently, data has an aspect of duality. We want reliable, mundane, fully anticipated data that simply confirms what we already know, but the unexpected is what makes collecting the data useful in the first place.

Still, you don't want data that is so far out of the ordinary that it becomes almost frightening to review. Balance needs to be maintained when obtaining data. The data must fit within certain limits (as described in the "Manicuring the Data" section, later in this chapter). It must also meet specific criteria as to truth value (as described in the "Considering the Five Mistruths in Data" section, later in this chapter). The data must also come at expected intervals, and all the fields of the incoming data record must be complete.

REMEMBER

To some extent, data security also affects data reliability. Data consistency comes in several forms. When the data arrives, you can ensure that it falls within expected ranges and appears in a particular form. However, after you store the data, the reliability can decrease unless you ensure that the data remains in the expected form. An entity fiddling with the data affects reliability, making the data suspect and potentially unusable for analysis later. Ensuring data reliability means that after the data arrives, no one tampers with it to make it fit within an expected domain (making it mundane as a result).

Making human input more reliable

Humans make mistakes — it's part of being human. In fact, expecting that humans won't make mistakes is unreasonable. Yet, many application designs assume that humans somehow won't make mistakes of any sort. The design expects that everyone will simply follow the rules. Unfortunately, the vast majority of users are guaranteed to not even read the rules because most humans are also lazy or too pressed for time when it comes to doing things that don't really help them directly.

Consider the entry of a state into a form. If you provide just a text field, some users might input the entire state name, such as Kansas. Of course, some users will make a typo or capitalization error and come up with Kanzuz, Kansus, or kAN-SAS. Setting these errors aside, people and organizations also have various approaches to performing tasks. Someone in the publishing industry might use the Associated Press (AP) style guide and input Kan. Someone who is older and used to the Government Printing Office (GPO) guidelines might input Kans. instead. Other abbreviations are used as well. The U.S. Post Office (USPS) uses KS, but the U.S. Coast Guard uses KA. Meanwhile, the International Standards Organization (ISO) form goes with US-KS. Mind you, this is just a state entry, which is reasonably straightforward — or so you thought before reading this section. Clearly, because the state isn't going to change names anytime soon, you could simply provide a drop-down list box on the form for choosing the state in the required format, thereby eliminating differences in abbreviation use, typos, and capitalization errors in one fell swoop.

Drop-down list boxes work well for an amazing array of data inputs, and using them ensures that human input into those fields becomes extremely reliable because the human has no choice but to use one of the default entries. Of course, the human can always choose the incorrect entry, which is where double-checks come into play. Some newer applications compare the zip code to the city and state entries to see whether they match. When they don't match (sometimes it's just a matter of capitalization), the user is asked again to provide the correct input. This double-check verges on being annoying, but the user is unlikely to see it very often, so it shouldn't become too annoying.

Even with cross-checks and static entries, humans still have plenty of room for making mistakes. For example, entering numbers can be problematic. When a user needs to enter 2.00, you might see 2, or 2.0, or 2., or any of a variety of other entries. Fortunately, parsing the entry and reformatting it will fix the problem, and you can perform this task automatically, without the user's aid. (Unfortunately, some online sites want you to enter information like credit cards with dashes, some with spaces, and some without any spacing at all, which makes for a very confusing session when the application doesn't fix the entry automatically.)

Unfortunately, reformatting won't correct an errant numeric input. You can partially mitigate such errors by including range checks. A customer can't buy −5 bars of soap. And, unless the customer is really dirty or owns a wombat farm, entering 50,000 bars of soap would likely be a mistake, too. The legitimate way to show that the customer is returning the bars of soap is to process a return, not a sale. However, the user might have simply made an error, and you can provide a message stating the proper input range for the value.

Using automated data collection

Some people think that automated data collection solves all the human input issues associated with datasets. In fact, automated data collection does provide a number of benefits:

» Better consistency

» Improved reliability

» Lower probability of missing data

» Enhanced accuracy

» Reduced variance for things like timed inputs

Unfortunately, to say that automated data collection solves every issue is simply incorrect. Automated data collection still relies on sensors, applications, and computer hardware designed by humans that provide access only to the data that humans decide to allow. Because of the limits that humans place on the characteristics of automated data collection, the outcome often provides less helpful information than hoped for by the designers. Consequently, automated data collection is in a constant state of flux as designers try to solve the input issues.

Automated data collection also suffers from both software and hardware errors present in any computing system, but with a higher potential for *soft issues* (which arise when the system is apparently working but isn't providing the desired result) than other kinds of computer-based setups. When the system works, the reliability of the input far exceeds human abilities. However, when soft issues occur, the system often fails to recognize, as a human might, that a problem exists, and therefore the dataset could end up containing more mediocre or even bad data.

Collecting personal data ethically

For some people, anything that appears on the Internet is automatically considered public domain — including people's faces and all their personal information. The fact is that you should consider everything as being copyrighted and not available for use in a public domain manner to use data safely. Even people who realize that material is copyrighted will often fall back on fair-use principles (as explained in "Using Copyrighted Material" at Baylor University.edu). Fair use can be a very tricky subject, as witnessed by the Author's Guild v. Google case (see "The Most Important Court Decision For Data Science and Machine Learning" at Towards Data Science.com) that was finally decided in favor of Google, but only because Google had met some very strict requirements. In addition, this kind of fair use is about books, not people.

The problem with considering fair use alone is that it's also essential to consider a person's right to privacy (you can read about various laws in "Internet privacy laws revealed — how your personal information is protected online" at Thomson Reuters Legal.com). Consequently, it shouldn't surprise anyone that a major ruckus arose when companies started scraping images of people wearing masks on the Internet without obtaining any permission whatsoever (see "Your face mask selfies could be training the next facial recognition tool" at Cnet.com). In fact, Facebook is being sued over its misuse of user data (see "$35B face data lawsuit against Facebook will proceed" at TechCrunch.com).

The right to privacy has also created a new industry for making a person's face less useful to companies who are determined to get free data without permission by using any means possible (see the *New York Times* article "This Tool Could Protect Your Photos From Facial Recognition"). The fact is, no matter where you stand on the free-use issue, you still need to consider the ethical use of data that you obtain no matter what the source might be. Here are some considerations to keep in mind as you collect personal data ethically:

>> **Obtaining permission:** Some research will require you to be able to identify persons used within a dataset. Going out and grabbing Personally Identifiable Information (PII) isn't a good way to gather data. For one thing, you can't be sure that the information is either complete or correct, so any analysis you perform is suspect. For another thing, you could encounter the messy and costly consequences of legal actions. The best way to obtain data with PII is to ask permission. You can find a number of resources online for asking permission, for example at the government level, by finding the right resource, such as "How to Obtain a Consumer's Authorization before Gaining Access to Personally Identifiable Information (PII)."

>> **Using sanitization techniques:** *Data sanitization* involves removing personal information, such as name, address, telephone number, ID, and so on from a dataset so that identifying a particular individual in a dataset becomes impossible. In addition to text and dataset variables, you must consider every kind of data. For instance, if you are working with collections of photos, it is paramount that you take steps to blur faces and remove car plates from images. Oddly enough, if you perform a Google search using *sanitization* as a key term, you still get many links dealing with cleaning. Adding *privacy* as another key term helps find the sorts of articles you actually need. Even so, you may find that you're not the only one who is confused about the process.

>> **Avoiding Data Inference:** When collecting data, some users will refuse to share personally identifiable information, such as gender and age. One recommendation is to infer this information when a user's picture or other information is available. Unfortunately, names that are associated with one gender in a particular culture may be assigned to the other gender in other

cultures. The problem with age inference is even more profound. For example, a machine learning algorithm will likely infer the wrong age for an albino, which can affect as many as one in 3,000 individuals, depending on the part of the world the data comes from (see details in "Information Bulletin – What is Albinism?" at NOAH.com.)

>> **Avoiding generalizations:** Many fields of study today try to incorrectly apply statistics and machine learning outcomes, with the result that an individual ends up being mistreated in some manner. It's essential to remember that statistics apply to groups, not to individuals.

Manicuring the Data

Some people use the term *manipulation* when speaking about data, giving the impression that the data is somehow changed in an unscrupulous or devious manner. Perhaps a better term would be *manicuring*, which makes the data well shaped and lovely. No matter what term you use, however, raw data seldom meets the requirements for processing and analysis. To get something out of the data, you must manicure it to meet specific needs. The following sections discuss data manicuring needs.

Dealing with missing data

To answer a given question correctly, you must have all the facts. You can guess the answer to a question without all the facts, but then the answer is just as likely to be wrong as correct. Often, someone who makes a decision, essentially answering a question, without all the facts is said to jump to a conclusion. When analyzing data, you have probably jumped to more conclusions than you think because of missing data. A *data record*, one entry in a *dataset* (which is all the data), consists of *fields* that contain facts used to answer a question. Each field contains a single kind of data that addresses a single fact. If that field is empty, you don't have the data you need to answer the question using that particular data record.

REMEMBER

As part of the process of dealing with missing data, you must know that the data is missing. Identifying that your dataset is missing information can actually be quite hard because it requires you to look at the data at a low level — something that most people aren't prepared to do and is time consuming even if you do have the required skills. Often, your first clue that data is missing is the preposterous answers that your questions get from the algorithm and associated dataset. When the algorithm is the right one to use, the dataset must be at fault. Here are some issues to consider:

>> **Essential data missing:** A problem can occur when the data collection process doesn't include all the data needed to answer a particular question. Sometimes you're better off to actually drop a fact rather than use a considerably damaged fact.

>> **Some data missing:** Less damaged fields can have data missing in one of two ways, randomly or sequentially, as described here:

- **Randomly missing data is often the result of human or sensor error.** Fixing randomly missing data is easiest. You can use a simple median or average value as a replacement. No, the dataset isn't completely accurate, but it will likely work well enough to obtain a reasonable answer.

- **Sequentially missing data occurs during some type of generalized failure.** Fixing sequentially missing data is significantly harder, if not impossible, because you lack any surrounding data on which to base any sort of guess. If you can find the cause of the missing data, you can sometimes reconstruct it.

Considering data misalignments

Data might exist for each of the data records in a dataset, but it might not align with other data in other datasets you own. For example, the numeric data in a field in one dataset might be a floating-point type (with decimal point), but an integer type in another dataset. Before you can combine the two datasets, the fields must contain the same type of data.

All sorts of other kinds of misalignment can occur. For example, date fields are notorious for being formatted in various ways. To compare dates, the data formats must be the same. However, dates are also insidious in their propensity for looking the same, but not being the same. For example, dates in one dataset might use Greenwich Mean Time (GMT) as a basis, while the dates in another dataset might use some other time zone. Before you can compare the times, you must align them to the same time zone. It can become even weirder when dates in one dataset come from a location that uses Daylight Saving Time (DST), but dates from another location don't.

Even when the data types and format are the same, other data misalignments can occur. For example, the fields in one dataset may not match the fields in the other dataset. In some cases, these differences are easy to correct. One dataset may treat first and last name as a single field, while another dataset might use separate fields for first and last name. The answer is to change all datasets to use a single field or to change them all to use separate fields for first and last name. Unfortunately, many misalignments in data content are harder to figure out. In fact, it's entirely possible that you might not be able to figure them out at all. However, before you give up, consider these potential solutions to the problem:

>> Calculate the missing data from other data that you can access.

>> Locate the missing data in another dataset.

>> Combine datasets to create a whole that provides consistent fields.

>> Collect additional data from various sources to fill in the missing data.

>> Redefine your question so that you no longer need the missing data.

Separating useful data from other data

Some organizations are of the opinion that they can never have too much data, but an excess of data becomes as much a problem as not enough. To solve problems efficiently, an AI requires just enough data. Defining the question that you want to answer concisely and clearly helps, as does using the correct algorithm (or algorithm ensemble). Of course, the major problems with having too much data are that finding the solution (after wading through all that extra data) takes longer, and sometimes you get confusing results because you can't see the forest for the trees.

WARNING

As part of creating the dataset you need for analysis, you make a copy of the original data rather than modify it. Always keep the original, raw data pure so that you can use it for other analysis later. In addition, creating the right data output for analysis can require a number of tries because you may find that the output doesn't meet your needs. The point is to create a dataset that contains only the data needed for analysis, but keep in mind that the data may need specific kinds of pruning to ensure the desired output.

Considering the Five Mistruths in Data

Humans are used to seeing data for what it is in many cases: an opinion. In fact, in some cases, people skew data to the point where it becomes useless, a *mistruth*. A computer can't tell the difference between truthful and untruthful data — all it sees is data. One of the issues that make it hard, if not impossible, to create an AI that actually thinks like a human is that humans can work with mistruths and computers can't. The best you can hope to achieve is to see the errant data as outliers and then filter it out, but that technique doesn't necessarily solve the problem because a human would still use the data and attempt to determine a truth based on the mistruths that are there.

WARNING

A common thought about creating less contaminated datasets is that instead of allowing humans to enter the data, collecting the data through sensors or other means should be possible. Unfortunately, sensors and other mechanical input methodologies reflect the goals of their human inventors and the limits of what the particular technology is able to detect. Consequently, even machine-derived or sensor-derived data is also subject to generating mistruths that are quite difficult for an AI to detect and overcome.

The following sections use a car accident as the main example to illustrate five types of mistruths that can appear in data. The concepts that the accident is trying to portray may not always appear in data, and they may appear in different ways than discussed. The fact remains that you normally need to deal with these sorts of things when viewing data.

Commission

Mistruths of commission are those that reflect an outright attempt to substitute truthful information for untruthful information. For example, when filling out an accident report, someone could state that the sun momentarily blinded them, making it impossible to see someone they hit. In reality, perhaps the person was distracted by something else or wasn't actually thinking about driving (possibly considering a nice dinner). If no one can disprove this theory, the person might get by with a lesser charge. However, the point is that the data would also be contaminated. The effect is that now an insurance company would base premiums on errant data.

REMEMBER

Although it would seem as if mistruths of commission are completely avoidable, often they aren't. Human tell "little white lies" to save others embarrassment or to deal with an issue with the least amount of personal effort. Sometimes a mistruth of commission is based on errant input or hearsay. In fact, the sources for errors of commission are so many that it really is hard to come up with a scenario where someone could avoid them entirely. All this said, mistruths of commission are one type of mistruth that someone can avoid more often than not.

Omission

Mistruths of omission are those where a person tells the truth in every stated fact, but leaves out an important fact that would change the perception of an incident as a whole. Thinking again about the accident report, say that you strike a deer, causing significant damage to your car. You truthfully say that the road was wet;

it was near twilight, so the light wasn't as good as it could be; you were a little late in pressing on the brake; and the deer simply ran out from a thicket at the side of the road. The conclusion would be that the incident is simply an accident.

However, you left out an important fact: You were texting at the time. If law enforcement knew about the texting, it would change the reason for the accident to inattentive driving. You might be fined, and the insurance adjuster would use a different reason when entering the incident into the database. As with the mistruth of commission, the resulting errant data would change how the insurance company adjusts premiums.

REMEMBER

Avoiding mistruths of omission is nearly impossible. Yes, people could purposely leave facts out of a report, but it's just as likely that they'll simply forget to include all the facts. After all, most people are quite rattled after an accident, so it's easy to lose focus and report only those truths that left the most significant impression. Even if a person later remembers additional details and reports them, the database is unlikely to ever contain a full set of truths.

Perspective

Mistruths of perspective occur when multiple parties view an incident from multiple vantage points. For example, in considering an accident involving a struck pedestrian, the person driving the car, the person getting hit by the car, and a bystander who witnessed the event would all have different perspectives. An officer taking reports from each person would understandably get different facts from each one, even assuming that each person tells the truth as each knows it. In fact, experience shows that this is almost always the case, and what the officer submits as a report is the middle ground of what each of those involved state, augmented by personal experience. In other words, the report will be close to the truth, but not close enough for an AI.

When dealing with perspective, it's important to consider vantage point. The driver of the car can see the dashboard and knows the car's condition at the time of the accident. This is information that the other two parties lack. Likewise, the person getting hit by the car has the best vantage point for seeing the driver's facial expression (intent). The bystander might be in the best position to see whether the driver made an attempt to stop, and assess issues such as whether the driver tried to swerve. Each party will have to make a report based on seen data without the benefit of hidden data.

WARNING

Perspective is perhaps the most dangerous of the mistruths because anyone who tries to derive the truth in this scenario will, at best, end up with an average of the various stories, which will never be fully correct. A human viewing the information can rely on intuition and instinct to potentially obtain a better approximation of the truth, but an AI will always use just the average, which means that the AI is always at a significant disadvantage. Unfortunately, avoiding mistruths of perspective is impossible because no matter how many witnesses you have to the event, the best you can hope to achieve is an approximation of the truth, not the actual truth.

There is also another sort of mistruth to consider, and it's one of perspective. Think about this scenario: You're a deaf person in 1927. Each week, you go to the theater to view a silent film, and for an hour or more, you feel like everyone else. You can experience the movie the same way everyone else does; there are no differences. In October of that year, you see a sign saying that the theater is upgrading to support a sound system so that it can display *talkies* — films with a sound track. The sign says that it's the best thing ever, and almost everyone seems to agree, except for you, the deaf person, who is now made to feel like a second-class citizen, different from everyone else and even pretty much excluded from the theater. In the deaf person's eyes, that sign is a mistruth; adding a sound system is the worst possible thing, not the best possible thing. The point is that what seems to be generally true isn't actually true for everyone. The idea of a general truth — one that is true for everyone — is a myth. It doesn't exist.

Bias

Mistruths of bias occur when someone is able to see the truth but because of personal concerns or beliefs is unable to actually see it. For example, when thinking about an accident, a driver might focus attention so completely on the middle of the road that the deer at the edge of the road becomes invisible. Consequently, the driver has no time to react when the deer suddenly decides to bolt out into the middle of the road in an effort to cross.

A problem with bias is that it can be incredibly hard to categorize. For example, a driver who fails to see the deer can have a genuine accident, meaning that the deer was hidden from view by shrubbery. However, the driver might also be guilty of inattentive driving because of incorrect focus. The driver might also experience a momentary distraction. In short, the fact that the driver didn't see the deer isn't the question; instead, it's a matter of why the driver didn't see the deer. In many cases, confirming the source of bias becomes important when creating an algorithm designed to avoid a bias source.

REMEMBER

Theoretically, avoiding mistruths of bias is always possible. In reality, however, all humans have biases of various types, and those biases will always result in mistruths that skew datasets. Just getting someone to actually look and then see something — to have it register in the person's brain — is a difficult task. Humans rely on filters to avoid information overload, and these filters are also a source of bias because they prevent people from actually seeing things.

Frame of reference

Of the five mistruths, frame of reference need not actually be the result of any sort of error, but one of understanding. A frame-of-reference mistruth occurs when one party describes something, such as an event like an accident, and because a second party lacks experience with the event, the details become muddled or completely misunderstood. Comedy routines abound that rely on frame-of-reference errors. One famous example is from Abbott and Costello, *Who's On First*, which you can find on YouTube.com. Getting one person to understand what a second person is saying can be impossible when the first person lacks experiential knowledge — the frame of reference.

Another frame-of-reference mistruth example occurs when one party can't possibly understand the other. For example, a sailor experiences a storm at sea. Perhaps it's a monsoon, but assume for a moment that the storm is substantial — perhaps life threatening. Even with the use of videos, interviews, and a simulator, the experience of being at sea in a life-threatening storm would be impossible to convey to someone who hasn't experienced such a storm firsthand; that person has no frame of reference.

REMEMBER

The best way to avoid frame-of-reference mistruths is to ensure that all parties involved can develop similar frames of reference. To accomplish this task, the various parties require similar experiential knowledge to ensure the accurate transfer of data from one person to another. However, when working with a dataset, which is necessarily recorded static data, frame-of-reference errors will still occur when the prospective viewer lacks the required experiential knowledge.

An AI will always experience frame-of-reference issues because an AI necessarily lacks the ability to create an experience. A databank of acquired knowledge isn't quite the same thing. The databank would contain facts, but experience is based on not only facts but also conclusions that current technology is unable to duplicate.

Defining the Limits of Data Acquisition

If you get the feeling that everyone is acquiring your data without thought or reason, you're right. In fact, organizations collect, categorize, and store everyone's data — seemingly without goal or intent. According to "Data Never Sleeps" at

Domo.com, the world is collecting data at an extraordinary rate every minute. Here are just some examples:

>> Zoom hosts 208,333 participants in meetings.

>> Users post 347,222 Instagram stories.

>> Microsoft Teams connects 52,083 users.

>> Users share 41,666,667 messages on WhatsApp.

>> People make 1,388,889 video/voice calls.

Data acquisition has become a narcotic for organizations worldwide, and some think that the organization that collects the most somehow wins a prize. However, data acquisition, in and of itself, accomplishes nothing. The book *The Hitchhiker's Guide to the Galaxy*, by Douglas Adams, illustrates this problem clearly. In this book, a race of supercreatures builds an immense computer to calculate the meaning of "life, the universe, and everything." The answer of 42 doesn't really solve anything, so some of the creatures complain that the collection, categorization, and analysis of all the data used for the answer hasn't produced a usable result. The computer — a sentient one, no less — tells the people receiving the answer that the answer is indeed correct, but they need to know the question in order for the answer to make sense. Data acquisition can occur in unlimited amounts, but figuring out the right questions to ask can be daunting, if not impossible.

REMEMBER

The main problem that any organization needs to address with regard to data acquisition is which questions to ask and why the questions are important. Tailoring data acquisition to answer the questions you need answered matters. For example, if you're running a shop in town, you might need questions like this answered:

>> How many people walk in front of the store each day?

>> How many of those people stop to look in the window?

>> How long do they look?

>> What time of day are they looking?

>> Do certain displays tend to produce better results?

>> Which of these displays actually cause people to come into the store and shop?

The list could go on, but the idea is that creating a list of questions that address specific business needs is essential. After you create a list, you must verify that each of the questions is actually important — that is, addresses a need — and then ascertain what sorts of information you need to answer the question.

WARNING

Of course, trying to collect all this data by hand would be impossible, which is where automation comes into play. Seemingly, automation would produce reliable, repeatable, and consistent data input. However, many factors in automating data acquisition can produce data that isn't particularly useful. For example, consider these issues:

>> Sensors can collect only the data that they're designed to collect, so you might miss data when the sensors used aren't designed for the purpose.

>> People create errant data in various ways (see the "Considering the Five Mistruths in Data" section, earlier in this chapter, for details), which means that data you receive might be false.

>> Data can become skewed when the conditions for collecting it are incorrectly defined.

>> Interpreting data incorrectly means that the results will also be incorrect.

>> Converting a real-world question into an algorithm that the computer can understand is an error-prone process.

Many other issues (enough to fill a book) need to be considered. When you combine poorly collected, ill-formed data with algorithms that don't actually answer your questions, you get output that may actually lead your business in the wrong direction, which is why AI is often blamed for inconsistent or unreliable results. Asking the right question, obtaining the correct data, performing the right processing, and then correctly analyzing the data are all required to make data acquisition the kind of tool you can rely on.

Considering Data Security Issues

This section discusses data security from the perspective of protecting data integrity, rather than keeping someone from stealing it or guarding privacy. Securing data doesn't mean placing it in a vault — assuming that doing so is even possible with data today. Data is useful only when it's accessible. Of course, the need to make data accessible means taking a risk that someone will do something you don't want done with the data. The following sections discuss a few data security issues you need to consider.

Understanding purposefully biased data

Bias appears in nearly every dataset available today, even custom-created datasets. The dataset is often biased because the collection methods are biased, the analysis methods are biased, and the data itself is biased. You often see articles online with titles like "8 Types Of Bias In Data Analysis and How to Avoid Them," which means that people recognize the existence of bias and want to mitigate it as much as possible. However, sometimes you find that the opposite is true; the people using the dataset purposely bias it in some manner. Here are some areas in which data becomes purposely biased:

» **Political:** Political maneuvering can become the source of data bias. Two groups with opposing opinions will use the same dataset and obtain two completely different outcomes that support their particular perspective. At issue are the records selected and the dataset features used to create an outcome. In other cases, a group will resort to techniques like using bogus respondents in polls (see "Assessing the Risks to Online Polls From Bogus Respondents" from Pew Research.org for details).

» **Medical:** When medical groups advertise for people to participate in trials of medications, procedures, and other needs, the group they get often doesn't represent the population as a whole, so the data is biased. For example, the article "Older Adults, Minorities Underrepresented in COVID-19 Vaccine Trials" at AARP.com points out that the vaccine trials didn't contain enough minorities and older adults, leading to data bias.

» **Legal:** The use of COMPAS to predict the potential for recidivism is another example of data and algorithm bias, as explained in "Injustice Ex Machina: Predictive Algorithms in Criminal Sentencing," at UCLA Law Review.org. The article points out so many flaws with COMPAS that the best idea might be to start from scratch, because the software is destroying people's lives at an unprecedented rate.

» **Hiring:** The use of datasets and well-rounded algorithms supposedly reduces the risk of bias in hiring and promoting individuals within an organization. According to "All the Ways Hiring Algorithms Can Introduce Bias" at Harvard Business Review.org, the opposite is too often true. The datasets become an amplification of biased hiring practices within an organization or within society as a whole.

» **Other:** Any time a dataset and its associated algorithms become influenced by bias, the outcome is less than ideal. The term *machine learning fairness* presents the idea that the outcome of any analysis should correctly represent the actual conditions within society (see "A Tutorial on Fairness in Machine Learning" at Towards Data Science.comfor details). If the outcome of an analysis doesn't match the result received afterward, the analysis is flawed and the data usually receives a lion's share of the blame.

Dealing with data-source corruption

Even if people don't cherry pick data or use data sources that fail to reflect the actual conditions in the world, as described in the previous section, data sources can become corrupt. For example, when seeing product reviews on a website, you can't be certain that

>> Real people created reviews.

>> Some people haven't voted more than once.

>> The person wasn't simply having an exceptionally bad (or less likely, good) day.

>> The reviews reflect a fair segment of society.

In fact, the reviews are likely so biased and corrupt that believing them at all becomes nearly impossible. Unfortunately, data-source corruption comes from many other sources:

>> A sensor might be bad, producing erroneous results.

>> A virus attack might cause data errors.

>> The database or other software contains a flaw.

>> Humans enter the data incorrectly into the database.

>> Acts of nature, such as lightning, cause momentary glitches in data collection.

You can rely on a number of approaches to deal with all sorts of data corruption. Storing data in the cloud tends to reduce problems associated with hardware, weather, or other issues that cause data loss. Ensuring that you have procedures and training in place, plus constant monitoring, can help reduce human errors. Active administrator participation and use of firewalls can reduce other sorts of data-source corruption.

REMEMBER

All these measures reflect what you can do locally. When performing screen scraping and other techniques to obtain data from online sources, data scientists must employ other measures to ensure that the data remains pure. Vouching for an online source isn't possible unless the source is vetted each time it's used.

Cancelling botnets with sinkholing

Botnets are coordinated groups of computers that focus on performing specific tasks, most of them nefarious. This short section focuses on botnets that feed a dataset erroneous data or take over accounts to modify the account information in certain ways. Whatever means is used, whatever the intent, botnets generally corrupt or bias data in ways that cause any kind of analysis to fail. One of the best methods for dealing with these botnets is to sinkhole them — that is, redirect them to a location where they can't do any harm. The *Wired* article "Hacker Lexicon: What Is Sinkholing?" provides techniques for performing this task.

Chapter **3**

Considering the Use of Algorithms

ata is a game changer in AI. Advances in AI hint that for some problems, choosing the right amount of data is more important than the right algorithm. For instance, in 2001, two researchers from Microsoft, Banko and Brill, in their memorable paper, "Scaling to Very Very Large Corpora for Natural Language Disambiguation," demonstrated that if you want a computer to create a model of a language, you don't need the smartest algorithm in town. After throwing more than one billion words within context at the problem, any algorithms will start performing incredibly well. This chapter helps you understand the relationship between algorithms and the data used to make them perform useful work.

However, no matter how much data you have, you still need an algorithm to make it useful. In addition, you must perform *data analysis* (a series of definable steps), to make data work correctly with the chosen algorithms. You don't get to take any shortcuts. Even though AI is intelligent automation, sometimes automation must take a back seat to analysis. Machines that learn by themselves are in the distant future. You won't find machines that know what's appropriate and can completely cut any human intervention today. The second half of this chapter helps you understand the role of expert systems, machine learning, deep learning, and applications such as AlphaGo in bringing future possibilities a little closer to reality.

Understanding the Role of Algorithms

An *algorithm* is a procedure that consists of a sequence of operations. Usually, a computer deals with these operations by either finding the correct solution to a problem in a finite time or telling you that no solution exists. Even though people have solved algorithms manually for literally thousands of years, doing so can consume huge amounts of time and require many numeric computations, depending on the complexity of the problem you want to solve. Algorithms are all about finding solutions, and the speedier and easier, the better. Algorithms have become hard-coded in the intelligence of humans who devised them, and any machine operating on algorithms cannot but reflect the intelligence embedded into such algorithmic procedures. AI provides the means to simulate the human in processing and solving existing algorithms, but AI can't replace humans or mimic human creativity in devising new algorithms.

People tend to recognize AI when a tool presents a novel approach and interacts with the user in a human-like way. Examples include digital assistants such as Siri, Alexa, Cortana, and Google Assistant. However, certain other common tools, such as GPS routers and specialized planners (like those used to avoid automotive collisions, auto-pilot airplanes, and arrange production plans) don't even look like AI because they're too common and taken for granted as they act behind the scenes. In addition, it's important to consider alternative forms of AI, such as smart thermostats that control the environment based on past usage and current environmental data, and smart garage door openers that automatically detect when you accidentally leave the door open after you leave for work.

This is clearly the *AI effect*, as named and described by Pamela McCorduck, an American author who wrote a notable history of AI, *Machines Who Think*, in 1979. (The version at Amazon.com is an updated version.) The AI effect states that people soon forget about successful, intelligent computer programs, which become silent actors while attention shifts to AI problems that still require resolution. The importance of classic algorithms to AI gets overlooked, and people start fantasizing about AI created from esoteric technology, or they equate it with recent advances, such as machine learning and deep learning.

Understanding what algorithm means

An algorithm always presents a series of steps, but it doesn't necessarily perform all these steps to solve a problem (some steps are optional or performed only under specific conditions). A group of related steps is an *operation*, such as the making tea operation being composed of these steps:

1. Pour water in the teapot.

2. Turn on the fire to heat the water in the teapot.

3. When water is heated, pour it in cup.

4. Place a teabag in the cup and steep the tea for the recommended time.

5. Remove teabag.

6. (Optional) Add sugar to tea.

7. (Optional) Add milk to tea.

8. Drink tea.

9. (Optional) Toss tea in sink when undrinkable. Watch sink melt.

The scope of algorithms is incredibly large. Operations may involve storing data, exploring it, and ordering or arranging it into data structures. You can find algorithms that solve problems in science, medicine, finance, industrial production and supply, and communication.

All algorithms contain sequences of operations to find the correct solution to a problem in a reasonable time (or report back if no solution is found). A subclass of algorithms, *heuristics*, produce good, but not necessarily perfect, solutions when time is more critical than finding the perfect solution. AI algorithms distinguish themselves from generic algorithms by solving problems whose resolution is considered typically (or even exclusively) the product of human intelligent behavior. AI algorithms tend to deal with complex problems, which are often part of the *NP-complete* class of problems (where NP is nondeterministic polynomial time) that humans routinely deal with by using a mix of rational approach and intuition. Here are just a few examples:

>> Scheduling problems and allocating scarce resources

>> Searching routes in complex physical or figurative spaces

>> Recognizing patterns in image vision (versus something like image restoration or image processing) or sound perception

>> Processing language (both text understanding and language translation)

>> Playing (and winning) competitive games

TIP

NP-complete problems distinguish themselves from other algorithmic problems because finding a solution for them in a reasonable time frame isn't yet possible. NP-complete isn't the kind of problem that you solve by trying all possible combinations or possibilities. Even if you had computers more powerful than those that exist today, a search for the solution would last almost forever. In a similar fashion, in AI, this kind of problem is called *AI-complete*.

Planning and branching: Trees and nodes

Planning helps you determine the sequence of actions to perform to achieve a certain goal. Deciding on the plan is a classic AI problem, and you find examples of planning in industrial production, resource allocation, and moving a robot inside a room. Starting from the present state, an AI determines all the possible actions from that state first. Technically, it *expands* the current state into a number of future states. Then it expands all the future states into their own future states, and so on. When you can't expand the states anymore and the AI stops the expansion, the AI has created a *state space*, which is composed of whatever could happen in the future. An AI can take advantage of a state space not just as a possible prediction (actually, it predicts everything, though some future states are more likely than others) but also because AI can use that state space to explore decisions it can make to reach its goal in the best way. This process is known as the *state-space search*.

Working with a state space requires use of both particular data structures and algorithms. The core data structures commonly used are trees and graphs. The favored algorithms used to efficiently explore graphs include breadth-first search or depth-first search.

Building a tree works in much the same way that a tree grows in the physical world. Each item you add to the tree is a *node*. Nodes connect to each other using links. The combination of nodes and links forms a structure that looks like a tree, as shown in Figure 3-1.

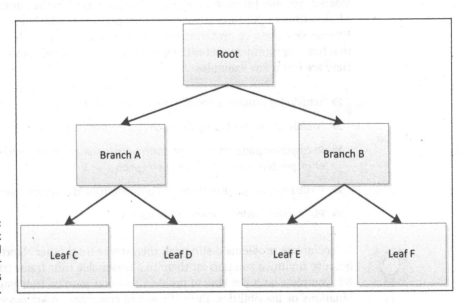

FIGURE 3-1:
A tree may look like its physical alternative or have its roots pointing upward.

Trees have one root node, just like a physical tree. The *root node* is the starting point for the processing you perform. Connected to the root are either branches or leaves. A *leaf node* is an ending point for the tree. *Branch nodes* support either other branches or leaves. The type of tree shown in Figure 3-1 is a binary tree because each node has, at most, two connections (but trees representing state spaces can have multiple branches).

In looking at the tree, Branch B is the *child* of the Root node. That's because the Root node appears first in the tree. Leaf E and Leaf F are both children of Branch B, making Branch B the *parent* of Leaf E and Leaf F. The relationship between nodes is important because discussions about trees often consider the child/parent relationship between nodes. Without these terms, discussions of trees could become quite confusing.

Extending the tree using graph nodes

A *graph* is a sort of a tree extension. As with trees, you have nodes that connect to each other to create relationships. However, unlike binary trees, a graph node can have more than one or two connections. In fact, graph nodes often have a multitude of connections, and, most important, nodes can connect in any direction, not just from parent to child. To keep things simple, though, consider the graph shown in Figure 3-2.

Graphs are structures that present a number of nodes (or vertexes) connected by a number of edges or arcs (depending on the representation). When you think about a graph, think about a structure like a map, where each location on the map is a node and the streets are the edges. This presentation differs from a tree, where each path ends up in a leaf node. Refer to Figure 3-2 to see a graph represented. Graphs are particularly useful when figuring out states that represent a sort of physical space. For instance, the GPS uses a graph to represent places and streets.

Graphs also add a few new twists that you might not have considered. For example, a graph can include the concept of directionality. Unlike a tree, which has parent/child relationships, a graph node can connect to any other node with a specific direction in mind. Think about streets in a city. Most streets are bidirectional, but some are one-way streets that allow movement in only one direction.

The presentation of a graph connection might not actually reflect the realities of the graph. A graph can designate a *weight* to a particular connection. The weight could define the distance between two points, define the time required to traverse the route, specify the amount of fuel used to travel the route, or provide other sorts of information.

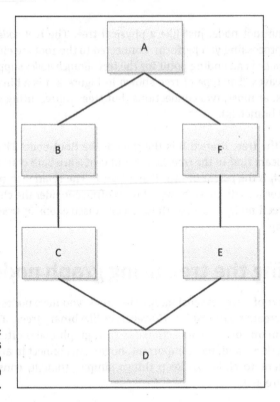

FIGURE 3-2:
Graph nodes
can connect to
each other in
myriad ways.

TIP

A tree is nothing more than a graph in which any two vertices are connected by exactly one path, and the tree doesn't allow cycles (to be able to get back to the parent from any child). Many graph algorithms apply only to trees.

Traversing the graph

Traversing a graph means to search (visit) each vertex (node) in a specific order. The process of visiting a vertex can include both reading and updating it. You discover unvisited vertexes as you traverse a graph. The vertex becomes discovered (because you just visited it) or processed (because the algorithm tried all the edges departing from it) after the search. The order of the search determines the kind of search performed:

>> **Uninformed (blind search):** The AI explores the state space without additional information except for the graph structure that it discovers as it traverses it. Here are two common blind-search algorithms, which are discussed in the sections that follow:

- **Breadth-first search (BFS):** Begins at the graph root and explores every node that attaches to the root. It then searches the next level, exploring each level in turn until it reaches the end. Consequently, in the example graph, the search explores from A to B and C before it moves on to explore D. BFS explores the graph in a systematic way, exploring vertexes around the starting vertex in a circular fashion. It begins by visiting all the vertexes that are a single step from the starting vertex; it then moves two steps out, then three steps out, and so on.

- **Depth-first search (DFS):** Begins at the graph root and then explores every node from that root down a single path to the end. It then backtracks and begins exploring the paths not taken in the current search path until it reaches the root again. At that point, if other paths to take from the root are available, the algorithm chooses one and begins the same search again. The idea is to explore each path completely before exploring any other path.

» **Informed (heuristic):** A heuristic finds or discovers the best method of traversing the graph based on rules of thumb (such as expert systems) or algorithms that use low-order polynomial time. It's an educated guess about a solution that points to the direction of a desired outcome but can't tell exactly how to reach it. It's like being lost in an unknown city and having people tell you a certain way to reach your hotel (but without precise instructions). Because this search is informed (even though it isn't precise), it can also estimate the remaining *cost* (time, resources, or other value that determines which route is better in a particular instance) to go from a particular state to a solution. Here are three common heuristic search algorithms (see the "Using local search and heuristics" section of this chapter and Chapter 10 for more details):

- **Best-first search:** An evaluation function assists in the search by determining the desirability of expanding a particular node based on the costs of the nodes that follow. The costs of each node are stored in a queue or other memory structure. Except for the foreknowledge of node cost, this solution works much like a BFS or DFS.

- **Greedy search:** Like a best-first search, the path to follow is informed by node costs. However, the greedy search looks only one node ahead, which saves processing time in the evaluation function, but doesn't always guarantee an optimal solution.

- **A* search:** An expansion of the best-first search which actually uses two costs: the cost to move from the starting point to another given position in the graph and the cost to move from that given node on the graph to the final destination.

Playing adversarial games

The interesting thing about state-space search is that it represents both AI's current functionality and future opportunities. This is the case with *adversarial games* (games in which one wins and the others lose) or with any similar situation in which players pursue an objective that conflicts with the goals of others. A simple game like tic-tac-toe presents a perfect example of a space search game that you may already have seen an AI play. In the 1983 film *WarGames*, the supercomputer WOPR (War Operation Plan Response) plays against itself at a blazing speed, yet it cannot win because the game is indeed simple, and if you use a state-space search, you won't ever lose.

You have nine cells to fill with X's and O's for each player. The first one to place three marks in a row (horizontal, vertical, or diagonal) wins. When building a state-space tree for the game, each level of the tree represents a game turn. The end nodes represent the final board state and determine a victory, draw, or defeat for the AI. Every terminal node has a higher score for winning, lower for drawing, and even lower or negative for losing. The AI propagates the scores to the upper nodes and branches using summation until reaching the starting node. The starting node represents the actual situation. Using a simple strategy enables you to traverse the tree: When it's AI's turn and you have to propagate the values of many nodes, you sum the maximum value (presumably because AI has to get the maximum result from the game); when it's the adversary's turn, you sum the minimum value instead. In the end, you get a tree whose branches are qualified by scores. When it's the AI's turn, it chooses its move based on the branch whose value is the highest because it implies expanding nodes with the highest possibility to win. Figure 3-3 shows a visual example of this strategy.

This approach is called the min-max approximation. Ronald Rivest, from the computer science laboratory at MIT, introduced it in 1987 (you can read his paper at https://people.csail.mit.edu/rivest/pubs/Riv87c.pdf). Since then, this algorithm and its variants have powered many competitive games, along with recent game-playing advances, such as AlphaGo from Google DeepMind, which uses an approach that echoes the min-max approximation (which is also found in the *WarGames* film of 1983).

TIP

Sometimes you hear about alpha-beta pruning as connected to min-max approximation. *Alpha-beta pruning* is a smart way to propagate values up the tree hierarchy in complex state spaces limiting computations. Not all games feature compact state-space trees; when your branches are in the number of millions, you need to prune them and shorten your calculations.

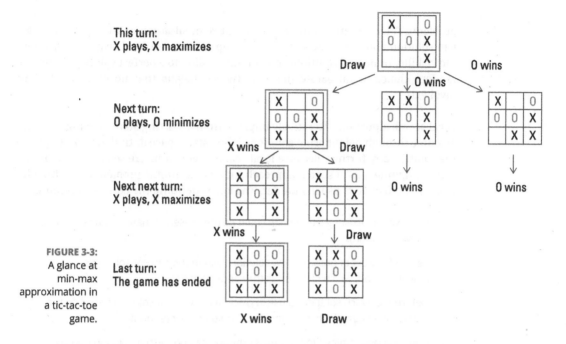

This turn:
X plays, X maximizes

Next turn:
O plays, O minimizes

Next next turn:
X plays, X maximizes

FIGURE 3-3:
A glance at
min-max
approximation in
a tic-tac-toe
game.

Last turn:
The game has ended

Draw

O wins

O wins

X wins

Draw

O wins

O wins

X wins

Draw

X wins

Draw

Using local search and heuristics

A lot goes on behind the state-space search approach. In the end, no machine, no matter how powerful, can enumerate all the possibilities that spring from a complex situation. This section continues with games because they're predictable and have fixed rules, whereas many real-world situations are unpredictable and lack clear rules, making games an optimistic and favorable setting.

Checkers, a relatively simple game compared to chess or Go, has 500 billion billion (500,000,000,000,000,000,000) possible board positions, a number which, according to computations by the mathematicians at Hawaii University, equates to all the grains of sand on Earth. It's true that fewer moves are possible as a game of checkers progresses. Yet the number to potentially evaluate at each move is too high. It took 18 years using powerful computers (see "Checkers Solved" at ScienceNetLinks.com) to compute all 500 billion billion possible moves. Just imagine how long it could take on a consumer's computer to work out even a smaller subset of moves. To be manageable, it should be a very small subset of all the potential moves.

Optimization using local search and heuristics helps by using constraints to limit the beginning number of possible evaluations (as in alpha pruning, where some computations are left out because they don't add anything to the search success). *Local search* is a general problem-solving approach that comprises a large range of algorithms that help you escape the exponential complexities of many NP problems. A local search starts from your present situation or an imperfect problem solution and moves away from it, a step at a time. A local search determines the viability of nearby solutions, potentially leading to a perfect solution, based on random choice or an astute heuristic (which means that no exact method is involved).

Local search algorithms iteratively improve from a starting state, moving one step at a time through neighboring solutions in the state space until they can't improve the solution any further. Because local search algorithms are so simple and intuitive, designing a local search approach for an algorithmic problem isn't difficult; making it effective is usually harder. The key is defining the correct procedure:

1. Start with an existing situation (it could be the present situation or a random or known solution).

2. Search for a set of possible new solutions within the current solution's neighborhood, which constitutes the candidates' list.

3. Determine which solution to use in place of the current solution based on the output of a heuristic that accepts the candidates' list as input.

4. Continue performing Steps 2 and 3 until you see no further solution improvement, which means that you have the best solution available.

Although easy to design, local search solutions may not find a solution in a reasonable time (you can stop the process and use the current solution) or produce a minimum-quality solution. You have no guarantee that a local search will arrive at a problem solution, but your chances do improve from the starting point when you provide enough time for the search to run its computations. It stops only after it can't find any further way to improve the solution. The secret is to determine the right neighborhood to explore. If you explore everything, you'll fall back to an exhaustive search, which implies an explosion of possibilities to explore and test.

Relying on a heuristic limits where you look based on a rule of thumb. Sometimes a heuristic is randomness, and such a solution, in spite of being a nonintelligent approach, can work fine. Few people, for instance, know that Roomba, the autonomous robotic vacuum cleaner created by three MIT graduates (see an example, iRobot Roomba, at Amazon.com), initially didn't plan its cleaning path but simply roamed around randomly. Yet it was considered a smart device by its owners and did an excellent cleaning job. (Intelligence is actually in the idea of using randomness to solve a problem that is otherwise too complex.)

Random choice isn't the only heuristic available. A local search can rely on more reasoned exploration solutions using well-devised heuristics to get directions:

>> **Hill climbing:** Relies on the observation that as a ball rolls down a valley, it takes the steepest descent. When it climbs a hill, a ball tends to take the most direct upward direction to reach the top, which is the one with the greatest inclination. The AI problem, therefore, is seen as a descent to a valley or an ascent to a mountaintop, and the heuristic is any rule that hints at the best downhill or uphill approach among the possible states of the state space. It's an effective algorithm, though sometimes it gets stuck in situations known as plateaus (intermediate valleys) and peaks (local maximum points).

>> **Twiddle (coordinate descent algorithms):** Similar to hill-climbing algorithms, but it explores all possible directions. It concentrates the search in the direction of the neighborhood that works best. As it does so, it calibrates its step, slowing down as it finds the discovery of better solutions difficult, until it reaches a stop.

>> **Simulated annealing:** Takes its name from a metallurgical technique that heats metal and then slowly cools it to soften the metal for cold working and to remove crystalline defects (see "Heat Treatment of Steels & Metals" at Bright Hub Engineering.com for details). Local search replicates this technique by viewing the solution search as an atomic structure that changes to improve its workability. The temperature is the game changer in the optimization process. Just as high temperatures make the structure of a material relax (solids melt and liquids evaporate at high temperatures), so high temperatures in a local search algorithm induce relaxation of the objective function, allowing it to prefer worse solutions to better ones. Simulated annealing modifies the hill-climbing procedure, keeping the objective function for neighbor solution evaluation, but allowing it to determine the search solution choice in a different way.

>> **Taboo search:** Uses memorization to remember which parts of the neighborhood to explore. When it seems to have found a solution, it tends to try to retrace to other possible paths that it didn't try in order to ascertain the best solution.

Using measures of direction (upward, downward) or temperature (controlled randomness), or simply restricting or retracing part of the search are all ways to effectively avoid trying everything and concentrating on a good solution. Consider, for instance, a robot walking. Guiding a robot in an unknown environment means avoiding obstacles to reach a specific target. It's both a fundamental and challenging task in artificial intelligence. Robots can rely on laser rangefinder (lidar) or sonar (which involves devices that use sound to see their environment) to navigate their surroundings. Yet, no matter the level of hardware sophistication, robots still need proper algorithms to

>> Find the shortest path to a destination (or at least a reasonably short one)

>> Avoid obstacles on the way

>> Perform custom behaviors such as minimizing turning or braking

A pathfinding algorithm helps a robot start in one location and reach a goal by using the shortest path between the two, anticipating and avoiding obstacles along the way. (Reacting after hitting a wall isn't sufficient.) Pathfinding is also useful when moving any other device to a target in space, even a virtual one, such as in a video game or web pages. When using pathfinding with a robot, the robot perceives movement as a flow of state spaces to the borders of its sensors. If the goal is not within range, the robot won't know where to go. Heuristics can point it in the right direction (for instance, it can know that the target is in the north direction) and help it to avoid obstacles in a timely fashion without having to determine all possible ways for doing so.

Discovering the Learning Machine

All the algorithmic examples so far are associated with AI because they're smart solutions that solve repetitive and well delimited, yet complex, problems requiring intelligence. They require an architect who studies the problem and chooses the right algorithm to solve it. Problem changes, mutations, or unusual characteristic displays can become a real problem for a successful execution of the algorithm. This is because learning the problem and its solution occur once when you train the algorithm. For instance, you can safely program an AI to solve Sudoku (a game in which you place numbers in a board according to certain rules, as explained at Learn-Sudoku.com). You can even provide flexibility that allows the algorithm to accept more rules or larger boards later. Peter Norvig, the director of research at Google, has written an interesting essay on this topic (http://norvig.com/sudoku.html) that demonstrates how wise use of DFS, limiting the number of computations (otherwise the computations may take practically forever), using constraints, and exploring smaller branches first can make Sudoku solutions possible.

Unfortunately, not all problems can rely on a Sudoku-like solution. Real-life problems are never set in simple worlds of perfect information and well-defined action. Consider the problem of finding a fraudster cheating on insurance claims, or the problem of diagnosing a medical disease. You have to contend with the following:

>> **A large set of rules and possibilities:** The number of possible frauds is incredibly high; many diseases have similar symptoms.

>> **Missing information:** Fraudsters can conceal information; doctors often rely on incomplete information (examinations may be missing).

>> **Problem rules aren't immutable:** Fraudsters discover new ways to arrange swindles or frauds; new diseases arise or are discovered.

To solve such problems, you can't use a predetermined approach, but rather need a flexible approach and must accumulate useful knowledge to face any new challenge. In other words, you continue learning, as humans do throughout their lives to cope with a changing and challenging environment.

Leveraging expert systems

Expert systems, a system of using rules to make decisions, were the first attempt to escape the realm of hard-coded algorithms and create more flexible and smart ways to solve real-life problems. The idea at the core of expert systems was simple and well suited at a time when storing and dealing with lots of data in computer memory was still costly. It may sound strange today, but in the 1970s, AI scientists such as Ross Quillian had to demonstrate how to build working language models based on a vocabulary of only 20 words, because computer memory of the time could hold only that much. Few options were available if a computer couldn't hold all the data, and a solution was to deal with key problem information and obtain it from humans who knew it best.

REMEMBER

Expert systems were experts not because they based their knowledge on their own learning process, but rather because they collected it from human experts who provided a predigested system of key information taken from studying books, learning from other experts, or discovering it by themselves. It was basically a smart way to externalize knowledge into a machine.

MYCIN: A beginning expert system

An example of one of the first systems of this kind is MYCIN, a system to diagnose blood-clotting diseases or infections caused by bacteria, such as bacteremia (when bacteria infect the blood) and meningitis (inflammation of the membranes that protect the brain and spinal cord). MYCIN recommended the right dosage of antibiotics by using well over 500 rules, and it relied, when needed, on the doctor using the system. When there wasn't enough information — for instance, lab tests were missing — MYCIN then started a consultative dialogue by asking relevant questions to reach a confident diagnosis and therapy.

Written in Lisp as a doctoral dissertation by Edward Shortliffe at Stanford University, MYCIN took more than five years to complete, and it performed better than any junior doctor, reaching the elevated diagnosis accuracy of an experienced doctor. It came from the same laboratory that devised DENDRAL, the first expert system ever created, a few years before. DENDRAL, which specializes in organic chemistry, is a challenging application in which brute-force algorithms proved unfeasible when faced with human-based heuristics that rely on field experience.

As for MYCIN's success, some issues arose. First, the terms of responsibility were unclear. (If the system were to provide a wrong diagnosis, who took responsibility?) Second, MYCIN had a usability issue because the doctor had to connect to MYCIN by using a remote terminal to the mainframe in Stanford, something quite difficult and slow at a time when the Internet was still at its infancy. MYCIN still proved its efficacy and usefulness in supporting human decisions, and it paved the way for many other expert systems that proliferated later in the 1970s and 1980s.

The components of expert systems

Generally, expert systems of the time were made of two distinct components: knowledge base and inference engine. The *knowledge base* retains knowledge as a collection of rules in the form of if-then statements (with *if* involving one or multiple conditions and *then* involving conclusion statements). These statements occurred in a symbolic form, differentiating between instances, (single events or facts), classes, and subclasses, which could all be manipulated using Boolean logic or sophisticated first-order logic, which comprises more possible operations.

TIP

First-order logic is a set of operations that goes beyond simply being bound to combine TRUE and FALSE assertions. For instance, it introduces concepts such as FOR ALL or THERE EXIST, allowing you to deal with statements that may be true but cannot be proved by the evidence you have at hand at that moment. You can read and discover more about this form of logic starting from this article at TechTarget.com, "First-order logic" (requires registration) or another one of the same title at Wikipedia.org (possibly less accurate and complete).

The *inference engine* is a set of instructions that tell the system how to manipulate the conditions based on Boolean logic set of operators such as AND, OR, NOT. Using this logic set, TRUE or FALSE symbolic conditions could combine into complex reasoning. (When TRUE, a rule is triggered or, technically, "fired"; when FALSE, the rule doesn't apply.)

Because the system was made at the core of a series of ifs (conditions) and thens (conclusions), and was nested and structured in layers, acquiring initial information helped rule out some conclusions while also helping the system interact with the user concerning information that could lead to an answer. When dealing with the inference engine, common operations by the expert systems were as follows:

>> **Forward chaining:** Available evidence triggered a series of rules and excluded others at each stage. The system initially concentrated on rules that could trigger an end conclusion by firing. This approach is clearly data driven.

>> **Backward chaining:** The system evaluates every possible conclusion and tries to prove each of them on the basis of the evidence available. This goal-driven approach helps determine which questions to pose and excludes entire sets of goals. MYCIN, described previously, used backward chaining; progressing from hypothesis backward to evidence is a common strategy in medical diagnosis.

>> **Conflict resolution:** If a system reaches more than one conclusion at the same time, the system favors the conclusion that has certain characteristics (in terms of impact, risk, or other factors). Sometimes the system consults the user and the resolution is realized based on user evaluations. For instance, MYCIN used a certainty factor that estimated the probability of diagnosis exactness.

One great advantage of such systems was to represent knowledge in a human-readable form, rendering the decision-making process transparent. If the system reaches a conclusion, it returns the rules used to reach that conclusion. The user can systematically review the work of the system and agree or review it for signs of input error. Moreover, expert systems were easy to program using languages such as Lisp, Prolog, or ALGOL. Users improved expert systems over time by adding new rules or updating existing rules. They could even be made to work through uncertain conditions by applying *fuzzy logic*, a kind of multivalued logic in which a value can contain anything between 0, or absolutely false, and 1, or absolutely true (see "Artificial Intelligence — Fuzzy Logic Systems" at TutorialsPoint.com for additional details). Fuzzy logic avoids the abrupt steps of triggering a rule based on a threshold. For instance, if a rule is set to trigger when the room is hot, the rule is not triggered at an exact temperature but rather when the temperature is around that threshold.

Expert systems witnessed their twilight at the end of the 1980s, and their development stopped, mostly for the following reasons:

>> The logic and symbolism of such systems proved limited in expressing the rules behind a decision, leading to the creation of custom systems, that is, falling back again on hard-coding rules with classical algorithms.

>> For many challenging problems, expert systems became so complex and intricate that they lost their appeal in terms of feasibility and economic cost.

>> Because data was becoming more diffuse and available, it made little sense to struggle to carefully interview, gather, and distill rare expert knowledge when the same (or even better) knowledge could be sifted from data.

Expert systems still exist. You can find them used in credit scoring, fraud detection, and other fields with the imperative to not just provide an answer but also clearly and transparently state the rules behind the decision in a way that the system user deems acceptable (as a subject expert would do). In addition, they're used in situations for which other forms of AI are too slow, such as some self-driving car applications (see "Expert Systems and AI Self-Driving Cars: Crucial Innovative Techniques" at aitrends.com for details).

Introducing machine learning

Solutions capable of learning directly from data without any predigestion to render it as symbols arose a few decades before expert systems. Some were statistical in nature; others imitated nature in different ways; and still others tried to generate autonomously symbolic logic in the form of rules from raw information. All these solutions derived from different schools and appeared under different names that today comprise *machine learning*. Machine learning is part of the world of algorithms, although, contrary to the many algorithms discussed so far, it's not intended as a series of predefined steps apt to solve a problem. As a rule, machine learning deals with problems that humans don't know how to detail into steps, but that humans naturally solve. An example of such a problem is recognizing faces in images or certain words in a spoken discussion. Machine learning is mentioned in almost every chapter of this book, but Chapters 9 to 11 are devoted to disclosing how major machine learning algorithms work, especially deep learning, which is the technology powering the new wave of AI applications that reaches the news headlines almost every day.

Touching new heights

The role of machine learning in the new wave of AI algorithms is to in part replace, in part supplement, existing algorithms. Machine learning works with activities that require intelligence from a human point of view but that aren't easy to formalize as a precise sequence of steps. A clear example of this role is the mastery displayed by a Go expert that, at a glance, understands the threats and opportunities of a board configuration and intuitively grasps the right moves. (Read the history of Go at https://www.usgo.org/brief-history-go.)

Go is an incredibly complex game for an AI. Chess has an average of 35 possible moves to evaluate in a board, and a game usually spans more than 80 moves, while a game of Go has about 140 moves to evaluate, and a game usually spans more than 240 moves. No computational power presently exists in the world to create a complete state space for a game of Go. Google's DeepMind team in London developed AlphaGo, a program that has defeated a number of top-ranked Go players (see `https://deepmind.com/research/alphago/` and `https://www.kdnuggets.com/2020/05/deepmind-gaming-ai-dominance.html`). The program doesn't rely on an algorithmic approach based on searching an immense state space, but instead uses the following:

>> A smart-search method based on random tests of a possible move. The AI applies a DFS multiple times to determine whether the first outcome found is a positive or negative one (an incomplete and partial state space).

>> A deep-learning algorithm processes an image of the board (at a glance) and derives both the best possible move in that situation (the algorithm is called the *policy network*) and an estimate of how likely the AI is to win the game using that move (the algorithm is called the *value network*).

>> A capability to learn by seeing past games by Go experts and by playing against itself. One version of the program, called AlphaGo Zero, can learn all by itself, without any human examples (see `https://deepmind.com/blog/alphago-zero-learning-scratch/`). This learning capability is called *reinforcement learning*.

Chapter **4**

Pioneering Specialized Hardware

In Chapter 1, you discover that one of the reasons for the failure of early AI efforts was a lack of suitable hardware. The hardware just couldn't perform tasks quickly enough for even mundane needs, much less something as complex as simulating human thought. This issue is described at some length in the movie *The Imitation Game* (see the description at Amazon.com), in which Alan Turing finally cracked the Enigma code by cleverly looking for a particular phrase, "Heil Hitler," in each message. Without that particular flaw in the way that operators used the Enigma, the computer equipment that Turing used would never have worked fast enough to solve the problem (and the movie had no small amount of griping about the matter). If anything, the historical account — what little of it is fully declassified — shows that Turing's problems were more profound than the movie expressed (see "Cracking the Uncrackable" at ScienceABC.com for details). Fortunately, standard, off-the-shelf hardware can overcome the speed issue for many problems today, which is where this chapter begins.

REMEMBER

To truly begin to simulate human thought requires specialized hardware, and even the best specialized hardware isn't up to the task today. Almost all standard hardware relies on the *von Neumann architecture* (the von Neumann computer model is explained at c-jump.com), which separates memory from computing, creating a wonderfully generic processing environment that just doesn't work well for some kinds of algorithms because the speed of the bus between the processor and memory creates a *von Neumann bottleneck*. The second part of this chapter helps you understand the various methods used to overcome the von Neumann bottleneck so that complex, data-intensive algorithms run faster.

Even with custom hardware specially designed to speed computations, a machine designed to simulate human thought can run only as fast as its inputs and outputs will allow. Consequently, people are working to create a better environment in which the hardware can operate. This need can be addressed in a number of ways, but this chapter looks at two: enhancing the capabilities of the underlying hardware, and using specialized sensors. These changes to the hardware environment work well, but as the following material explains, it still isn't enough to build a human brain.

Ultimately, hardware is useless, even with enhancements, if the humans who rely on it can't interact with it effectively. The final sections of this chapter describe techniques for making those interactions more efficient. Of special importance now is the use of Deep Learning Processors (DLPs), which are designed specifically to work with deep learning algorithms. However, there are also more mundane approaches that are simply the result of the combination of enhanced output and clever programming. Just as Alan Turing used a trick to make his computer seemingly do more than it was able to do, these techniques make modern computers look like miracle workers. In fact, the computer understands nothing; all the credit goes to the persons who program the computer.

Relying on Standard Hardware

Most AI projects that you create will at least begin with standard hardware because modern off-the-shelf components actually provide significant processing power, especially when compared to components from the 1980s when AI first began to produce usable results. Consequently, even if you can't ultimately perform production-level work by using standard hardware, you can get far enough along with your experimental and preproduction code to create a working model that will eventually process a full dataset.

Understanding the standard hardware

The *architecture* (structure) of the standard PC hasn't changed since John von Neumann first proposed it in 1946 (see the article "John von Neumann: The Father of the Modern Computer" at https://www.maa.org/external_archive/devlin/devlin_12_03.html for details). Reviewing the history at https://lennartb.home.xs4all.nl/coreboot/col2.html shows you that the processor connects to memory and peripheral devices through a bus in PC products as early as 1981 (and long before). All these systems use the von Neumann architecture because this architecture provides significant benefits in modularity. Reading the history tells you that these devices allow upgrades to every component as individual decisions, allowing increases in *capability*. For example, within limits, you can increase the amount of memory or storage available to any PC. You can also use advanced peripherals. However, all these elements connect through a bus.

REMEMBER

That a PC becomes more capable doesn't change the facts of its essential architecture. So, the PC you use today has the same architecture as devices created long ago; they're simply more capable. In addition, the form factor of a device doesn't affect its architecture, either. The computers in your car rely on a bus system for connectivity that directly relies on the von Neumann architecture. (Even if the kind of bus is different, the architecture is the same.) Lest you think any device remains unaffected, look at the block diagram for a Blackberry at `http://mobilesaudi.blogspot.com/2011/10/all-blackberry-schematic-complete.html`. It, too, relies on a von Neumann setup. Consequently, almost every device you can conceive of today has a similar architecture, despite having different form factors, bus types, and essential capabilities.

Describing standard hardware deficiencies

The ability to create a modular system does have significant benefits, especially in business. The ability to remove and replace individual components keeps costs low while allowing incremental improvements in both speed and efficiency. However, as with most things, there is no free lunch. The modularity provided by the von Neumann architecture comes with some serious deficiencies:

>> **von Neumann bottleneck:** Of all the deficiencies, the von Neumann bottleneck is the most serious when considering the requirements of disciplines such as AI, machine learning, and even data science. You can find this particular deficiency discussed in more detail in the "Considering the von Neumann bottleneck" section, later in this chapter.

>> **Single points of failure:** Any loss of connectivity with the bus necessarily means that the computer fails immediately, rather than gracefully. Even in systems with multiple processors, the loss of a single processor, which should simply produce a loss of capability, instead inflicts complete system failure. The same problem occurs with the loss of other system components: Instead of reducing functionality, the entire system fails. Given that AI often requires continuous system operation, the potential for serious consequences escalates with the manner in which an application relies on the hardware.

>> **Single-mindedness:** The von Neumann bus can either retrieve an instruction or retrieve the data required to execute the instruction, but it can't do both. Consequently, when data retrieval requires several bus cycles, the processor remains idle, reducing its ability to perform instruction-intensive AI tasks even more.

>> **Tasking:** When the brain performs a task, a number of synapses fire at one time, allowing simultaneous execution of multiple operations. The original von Neumann design allowed just one operation at a time, and only after the system retrieved both the required instruction and data. Computers today typically have multiple cores, which allow simultaneous execution of operations in each core. However, application code must specifically address this requirement, so the functionality sometimes remains unused.

EXAMINING THE HARVARD ARCHITECTURE DIFFERENCE

You may encounter the Harvard architecture during your hardware travels because some systems employ a modified form of this architecture to speed processing. Both the von Neumann architecture and Harvard architecture rely on a bus topology. However, when working with a von Neumann architecture system, the hardware relies on a single bus and a single memory area for both instructions and data, whereas the Harvard architecture relies on individual buses for instructions and data, and can use separate physical memory areas (see the comparison in "Difference between Von Neumann and Harvard Architecture" at GeeksforGeeks.org). The use of individual buses enables a Harvard architecture system to retrieve the next instruction while waiting for data to arrive from memory for the current instruction, thereby making the Harvard architecture both faster and more efficient. However, reliability suffers because now you have two failure points for each operation: the instruction bus and the data bus.

Microcontrollers, such as those that power your microwave, often use the Harvard architecture. In addition, you might find it in some unusual places for a specific reason. The iPhone and Xbox 360 both use modified versions of the Harvard architecture that rely on a single memory area (rather than two), but still rely on separate buses. The reason for using the architecture in this case is Digital Rights Management (DRM). You can make the code area of memory read-only so that no one can modify it or create new applications without permission. From an AI perspective, this can be problematic because one of an AI's capabilities is to write new algorithms (executable code) as needed to deal with unanticipated situations. Because PCs rarely implement a Harvard architecture in its pure form or as its main bus construction, the Harvard architecture doesn't receive much attention in this book.

Relying on new computational techniques

Reading literature about how to perform tasks using AI can feel like you're seeing a marketer on TV proclaiming, "It's new! It's improved! It's downright dazzling!" So it shouldn't surprise you much that people are always coming up with ways to make the AI development experience faster, more precise, and better in other ways. The problem is that many of these new techniques are untested, so they might look great, but you have to think about them for a while.

One way around the various issues surrounding AI computational speed is to create new techniques for performing tasks. Although many data scientists rely on the Graphical Processing Unit (GPU) to speed execution of complex code, the article "The startup making deep learning possible without specialized hardware" at MIT Technology Review.com describes another approach, based on a product called Neural Magic (https://neuralmagic.com), which essentially compresses data to make a CPU more efficient. Neural Magic also keeps costs lower than using specialized hardware. (The more specialized the hardware, the higher the costs.)

WARNING

Reading the fine print with any new technology is always important, however, and this is the case with Neural Magic. The process for using the Neural Magic approach still involves training the model on hardware robust enough to perform the task, which usually means relying on GPUs. In addition, you now take the additional step of converting the model using Neural Magic to run on a standard CPU. So, the Neural Magic approach really isn't an option for someone who is experimenting. Anyone using Neural Magic already has a well-developed application and simply wants to run it on a low-cost machine. In addition, Neural Magic is currently used only for *computer vision* tasks (for which the computer relies on cameras to capture images and then interprets those images mathematically to do things like categorize objects), which is a somewhat smallish part of AI as a whole.

The advantage of using the Neural Magic approach is that an organization can buy just a few high-cost machines to perform research and create an application. It can then run the resulting application on as many low-cost systems as needed to satisfy user requirements. The big payoff is that these systems need not rely on desktop technology, but can use mobile devices as well, so the application can run anywhere. Consequently, this is a valuable approach within the limits of the technology it currently uses.

Another new approach relies on using hash tables instead of matrices to model problems. According to the "CPU algorithm trains deep neural nets up to 15 times faster than top GPU trainers" article at TechXplore.com, the Sub-Linear Deep Learning Engine (SLIDE) can train models using commodity processors rather than using GPUs. Beside using hash tables in place of matrix multiplication, using SLIDE also eliminates some of the more wasteful elements of training a model (see the KD-nuggets.com article "Deep Learning Breakthrough: a sub-linear deep learning algorithm that does not need a GPU?"). The problem with this new approach (as with many new approaches) is that it requires a complete change in how tasks are performed. Obviously, organizations won't be happy about throwing out millions of dollars in existing development to try something new. The white paper "SLIDE : In Defense of Smart Algorithms over Hardware Acceleration for Large-Scale Deep Learning Systems" at arXiv.org provides a more formal discussion of this new methodology.

CONSIDERING ALAN TURING'S BOMBE MACHINE

Alan Turing's Bombe machine wasn't any form of AI. In fact, it isn't even a real computer. It broke Enigma cryptographic messages, and that's it. However, it did provide food for thought for Turing, which eventually led to a paper entitled "Computing Machinery and Intelligence." Turing published that paper, which describes the imitation game, in the 1950s (*The Imitation Game* movie is a depiction of the events surrounding the creation of this game). However, the Bombe itself was actually based on a Polish machine called the Bomba.

Even though some sources imply that Alan Turing worked alone, the Bombe was produced with the help of many people, most especially Gordon Welchman. Turing also didn't spring from a vacuum, ready-made to break German encryption. His time at Princeton was spent with greats like Albert Einstein and John von Neumann (who would go on to invent the concept of computer software). The papers Turing wrote inspired these other scientists to experiment and see what is possible.

Specialized hardware of all sorts will continue to appear as long as scientists are writing papers, bouncing ideas off of each other, creating new ideas of their own, and experimenting. When you see movies or other media, assuming that they're historically accurate at all, don't leave with the feeling that these people just woke up one morning, proclaimed, "Today, I will be brilliant!" and went on to do something marvelous. Everything builds on something else, so history is important because it helps show the path followed and illuminates other promising paths — those not followed.

Using GPUs

After creating a prototypical setup to perform the tasks required to simulate human thought on a given topic, you may need additional hardware to provide sufficient processing power to work with the full dataset required of a production system. Many ways are available to provide such processing power, but a common way is to use Graphic Processing Units (GPUs) in addition to the central processor of a machine. The following sections describe the problem domain that a GPU addresses, what precisely the term GPU means, and why a GPU makes processing faster.

Considering the von Neumann bottleneck

The von Neumann bottleneck is a natural result of using a bus to transfer data between the processor, memory, long-term storage, and peripheral devices. No matter how fast the bus performs its task, overwhelming it — that is, forming a bottleneck that reduces speed — is always possible. Over time, processor speeds continue to increase while memory and other device improvements focus on density — the capability to store more in less space. Consequently, the bottleneck becomes more of an issue with every improvement, causing the processor to spend a lot of time being idle.

Within reason, you can overcome some of the issues that surround the von Neumann bottleneck and produce small, but noticeable, increases in application speed. Here are the most common solutions:

>> **Caching:** When problems with obtaining data from memory fast enough with the von Neumann architecture became evident, hardware vendors quickly responded by adding localized memory that didn't require bus access. This memory appears external to the processor but as part of the processor package. High-speed cache is expensive, however, so cache sizes tend to be small.

>> **Processor caching:** Unfortunately, external caches still don't provide enough speed. Even using the fastest RAM available and cutting out the bus access completely doesn't meet the processing capacity needs of the processor. Consequently, vendors started adding internal memory — a cache smaller than the external cache, but with even faster access because it's part of the processor.

>> **Prefetching:** The problem with caches is that they prove useful only when they contain the correct data. Unfortunately, cache hits prove low in applications that use a lot of data and perform a wide variety of tasks. The next step in making processors work faster is to guess which data the application will require next and load it into a cache before the application requires it.

>> **Using specialty RAM:** You can get buried by RAM alphabet soup because there are more kinds of RAM than most people imagine. Each kind of RAM purports to solve at least part of the von Neumann bottleneck problem, and they do work — within limits. In most cases, the improvements revolve around the idea of getting data from memory and onto the bus faster. Two major (and many minor) factors affect speed: *memory speed* (how fast the memory moves data) and *latency* (how long it takes to locate a particular piece of data). You can read more about memory and the factors that affect it in "Different RAM Types and its uses" at Computer Memory Upgrade.net.

WARNING

As with many other areas of technology, hype can become a problem. For example, *multithreading,* the act of breaking an application or other set of instructions into discrete execution units that the processor can handle one at a time, is often touted as a means to overcome the von Neumann bottleneck, but it doesn't actually do anything more than add overhead (making the problem worse). Multithreading is an answer to another problem: making the application more efficient. When an application adds latency issues to the von Neumann bottleneck, the entire system slows. Multithreading ensures that the processor doesn't waste yet more time waiting for the user or the application, but instead has something to do all the time. Application latency can occur with any processor architecture, not just the von Neumann architecture. Even so, anything that speeds the overall operation of an application is visible to the user and the system as a whole.

Defining the GPU

The original intent of a GPU was to process image data quickly and then display the resulting image onscreen. During the initial phase of PC evolution, the CPU performed all the processing, which meant that graphics could appear slowly while the CPU performed other tasks. During this time, a PC typically came equipped with a *display adapter,* which contains little or no processing power. A display adapter merely converts the computer data into a visual form. In fact, using just one processor proved almost impossible after the PC moved past text-only displays or extremely simple 16-color graphics. However, GPUs didn't really make many inroads into computing until people began wanting 3D output. At this point, a combination of a CPU and a display adapter simply couldn't do the job.

A first step in this direction was taken by systems such as the Hauppauge 4860 (see details at Geekdot.com), which included a CPU and a special graphics chip (the 80860, in this case) on the motherboard. The 80860 has the advantage of performing calculations extremely fast (see "Intel 80860 (i860) CPU family" at CPU-World.com for details). Unfortunately, these multiprocessor, asynchronous systems didn't quite meet the expectations that people had for them (although they were incredibly fast for systems of the time) and they proved extremely expensive. Plus, there was the whole issue of writing applications that included that second (or subsequent) chip. The two chips also shared memory (which was abundant for these systems).

A GPU moves graphics processing from the motherboard to the graphics peripheral board. The CPU can tell the GPU to perform a task, and then the GPU determines the best method for doing so independently of the CPU. A GPU has a separate memory, and the data path for its bus is immense. In addition, a GPU can access the main memory for obtaining data needed to perform a task and to post results independently of the CPU. Consequently, this setup makes modern graphics displays possible.

TECHNICAL STUFF

However, what really sets a GPU apart is that a GPU typically contains hundreds or thousands of cores (see the article about supercharged computing at NVIDIA.com), contrasted with just a few cores for a CPU. (Eight cores is about the best that you get, even with the newer i9 processor, described in "11th Generation Intel Core i9 Processors" at Intel.com. According to the NVIDIA blog post at https://developer.nvidia.com/blog/nvidia-ampere-architecture-in-depth/, an A100 GPU can host up to 80GB of RAM and has up to 8,192 FP32 (single-precision floating-point format) CUDA (Compute Unified Device Architecture) Cores per full GPU. *CUDA* is a parallel computing platform and Application Programming Interface (API) developed by NVIDIA. Even though the CPU provides more general-purpose functionality, the GPU performs calculations incredibly fast and can move data from the GPU to the display even faster. This ability is what makes the special-purpose GPU a critical component in today's systems.

Considering why GPUs work well

As with the 80860 chip described in the previous section, the GPUs today excel at performing the specialized tasks associated with graphics processing, including working with vectors. All those cores performing tasks in parallel really speed AI calculations. For example, they're indispensable in creating compute-intensive AI models, like the Generative Adversarial Networks (GANs) that perform tasks like the ones described in the "18 Impressive Applications of Generative Adversarial Networks (GANs)" article at Machine Learning Mastery.com.

In 2011, the Google Brain Project (https://research.google.com/teams/brain/) trained an AI to recognize the difference between cats and people by watching movies on YouTube. However, to make this task work, Google used 2,000 CPUs in one of Google's giant data centers. Few people would have the resources required to replicate Google's work.

On the other hand, Bryan Catanzaro (NVIDIA's research team) and Andrew Ng (Stanford) were able to replicate Google's work using a set of 12 NVIDIA GPUs (see the "Accelerating AI with GPUs: A New Computing Model" post at the NVIDIA.com blog for details). After people understood that GPUs could replace a host of computer systems stocked with CPUs, they could start moving forward with a variety of AI projects. In 2012, Alex Krizhevsky (Toronto University) won the ImageNet computer image recognition competition using GPUs. In fact, a number of researchers have now used GPUs with amazing success (see "The 9 Deep Learning Papers You Need To Know About" at https://adeshpande3.github.io/The-9-Deep-Learning-Papers-You-Need-To-Know-About.html for details).

Working with Deep Learning Processors (DLPs)

Researchers engage in a constant struggle to discover better ways to train, verify, and test the models used to create AI applications. One of those ways is to use new computing techniques, as described in the "Relying on new computational techniques" section, earlier in this chapter. Another way is to throw more processing power at the problem, such as by using a GPU.

However, a GPU is beneficial only because it can perform matrix manipulation quickly, and on a massively parallel level. Otherwise, using a GPU can create problems as well, as discussed in the "Using GPUs" section of the chapter. So, the search for something better is ongoing, and you can find a veritable alphabet soup of processor types described on sites such as Primo.ai, with this page: "Processing Units - CPU, GPU, APU, TPU, VPU, FPGA, QPU." This resource page will acquaint you with all of the current processor types. However, you should start with the overview provided in the following sections because it's easy to get mired in the quicksand of too many options (and then your head explodes).

Defining the DLP

A Deep Learning Processor (DLP) is simply a specialized processor that provides some advantages in training, verifying, testing, and running AI applications. They try to create an environment in which AI applications run quickly even on smaller or less capable devices. Most DLPs follow a similar pattern by providing

>> Separate data and code memory areas

>> Separate data and code buses

>> Specialized instruction sets

>> Large on-chip memory

>> Large buffers to encourage data reuse patterns

In 2014, Tianshi Chen (and others) proposed the first DLP, called DianNoa (Chinese for *electric brain*), in a white paper at http://novel.ict.ac.cn/ychen/pdf/DianNao.pdf. Of course, a first attempt is never good enough, so there is a whole family of DianNoa chips: DaDianNao, ShiDianNao, and PuDianNao (and possibly others).

REMEMBER

Since these first experiments with DLPs, the number and types of DLPs have soared, but most of these endeavors are currently part of university research efforts. The exceptions are the Neural Processing Unit (NPU) created by Huawei (https://developer.huawei.com/consumer/en/doc/2020314) and Samsung (https://news.samsung.com/global/samsung-electronics-introduces-a-high-speed-low-power-npu-solution-for-ai-deep-learning) for mobile devices, and the Tensor Processing Unit (TPU) created by Google (https://cloud.google.com/tpu/docs/tpus) specifically for use with TensorFlow (https://www.tensorflow.org/). These two DLP types are described next.

Using the mobile Neural Processing Unit (NPU)

A number of mobile devices, notably those by Huawei and Samsung, have a Neural Processing Unit (NPU) in addition to a general CPU to perform AI predictive tasks using models such as Artificial Neural Networks (ANNs) and Random Forests (RFs). You can't use an NPU for general computing needs because it's so specialized. However, an NPU characteristically performs up to ten times faster than a GPU does for the same task. An NPU is specialized in these ways:

>> It accelerates the running of predefined models (as contrasted to training, verification, and testing)

>> It's designed for use with small devices

>> It consumes little power when contrasted to other processor types

>> It uses resources, such as memory, efficiently

Because the precise boundaries between processor types are hard to define, you might see a number of NPU look-alikes or alternatives classified as NPUs. However, here is a list of processors that you can currently classify as true NPUs:

>> Ali-NPU, by Alibaba

>> Ascend, by Huawei

>> Neural Engine, by Apple

>> Neural Processing Unit (NPU), by Samsung

>> NNP, Myriad, EyeQ, by Intel

>> NVDLA (mostly used for Internet of Things [IoT] devices), by NVIDIA

Accessing the cloud-based Tenser Processing Unit (TPU)

Google specifically designed the Tensor Processing Unit (TPU) in 2015 to more quickly run applications built on the TensorFlow framework. It represents a true chip specialization in that you can't use it effectively without TensorFlow. However, it's different in another way in that it's an Application-Specific Integrated Circuit (ASIC), rather than a full-blown CPU-type chip. The differences are important:

>> An ASIC can perform only one task, and you can't change it.

>> Because of its specialization, an ASIC is typically much less expensive than a CPU.

>> Most ASIC implementations are much smaller than the same implementation created with a CPU.

>> Compared to a CPU implementation, an ASIC is more power efficient.

>> ASICs are incredibly reliable.

Creating a Specialized Processing Environment

Deep learning and AI are both non-von Neumann processes, according to many experts, including Massimiliano Versace, CEO of Neurala Inc. (https://www. neurala.com/). Because the task the algorithm performs doesn't match the underlying hardware, all sorts of inefficiencies exist, hacks are required, and obtaining a result is much harder than it should be. Therefore, designing hardware that matches the software is quite appealing. The Defense Advanced Research Projects Agency (DARPA) undertook one such project in the form of Systems of Neuromorphic Adaptive Plastic Scalable Electronics (SyNAPSE). The idea behind this approach is to duplicate nature's approach to solving problems by combining memory and processing power, rather than keeping the two separate. They actually built the system (it was immense), and you can read more about it at `https://www.darpa.mil/program/systems-of-neuromorphic-adaptive-plastic-scalable-electronics` and `https://www.darpa.mil/news-events/2014-08-07`.

The SyNAPSE project did move forward. IBM built a smaller system by using modern technology that was both incredibly fast and power efficient (see `https://www.research.ibm.com/articles/brain-chip.shtml`). The only problem is that no one is buying them. Just as many people would argue that Betamax was a better way of storing data than VHS, VHS won out on cost, ease of use, and compelling features (see "Betamax vs. VHS: How Sony Lost the Original Home Video Format War" at GIZMODO.com). The same holds true for IBM's SyNAPSE offering, True-North. It has been hard to find people who are willing to pay the higher price, programmers who can develop software using the new architecture, and products that genuinely benefit from the chip. Consequently, a combination of CPUs and GPUs, even with its inherent weaknesses, continues to win out.

Increasing Hardware Capabilities

The CPU still works well for business systems or in applications in which the need for general flexibility in programming outweighs pure processing power. However, GPUs are now the standard for various kinds of data science, machine learning, AI, and deep learning needs. Of course, everyone is constantly looking for the next big thing in the development environment. Both CPUs and GPUs are production-level processors. In the future, you may see one of two kinds of processors used in place of these standards:

>> **Application-Specific Integrated Circuits (ASICs):** In contrast to general processors, a vendor creates an ASIC for a specific purpose. An ASIC solution offers extremely fast performance using very little power, but it lacks flexibility. You can find an example of an ASIC earlier in this chapter in the form of a TPU (see the "Accessing the cloud-based Tenser Processing Unit (TPU)" section for details).

>> **Field Programmable Gate Arrays (FPGAs):** As with an ASIC, a vendor generally crafts an FPGA for a specific purpose. However, contrary to an ASIC, you can program an FPGA to change its underlying functionality. An example of an FPGA solution is Microsoft's Brainwave, which is used for deep learning projects (see "Microsoft Brainwave aims to accelerate deep learning with FPGAs" at TechCrunch.com).

REMEMBER

The battle between ASICs and FPGAs promises to heat up, with AI developers emerging as the winner. For the time being, Microsoft and FPGAs appear to have taken the lead (see "Microsoft: FPGA Wins Versus Google TPUs For AI" at Moor Insights & Strategy.com). The point is that technology is fluid, and you should expect to see new developments. The article "AI Chips Technology Trends & Landscape (GPU + TPU + FPGA + Startups)," by Jonathan Hui, provides an even better idea of just how much things are changing.

Vendors are also working on entirely new processing types, which may or may not actually work as expected. For example, Graphcore is working on an Intelligence Processing Unit (IPU), as described at `https://www.prnewswire.com/news-releases/sequoia-backs-graphcore-as-the-future-of-artificial-intelligence-processors-300554316.html`. The company has developed the line of processors shown at `https://www.graphcore.ai/products/ipu`. However, you have to take the news of these new processors with a grain of salt, given the hype that has surrounded the industry in the past. When you see real applications from large companies such as Google and Microsoft, you can start to feel a little more certain about the future of the technology involved.

Adding Specialized Sensors

An essential component of AI is the capability of the AI to simulate human intelligence using a full set of senses. Input provided through senses helps humans develop the various kinds of intelligence described in Chapter 1. A human's senses provide the right sort of input to create an intelligent human. Even assuming that it becomes possible for an AI to fully implement all seven kinds of intelligence, it still requires the right sort of input to make that intelligence functional.

Humans typically have five senses with which to interact with the environment: sight, sound, touch, taste, and hearing. Oddly enough, humans still don't fully understand their own capabilities, so it's not too surprising that computers lag when it comes to sensing the environment in the same way that humans do. For example, until recently, taste comprised only four elements: salt, sweet, bitter, and sour. However, two more tastes now appear on the list: umami and fat (see "Sweet, Sour, Salty, Bitter, Umami . . . And Fat?" at FiveThirtyEight.com for details). Likewise, some women are tetrachromats (https://concettaantico.com/tetrachromacy/), who can see 100,000,000 colors rather than the more usual 1,000,000. (Only women can be tetrachromats because of the chromosomal requirements.) Knowing how many women have this capability isn't even possible yet, but some sources have the number as high as 20 percent; see http://sciencevibe.com/2016/12/11/the-women-that-see-100-million-colors-live-in-a-different-world/ for details.

The use of filtered static and dynamic data enables an AI to interact with humans in specific ways today. For example, consider Alexa, the Amazon device that apparently hears you and then says something back. Even though Alexa doesn't actually understand anything you say, the appearance of communication is quite addicting and encourages people to anthropomorphize these devices. To perform its task at all, Alexa requires access to a special sensor: a microphone that allows it to hear. Actually, Alexa has a number of microphones to help it hear well enough to provide the illusion of understanding. Unfortunately, as advanced as Alexa is, it can't see, feel, touch, or taste anything, which makes it far from human in even the smallest ways.

TIP

In some cases, humans actually want their AI to have superior or different senses. An AI that detects motion at night and reacts to it might rely on infrared rather than normal vision. In fact, the use of alternative senses is one of the valid uses for AI today. The capability to work in environments that people can't work in is one reason that some types of robots have become so popular, but working in these environments often requires that the robots have, or be connected to, a set of nonhuman sensors. Consequently, the topic of sensors actually falls into two categories (neither of which is fully defined): human-like sensors and alternative environment sensors.

Devising Methods to Interact with the Environment

An AI that is self-contained and never interacts with the environment is useless. Of course, that interaction takes the form of inputs and outputs. The traditional method of providing inputs and outputs is directly through data streams that the computer can understand, such as datasets, text queries, and the like. However, these approaches are hardly human friendly, and they require special skills to use.

REMEMBER

Interacting with an AI is increasingly occurring in ways that humans understand better than they do direct computer contact. For example, input occurs through a series of microphones when you ask Alexa a question. The AI turns the keywords in the question into tokens it can understand. These tokens then initiate computations that form an output. The AI tokenizes the output into a human-understandable form: a spoken sentence. You then hear the sentence as Alexa speaks to you through a speaker. In short, to provide useful functionality, Alexa must interact with the environment in two different ways that appeal to humans, but which Alexa doesn't actually understand.

Interactions can take many forms. In fact, the number and forms of interaction are increasing continually. For example, an AI can now smell (see "Artificial intelligence grows a nose" at ScienceMag.org). However, the computer doesn't actually smell anything. Sensors provide a means to turn chemical detection into data that the AI can then use in the same way that it does all other data. The capability to detect chemicals isn't new; the ability to turn the analysis of those chemicals isn't new; nor are the algorithms used to interact with the resulting data new. What is new is the datasets used to interpret the incoming data as a smell, and those datasets come from human studies. An AI's "nose" has all sorts of possible uses. For example, think about the AI's capability to use a nose when working in some dangerous environments, such as to smell a gas leak before being able to see it by using other sensors.

Physical interactions are also on the rise. Robots that work in assembly lines are old hat, but consider the effects of robots that can drive. These are larger uses of physical interaction. Consider also that an AI can react in smaller ways. Hugh Herr, for example, uses an AI to provide interaction with an intelligent foot, as described in "Is This the Future of Robotic Legs?" at Smithsonian Magazine.com and "New surgery may enable better control of prosthetic limbs" at MIT News. edu. This dynamic foot provides a superior replacement for people who have lost their real foot. Instead of the static sort of feedback that a human gets from a standard prosthetic, this dynamic foot actually provides the sort of active feedback that humans are used to obtaining from a real foot. For example, the amount of pushback from the foot differs when walking uphill than walking downhill. Likewise, navigating a curb requires a different amount of pushback than navigating a step.

The point is that as AI becomes more able to perform complex calculations in smaller packages with ever-larger datasets, the capability of an AI to perform interesting tasks increases. However, the tasks that the AI performs may not currently have a human category. You may not ever truly interact with an AI that understands your speech, but you may come to rely on an AI that helps you maintain life or at least make it more livable.

2

Considering the Uses of AI in Society

Work with AI in computer applications.

Use AI to automate common processes.

Consider how AI addresses medical needs.

Define methods to allow human interaction.

Chapter **5**

Seeing AI Uses in Computer Applications

You have likely used AI in some form in many of the computer applications you rely on for your work. For example, talking to your smartphone requires the use of a speech recognition AI. Likewise, an AI filters out all that junk mail that could arrive in your Inbox. The first part of this chapter discusses AI application types, many of which will surprise you, and the fields that commonly rely on AI to perform a significant number of tasks. You also discover a source of limitations for creating AI-based applications, which helps you understand why sentient robots may not ever happen — or not with the currently available technology, at least.

However, regardless of whether AI ever achieves sentience, the fact remains that AI does perform a significant number of useful tasks. The two essential ways in which AI currently contributes to human needs are through corrections and suggestions. You don't want to take the human view of these two terms. A correction isn't necessarily a response to a mistake. Likewise, a suggestion isn't necessarily a response to a query. For example, consider a driving-assisted car (one in which the AI assists rather than replaces the driver). As the car moves along, the AI can make small corrections that allow for driving and road conditions, pedestrians, and a wealth of other issues in advance of an actual mistake. The AI takes a proactive approach to an issue that may or may not occur. Likewise, the AI can suggest a certain path to the human driving the car that may present the greatest likelihood of success, only to change the suggestion later based on new conditions. The second part of the chapter considers corrections and suggestions separately.

The third main part of the chapter discusses potential AI errors. An error occurs whenever the result is different from expected. The result may be successful, but it might remain unexpected. Of course, outright errors occur, too: An AI may not provide a successful result. Perhaps the result even runs counter to the original goal (possibly causing damage). If you get the idea that AI applications provide gray, rather than black or white, results, you're well on the road to understanding how AI modifies typical computer applications, which do, in fact, provide either an absolutely correct or absolutely incorrect result.

Introducing Common Application Types

Just as the only thing that limits the kinds of procedural computer application types is the imagination of the programmer, so may AI applications appear in any venue for just about any purpose, most of which no one has thought of yet. In fact, the flexibility that AI offers means that some AI applications may appear in places other than those for which the programmer originally defined them. In fact, someday AI software may well write its own next generation (see "AI Software Learns to Make AI Software" at MIT Technology Review.com for details). The GPT-3 tool (https://openai.com/blog/openai-api/ and https://arxiv.org/abs/2005.14165) writes a considerable number of document types today, including code (see "This AI Could Bring Us Computers That Can Write Their Own Software" at SingularityHub.com). However, to obtain a better idea of just what makes AI useful in applications, it helps to view the most commonly applied uses for AI today (and the potential pitfalls associated with those uses), as described in the sections that follow.

Using AI in typical applications

You might find AI in places where it's hard to imagine using an AI. For example, your smart thermostat for controlling home temperature could contain an AI if the thermostat is complex enough (see "Best smart thermostats 2020" at NBC News.comfor details). The use of AI, even in these particularly special applications, really does make sense when the AI is used for things that AI does best, such as tracking preferred temperatures over time to automatically create a temperature schedule. Here are some of the more typical uses for AI that you'll find in many places:

- Artificial creativity

- Computer vision, virtual reality, and image processing

- Diagnosis (artificial intelligence)

- Face recognition

- Game artificial intelligence, computer game bot, game theory, and strategic planning

- Handwriting recognition

- Natural language processing, translation, and chatterbots

- Nonlinear control and robotics

- Optical character recognition

- Speech recognition

The AI exploit with the greatest potential for creating serious problems, however, is the *deep fake* (the impersonation of someone by an AI to say or do things that the real person would never do). The article "The Year Deepfakes Went Mainstream" at MIT Technology Review.com describes the technology in some detail. However, reading about a deep fake and seeing one in action are two different things. Watch the deep fake of former President Obama at YouTube.com and you begin to understand the truly evil purposes to which some people can apply AI. Of course, this new use of AI is creating serious problems for the court system, as described in "Courts and lawyers struggle with growing prevalence of deepfakes" at ABA Journal.com. If you want to see how that deep fake actually works, watch the video "How the Obama / Jordan Peele DEEPFAKE actually works | Ian Hislop's Fake News – BBC" at YouTube.com.

AI EXPLOITS

Not every use of AI is aboveboard and honest. Hackers can use AI hacks to attack AI applications to force them to perform in ways that the creator never envisioned, as described in "AI and ML Misuses and Abuses at Present" at TrendMicro.com. Some of these exploits are quite devious. It's now possible to find thermostats with a machine learning application controlling them, as described in "Swiss Researchers Create Machine Learning Thermostat" at RTInsights.com. It turns out that some researchers have found a way to hack a smart thermostat, as described in "#DefCon: Thermostat Control Hacked to Host Ransomware" at InfoSecurity Magazine.com. Now, imagine what would happen if the thermostat somehow connected to someone's network, perhaps for the purpose of recording statistics, and you see that a machine learning controlled thermostat really can be a security threat. AI makes unbelievably exotic attacks quite possible.

Realizing AI's wide range of fields

Applications define specific kinds of uses for AI. You can also find AI used more generically in specific fields of expertise. The following list contains the fields where AI most commonly makes an appearance:

>> Artificial life

>> Automated reasoning

>> Automation

>> Biologically Inspired Computing

>> Concept mining

>> Data mining

>> Email spam filtering

>> Hybrid intelligent system

>> Intelligent agent and intelligent control

>> Knowledge representation

>> Litigation

>> Robotics: behavior-based robotics, cognition, cybernetics, developmental robotics (epigenetic), and evolutionary robotics

>> Semantic web

Considering the Chinese Room argument

In 1980, John Searle wrote an article entitled "Minds, Brains, and Programs" that was published in *Behavioral and Brain Sciences*. The emphasis of this article is on refuting the Turing test, in which a computer can fool a human into thinking that the computer is a human (rather than a computer) by using a series of questions (see the article at https://www.abelard.org/turpap/turpap.php for details). The basic assumption is that functionalism, or the capability to simulate specific characteristics of the human mind, isn't the same as actually thinking.

The Chinese Room argument, as this thought experiment is called, relies on two tests. In the first test, someone creates an AI that can accept Chinese characters, use a set of rules to create a response from those characters, and then output the response using Chinese characters. The question is about a story — the AI must interpret the questions put to it such that the answer reflects actual story content and not just some random response. The AI is so good that no one outside the room can tell that an AI is performing the required tasks. The Chinese speakers are completely fooled into thinking that the AI really can read and understand Chinese.

In the second test, a human who doesn't speak Chinese is given three items that mimic what the computer does. The first is a script that contains a large number of Chinese characters; the second is a story in Chinese; and the third is a set of rules for correlating the first item to the second. Someone sends in a set of questions, written in Chinese, that the human makes sense of by using the set of rules to find the location in the story containing the answer based on an interpretation of the Chinese characters. The answer is the set of Chinese characters that correlate to the question based on the rules. The human gets so good at this task that no one can perceive the lack of understanding of the Chinese language.

The purpose of the two tests is to demonstrate that the capability to use formal rules to produce a result (syntax) is not the same as actually understanding what someone is doing (semantics). Searle postulated that syntax doesn't suffice for semantics, yet this is what some people who implement an AI are trying to say when it comes to creating various rule-based engines, such as the Script Applier Mechanism (SAM); see "Sam--A Story Understander. Research Report No. 43" at Eric.ed.gov for details.

The underlying issue pertains to having a strong AI, one that actually understands what it's trying to do, and a weak AI, one that is simply following the rules. All AI today is weak AI; it doesn't actually understand anything. What you see is clever programming that simulates thought by using rules (such as those implicit in algorithms). Of course, much controversy arises over the idea that no matter how complex machines become, they won't actually develop brains, which means that they'll never understand. The Searle assertion is that AI will remain weak. You can see a discussion of this topic at `http://www.iep.utm.edu/chineser/`. The arguments and counterarguments are interesting to read because they provide significant insights into what truly comes into play when creating an AI.

Seeing How AI Makes Applications Friendlier

You can view the question of application friendliness addressed by AI in a number of different ways. At its most basic level, an AI can provide anticipation of user input. For example, when the user has typed just a few letters of a particular word, the AI guesses the remaining characters. By providing this service, the AI accomplishes several goals:

>> The user becomes more efficient by typing fewer characters.

>> The application receives fewer errant entries as the result of typos.

>> The user and application both engage in a higher level of communication by prompting the user with correct or enhanced terms that the user might not otherwise remember, avoiding alternative terms that the computer may not recognize.

An AI can also learn from previous user input in reorganizing suggestions in a way that works with the user's method of performing tasks. This next level of interaction falls within the realm of suggestions described in the "Making Suggestions" section, later in this chapter. Suggestions can also include providing the user with ideas that the user might not have considered otherwise.

WARNING

Even in the area of suggestions, humans may begin to think that the AI is thinking, but it isn't. The AI is performing an advanced form of pattern matching as well as analysis to determine the probability of the need for a particular input. The "Considering the Chinese Room argument" section, earlier in this chapter, discusses the difference between weak AI, the kind found in every application today, and strong AI, something that applications may eventually achieve.

Using an AI also means that humans can now exercise other kinds of intelligent input. The example of voice is almost overused, but it remains one of the more common methods of intelligent input. However, even if an AI lacks the full range of senses, as described in Chapter 4, it can provide a wide variety of nonverbal intelligent inputs. An obvious choice is visual, such as recognizing the face of its owner or a threat based on facial expression. However, the input could include a monitor, possibly checking the user's vital signs for potential problems. In fact, an AI could use an enormous number of intelligent inputs, most of which aren't even invented yet.

Currently, applications generally consider just these first three levels of friendliness. As AI intelligence increases, however, it becomes essential for an AI to exhibit Friendly Artificial Intelligence (FAI) behaviors consistent with an Artificial General Intelligence (AGI) that has a positive effect on humanity. AI has goals, but those goals may not align with human ethics, and the potential for misalignment causes angst today. An FAI would include logic to ensure that the AI's goals remain aligned with humanity's goals, similar to the three laws found in Isaac Asimov's books (see "Isaac Asimov's 'Three Laws of Robotics'" at webhome.auburn.edu), which you find discussed in more detail in Chapter 12. However, many say that the three laws are just a good starting point and that we need further safeguards (see

"After 75 years, Isaac Asimov's Three Laws of Robotics need updating" The Conversation.com.

TIP

Of course, all this discussion about laws and ethics could prove quite confusing and difficult to define. A simple example of FAI behavior would be that the FAI would refuse to disclose personal user information unless the recipient had a need to know. In fact, an FAI could go even further by pattern matching human input and locating potential personal information within it, notifying the user of the potential for harm before sending the information anywhere. The point is that an AI can significantly change how humans view applications and interact with them.

Performing Corrections Automatically

Humans constantly correct everything. It isn't a matter of everything being wrong. Rather, it's a matter of making everything slightly better (or at least trying to make it better). Even when humans manage to achieve just the right level of rightness at a particular moment, a new experience brings that level of rightness into question because now the person has additional data by which to judge the whole question of what constitutes right in a particular situation. To fully mimic human intelligence, AI must also have this capability to constantly correct the results it provides, even if the current results would provide a positive result. The following sections discuss the issue of correctness and examine how automated corrections sometimes fail.

Considering the kinds of corrections

When most people think about AI and correction, they think about the spell checker or grammar checker. A person makes a mistake (or at least the AI thinks so) and the AI corrects this mistake so that the typed document is as accurate as possible. Of course, humans make lots of mistakes, so having an AI to correct them is a good idea.

Corrections can take all sorts of forms, and they don't necessarily mean that an error has occurred or will occur in the future. For example, a car could assist a driver by making constant lane position corrections. The driver might be well within the limits of safe driving, but the AI could provide these micro-corrections to help ensure that the driver remains safe.

Taking the whole correction scenario further, imagine that the car in front of the car containing the AI makes a sudden stop because of a deer in the road. The driver of the current car hasn't committed any sort of error. However, the AI can react faster than the driver can and acts to stop the car as quickly and safely as possible to address the now-stopped car in front of it.

Seeing the benefits of automatic corrections

When an AI sees a need for a correction, it can either ask the human for permission to make the correction or make the change automatically. For example, when someone uses speech recognition to type a document and makes an error in grammar, the AI should ask permission before making a change because the human may have actually meant the word, or the AI may have misunderstood what the human meant.

However, sometimes it's critical that the AI provide a robust enough decision-making process to perform corrections automatically. For example, when considering the lane position scenario from the previous section, the AI doesn't have time to ask permission; it must apply the brake immediately or the human could die from the crash. Automatic corrections have a definite place when working with an AI, assuming that the need for a decision is critical and the AI is robust.

Understanding why automated corrections don't work

As related in the "Considering the Chinese Room argument" section, earlier in this chapter, an AI can't actually understand anything. Without understanding, it doesn't have the capability to compensate for an unforeseen circumstance. In this case, the unforeseen circumstance relates to an unscripted event, one in which the AI can't accumulate additional data or rely on other mechanical means to solve. A human can solve the problem because a human understands the basis of the problem and usually enough of the surrounding events to define a pattern that can help form a solution. In addition, human innovation and creativity provides solutions where none are obvious through other means. Given that an AI currently lacks both innovation and creativity, the AI is at a disadvantage in solving specific problem domains.

To put this issue into perspective, consider the case of a spelling checker. A human types a perfectly legitimate word that doesn't appear in the dictionary used by the AI for making corrections. The AI often substitutes a word that looks close to the specified word but is still incorrect. Even after the human checks the document, retypes the correct word, and then adds it to the dictionary, the AI is still apt to make a mistake. For example, the AI could treat the abbreviation *CPU* differently from *cpu* because the former is in uppercase and the latter appears in lowercase. A human would see that the two abbreviations are the same and that, in the second case, the abbreviation is correct but may need to appear in uppercase instead.

Making Suggestions

A suggestion is different from a command. Even though some humans seem to miss the point entirely, a suggestion is simply an idea put forth as a potential solution to a problem. Making a suggestion implies that other solutions could exist and that accepting a suggestion doesn't mean automatically implementing it. In fact, the suggestion is only an idea; it may not even work. Of course, in a perfect world, all suggestions would be good suggestions — at least possible solutions to a correct output, which is seldom the case in the real world. The following sections describe the nature of suggestions as they apply to an AI.

Getting suggestions based on past actions

The most common way that an AI uses to create a suggestion is by collecting past actions as events and then using those past actions as a dataset for making new suggestions. For example, someone purchases a Half-Baked Widget every month for three months. It makes sense to suggest buying another one at the beginning of the fourth month. In fact, a truly smart AI might make the suggestion at the right time of the month. For example, if the user makes the purchase between the third and the fifth day of the month for the first three months, it pays to start making the suggestion on the third day of the month and then move onto something else after the fifth day.

Humans output an enormous number of clues while performing tasks. Unlike humans, an AI actually pays attention to every one of these clues and can record them in a consistent manner to create *action data*. The action data varies by the task being performed; it could include things like interactions with a device, sequences for making selections, body position, facial expression, manner of expression (such as attitude), and so on. By collecting action data consistently, an AI can provide suggestions based on past actions with a high degree of accuracy in many cases.

Getting suggestions based on groups

Another common way to make suggestions relies on group membership. In this case, group membership need not be formal. A group could consist of a loose association of people who have some minor need or activity in common. For example, a lumberjack, a store owner, and a dietician could all buy mystery books. Even though they have nothing else in common, not even location, the fact that all three like mysteries makes them part of a group. An AI can easily spot patterns like this that might elude humans, so it can make good buying suggestions based on these rather loose group affiliations.

Groups can include ethereal connections that are temporary at best. For example, all the people who flew flight 1982 out of Houston on a certain day could form a group. Again, no connection whatsoever exists between these people except that they appeared on a specific flight. However, by knowing this information, an AI could perform additional filtering to locate people within the flight who like mysteries. The point is that an AI can provide good suggestions based on group affiliation even when the group is difficult (if not impossible) to identify from a human perspective.

Obtaining the wrong suggestions

Anyone who has spent time shopping online knows that websites often provide suggestions based on various criteria, such as previous purchases or even searches. Unfortunately, these suggestions are often wrong because the underlying AI lacks understanding. For example, if you're an author of a book and you look at your book's statistics on Amazon, the Amazon AI will consistently recommend that you buy copies of your book no matter what you might want to do about it. As another example, when someone makes a once-in-a-lifetime purchase of a Super-Wide Widget, a human would likely know that the purchase is indeed once in a lifetime because it's extremely unlikely that anyone will need two. However, the AI doesn't understand this fact. So, unless a programmer specifically creates a rule specifying that Super-Wide Widgets are a once-in-a-lifetime purchase, the AI may choose to keep recommending the product because sales are understandably small. In following a secondary rule about promoting products with slower sales, the AI behaves according to the characteristics that the developer provided for it, but the suggestions it makes are outright wrong.

Besides rule-based or logic errors in AIs, suggestions can become corrupted through data issues. For example, a GPS could make a suggestion based on the best possible data for a particular trip. However, road construction might make the suggested path untenable because the road is closed. Of course, many GPS applications do consider road construction, but they sometimes don't consider other issues, such as a sudden change in the speed limit or weather conditions that make a particular path treacherous. Humans can overcome a lack of data through innovation, such as by using the less traveled road or understanding the meaning of detour signs.

When an AI manages to get past the logic, rule, and data issues, it sometimes still makes bad suggestions because it doesn't understand the correlation between certain datasets in the same way a human does. For example, the AI may not know to suggest paint after a human purchases a combination of pipe and drywall when making a plumbing repair. The need to paint the drywall and the surrounding area after the repair is obvious to a human because a human has a sense of aesthetics that the AI lacks. The human makes a correlation between various products that isn't obvious to the AI.

Considering AI-based Errors

An outright error occurs when the result of a process, given specific inputs, isn't correct in any form. The answer doesn't provide a suitable response to a query. It isn't hard to find examples of AI-based errors. For example, "AI image recognition fooled by single pixel change" at BBC News.com describes how a single pixel difference in a picture fools a particular AI. Errors can also lead to attacks, such as those described in the "AI Exploits" sidebar, earlier in the chapter. You can read more about the impact of adversarial attacks on AI in "Image-scaling attacks highlight dangers of adversarial machine learning" at TechTalks.com and in "One Pixel Attack for Fooling Deep Neural Networks" at ResearchGate.net. The point is that AI still has a high error rate in some circumstances, and the developers working with the AI are usually unsure why the errors even occur.

The sources of errors in AI are many. However, as noted in Chapter 1, AI can't even emulate all seven forms of human intelligence, so mistakes are not only possible but also unavoidable. Much of the material in Chapter 2 focuses on data and its impact on AI when the data is flawed in some way. In Chapter 3, you also find that even the algorithms that AI uses have limits. Chapter 4 points out that an AI doesn't have access to the same number or types of human senses. As the TechCrunch.com article "Artificial intelligence is not as smart as you (or Elon Musk) think" notes, many of the seemingly impossible tasks that AI performs today are the result of using brute-force methods rather than anything even close to actual thinking.

A major problem that's becoming more and more evident is that corporations often gloss over or even ignore problems with AI. The emphasis is on using an AI to reduce costs and improve productivity, which may not be attainable. The Bloomberg.com article "The Limits of Artificial Intelligence" discusses this issue in some detail. One of the more interesting, but disturbing, examples of a corporate entity going too far with an AI is Microsoft's Tay which was maliciously trained to provide racist, sexist, and pornographic remarks in front of a large crowd during a presentation (see "Microsoft's chatbot gone bad, Tay, makes MIT's annual list of biggest technology fails" at GeekWire.com).

REMEMBER

The valuable nugget of truth to take from this section isn't that AI is unreliable or unusable. In fact, when coupled with a knowledgeable human, AI can make its human counterpart fast and efficient. AI can enable humans to reduce common or repetitive errors. In some cases, AI mistakes can even provide a bit of humor in the day. However, AI doesn't think, and it can't replace humans in many dynamic situations today. AI works best when a human reviews important decisions, or the environment is so static that good results are predictably high (well, as long as a human doesn't choose to confuse the AI).

Chapter **6**

Automating Common Processes

C hapter 5 considers the use of AI in an *application*, which is a situation in which a human interacts with the AI in some meaningful way, even if the human is unaware of the presence of the AI. The goal is to help humans do something faster, easier, or more efficiently, or to meet some other need. A *process* that includes an AI is different because the AI is now working to assist a human or perform some other task without direct intervention. The first section of this chapter addresses how processes help humans. Given that boredom is possibly the worst-case human scenario (just think of all the negative things that happen when humans are bored), this chapter views the AI process for humans from a boredom perspective.

One of the ways AI has been in use the longest is industrial utilization, such as manufacturing processes, to eventually allow for Industry 4.0 implementation (see "What is Industry 4.0?" at TWI Global.com for details). Consider all the robots that now power the factories across the world. Even though AI-powered automation replaces humans, it also keeps humans safer by performing tasks generally considered dangerous. Oddly enough, one of the most significant causes of industrial accidents and a wealth of other problems is boredom, as explained in "Boredom at work" at The Psychologist.bps.org.uk. The article "How to make your boredom work for you" at Fast Company.com does try to turn things around, but still, boredom can be and is dangerous. Robots can perform those repetitive jobs consistently and without getting bored (although you might see an occasional yawn).

Just in case you haven't had enough about boredom yet, you can also read something about it in the third section of the chapter, which discusses some of the newest areas in which AI excels —making environments of all sorts safer. In fact, just in the automotive industry, you can find myriad ways in which the use of AI is making things better (see "Artificial Intelligence Reshaping the Automotive Industry" at Future Bridge.com for details).

REMEMBER

The point of this chapter is that AI works well in processes, especially those processes during which humans tend to get bored, causing them to make a mistake when the AI likely wouldn't. Of course, an AI can't eliminate every source of lost efficiency, disinterest, and safety issue. For one thing, humans can choose to ignore the AI's help, but the nature of the limitations goes much deeper than that. As discussed in previous chapters (especially Chapter 5), an AI doesn't understand; it can't provide creative or innovative solutions to problems, so some problems aren't solvable by an AI, no matter how much effort someone puts into creating it.

Developing Solutions for Boredom

Polls often show what people *think* they want, rather than what they do want, but they're still useful. When college graduates were polled to see what kind of life they wanted, not one of them said, "Oh please, let me be bored!" (check out "What Kind of Life Do You Want to Live?" at Huffington Post.com). In fact, you could possibly poll just about any group and not come up with a single boring response. Most humans (saying "all" would likely result in an avalanche of email, with examples) don't want to be bored. In some cases, AI can work with humans to make life more interesting — for the human, at least. The following sections discuss solutions for human boredom that AI can provide (and a few that it can't).

Making tasks more interesting

Any occupation, be it personal or for an organization, has certain characteristics that attract people and make them want to participate in it. Obviously, some occupations, such as taking care of your own children, pay nothing, but the satisfaction of doing so can be incredibly high. Likewise, working as a bookkeeper may pay quite well but not offer much in the way of job satisfaction. Various polls (such as this one in "The 2019 Jobs Rated Report" at CareerCast.com" and articles such as "Which is the key to happiness: High salary or job satisfaction?" at Engineering and Technology Jobs.org talk about the balance of money and satisfaction, but reading them often proves confusing because the basis for making a determination is ambiguous. However, most of these sources agree that after a human makes a certain amount of money, satisfaction becomes the key to maintaining interest in the occupation (no matter what that occupation might be). Of course, figuring out what comprises job satisfaction is nearly impossible, but interest remains high on the list. An interesting occupation will always have higher satisfaction potential.

TIP

The problem is not one of necessarily changing jobs, then, but of making the job more interesting as a means to avoid boredom. An AI can effectively help this process by removing repetition from tasks. However, examples such as Amazon's Alexa and Google's Home do provide other alternatives. The feeling of loneliness that can pervade the home, workplace, car, and other locations is a strong creator of boredom. When humans begin to feel alone, depression sets in and boredom is often just a step away. Creating applications that use the Alexa interface (see `https://developer.amazon.com/`) or Actions on the Google API (see `https://developers.google.com/actions/`) to simulate human interaction of the appropriate sort can improve the workplace experience. More important, developing smart interfaces of this sort can help humans perform a wealth of mundane tasks quickly, such as researching information and interacting with smart devices, not just light switches (see "How to control your lights with Amazon Echo" at iMore.com and `https://store.google.com/product/google_home` for details).

Helping humans work more efficiently

Most humans, at least the forward-thinking ones, have some ideas of how they'd like an AI to make their lives better by eliminating tasks that they don't want to do. The poll in "Which tasks in your job would you like to be automated by AI?" at blog.devolutions.net shows some of the more interesting ways that they wish AI could improve their lives:. Many of them are mundane, but notice the ones like detecting when a significant other is unhappy and sending flowers. It probably won't work, but it's an interesting idea nonetheless.

The point is that humans will likely provide the most interesting ideas on how to create an AI that specifically addresses their needs. In most cases, serious ideas will work well for other users, too. For example, automating trouble tickets is something that could work in a number of different industries. If someone were to come up with a generic interface, with a programmable back end to generate the required custom trouble tickets, the AI could save users a lot of time and ensure future efficiencies by ensuring that trouble tickets consistently record the required information.

COUNTER INTELLIGENCE IN WORK

Few people like things to be hard; most of us want to ease into work and come out with a sense of satisfaction each day. However, some new articles and white papers seem to indicate that adding AI to the workplace actually makes things harder. Consider this article from *The Atlantic*, "AI Is Coming for Your Favorite Menial Tasks"). However, the article isn't actually about menial tasks. It's more about AI sucking all the fun out of a person's job and leaving only the most stressful elements that only a human can effectively deal with. The article considers the other side of the coin: instances when automation makes a person's job significantly more difficult and definitely less satisfying, and the human isn't even getting paid more to do it. More important, the human's chance of making the right decision because all the decisions are hard ones also drops, which can then give management the impression that a worker is suddenly losing interest or simply not focusing. At some point, a balance will have to be struck between what AI does and what humans do to maintain job satisfaction. Current AI design doesn't consider this aspect of human need at all, but it will be a requirement in the future.

Understanding how AI reduces boredom

Boredom comes in many packages, and humans view these packages in different ways. There is the boredom that comes from not having required resources, knowledge, or other needs met. Another kind of boredom comes from not knowing what to do next when activities don't follow a specific pattern. An AI can help with the first kind of boredom; it can't help with the second. This section considers the first kind of boredom. (The next section considers the second kind.)

REMEMBER

Access to resources of all sorts helps reduce boredom by allowing humans to be creative without the mundane necessity of acquiring needed materials. Here are some ways in which an AI can make access to resources easier:

>> Searching for needed items online

>> Ordering needed items automatically

>> Performing sensor and other data-acquisition monitoring

>> Managing data

>> Accomplishing mundane or repetitive tasks

Considering how AI can't reduce boredom

As noted in previous chapters, especially Chapters 4 and 5, an AI is not creative or intuitive. So, asking an AI to think of something for you to do is unlikely to produce satisfying results. Someone could program the AI to track the top ten things you like to do and then select one of them at random, but the result still won't be satisfying because the AI can't take aspects like your current state of mind into account. In fact, even with the best facial expression recognition software, an AI will lack the capability to interact with you in a manner that will produce any sort of satisfying result.

An AI also can't motivate you. Think about what happens when a friend comes by to help motivate you (or you motivate the friend). The friend actually relies on a combination of intrapersonal knowledge (empathizing by considering how it feels to be in your situation) and interpersonal knowledge (projecting creative ideas on how to obtain a positive emotional response from you). An AI won't have any of the first kind of knowledge and only extremely limited amounts of the second kind of knowledge, as described in Chapter 1. Consequently, an AI can't reduce your boredom through motivational techniques.

TIP

Boredom may not always be a bad thing, anyway. A number of recent studies have shown that boredom actually helps promote creative thought, which is the direction that humans need to go (see "Being Bored Can Be Good for You—If You Do It Right" at Time.com and "The Science behind How Boredom Benefits Creative Thought" at Fast Company.com as examples). Despite the myriad articles on how AI is going to take jobs away, it's important to consider that the jobs that AI is taking are, in themselves, often boring and leave humans no time to create. Even today, humans could find productive, creative, jobs to do if they really thought about it. The article "7 Surprising Facts About Creativity, According To Science" at Fast Company.com discusses the role of daydreaming when bored in enhancing creativity. In the future, if humans really want to reach for the stars and do other amazing things, creativity will be essential, so the fact that AI can't reduce your boredom is actually a good thing.

Working in Industrial Settings

Any industrial setting is likely to have safety hazards, no matter how much time, effort, and money is thrown at the problem. You can easily find articles such as this one, "A Guide to the Most Common Workplace Hazards" at High Speed Training.co.uk, which describes common safety hazards found in industrial settings. Although humans cause many of these problems and boredom makes them worse, the actual environment in which the humans are working causes a great many issues. The following sections describe how automation can help humans live longer and better lives.

Developing various levels of automation

Automation in industrial settings is a lot older than you might think. Many people think of Henry Ford's assembly line as the starting point of automation (see "Ford's assembly line starts rolling" at History.com). In fact, the basics of automation began in 1104 AD in Venice (see "Trends in 21st Century Factory Automation" at Mouser.com),where 16,000 workers were able to build an entire warship in a single day. Americans repeated the feat of building warships extremely fast with modern ships during WWII (read about it in "World War II Shipbuilding in the San Francisco Bay Area" at nps.gov) by relying heavily on automation. In fact, there have been four industrial revolutions so far according to the Institute of Entrepreneurship Development ("The 4 Industrial Revolutions"). So automation has been around for a long time.

What hasn't been around for a long time is an AI that can actually help humans within the automation process. In many cases today, a human operator begins by outlining how to perform the task, creating a *job*, and then turns the job over to a computer. An example of one of several fairly new kinds of job is Robot Process Automation (RPA), which allows a human to train software to act in the stead of a human when working with applications (see "The Tools of the Future Today" at Valamis.com). Many companies are now offering RPA services, such as UiPath (https://www.uipath.com/rpa/robotic-process-automation). This process differs from scripting, such as the use of Visual Basic for Applications (VBA) in Microsoft Office, in that RPA isn't application specific and doesn't require coding. Many people find it surprising that there are actually ten levels of automation, nine of which can rely on an AI. The level you choose is dependent on your application:

1. A human operator creates a job and turns it over to a computer to implement.

2. An AI helps the human determine job options.

3. The AI determines the best job options and then allows the human to accept or reject the recommendation.

4. The AI determines the options, uses them to define a series of actions, and then turns the list of actions over to a human for acceptance or rejection of individual actions prior to implementation.

5. The AI determines the options, defines a series of actions, creates a job, and then asks for human approval before submitting the job to the computer.

6. The AI automatically creates the job and submits it to the computer's job queue, with the human operator acting as an intermediary in case the selected job requires termination prior to actual implementation.

7. The AI creates and implements the job and then tells the human operator what it did in case the job requires correction or reversal.

8. The AI creates and implements the job, telling the human what it did only when the human asks.

9. The AI creates and implements the job without providing any feedback unless a human needs to intervene, such as when an error occurs or the result isn't what was expected.

10. The AI initiates the need for the job, rather than waiting for the human to tell it to create the job. The AI provides feedback only when a human must intervene, such as when an error occurs. The AI can provide a level of error correction and manage unexpected results on its own.

Using more than just robots

When thinking about industry, most people think about automation: robots making stuff. However, society is actually in at least the fourth industrial revolution; we've had steam, mass production, automation, and now communication (see "Industrial Revolution - From Industry 1.0 to Industry 4.0" at Desouttertools.com for details). (Some people are already talking about a fifth level, personalization; see this LinkedIn post, "Industry 5.0-Future of Personalisation.") An AI requires information from all sorts of sources in order to perform tasks efficiently. It follows that the more information an industrial setting can obtain from all sorts of sources, the better an AI can perform (assuming that the data is also managed properly). With this multisourced idea in mind, industrial settings of all sorts now rely on an Industrial Communication Engine (ICE) to coordinate communication between all the various sources that an AI requires.

Robots do perform much of the actual work in an industrial setting, but you also need sensors to assess potential risks, such as storms. However, coordination is becoming ever more important to ensuring that operations remain efficient. For example, ensuring that trucks with raw materials arrive at the proper time, while other trucks that haul off finished goods are available when needed, are essential tasks for keeping warehouse floors running efficiently. The AI needs to know about the maintenance status of all equipment to ensure that the equipment receives the best possible care (to improve reliability); the AI also needs to know the times when the equipment is least needed (to improve efficiency). The AI would also need to consider issues such as resource cost. Perhaps gaining an advantage is possible by running certain equipment during evening hours when power is less expensive.

Relying on automation alone

Early examples of human-free factories included specialty settings, such as chip factories that required exceptionally clean environments. However, since that early beginning, automation has spread. Because of the dangers to humans and the cost of using humans to perform certain kinds of industrial tasks, you can find many instances today of common factories that require no human intervention at all (see "No Humans, Just Robots" at Singularity Hub.com for examples). The term for that type of industry is *lights-out manufacturing*, which is detailed in "Lights out Manufacturing. . .Is it Possible?" at the Syscon Plantstar blog.

REMEMBER

A number of technologies will at some point enable the performance of all factory-related tasks without human intervention (see https://waypointrobotics. com/blog/manufacturing-trends/ for examples). The point is that eventually society will need to find jobs, other than repetitive factory jobs, for humans to perform.

Creating a Safe Environment

One of the most often stated roles for AI, besides automating tasks, is keeping humans safe in various ways. Articles such as "7 Reasons You Should Embrace, Not Fear, Artificial Intelligence" at Futurism.com describe an environment in which AI acts as an intermediary, taking the hit that humans would normally take when a safety issue occurs. Safety takes all sorts of forms. Yes, AI will make working in various environments safer, but it'll also help create a healthier environment and reduce risks associated with common tasks, including surfing the Internet. The following sections offer an overview of the ways in which AI could provide a safer environment.

Considering the role of boredom in accidents

From driving or being at work, boredom increases accidents of all sorts (see "Distracted Driving Survey 2021: Drivers confess to bad behavior" at Insurance.com and "Job Boredom a Workplace Hazard?" at Risk and Insurance.com). In fact, anytime someone is supposed to perform a task that requires any level of focus and instead acts like they're half asleep, the outcome is seldom good. The problem is so serious and significant that you can find a wealth of articles on the topic, such as "Modelling human boredom at work: mathematical formulations and a probabilistic framework" at Emerald Insight.com. Solutions come in the form of articles like "Modeling job rotation in manufacturing systems: The study of employee's boredom and skill variations" at ResearchGate.net. Whether an accident actually occurs (or was a close call) depends on random chance. Imagine actually developing algorithms that help determine the probability of accidents happening because of boredom under certain conditions.

Using AI to avoid safety issues

No AI can prevent accidents owing to human causes, such as boredom. In a best-case scenario, when humans decide to actually follow the rules that AI helps create, the AI can only help avoid potential problems. Unlike with Asimov's robots, there are no three-laws protections in place in any environment; humans must choose to remain safe. With this reality in mind, an AI could help in these ways:

» Suggest job rotations (whether in the workplace, in a car, or even at home) to keep tasks interesting

» Monitor human performance in order to better suggest down time because of fatigue or other factors

» Assist humans in performing tasks to combine the intelligence that humans provide with the quick reaction time of the AI

» Augment human detection capabilities so that potential safety issues become more obvious

» Take over repetitive tasks so that humans are less likely to become fatigued and can participate in the interesting aspects of any job

Understanding that AI can't eliminate safety issues

Ensuring complete safety implies an ability to see the future. Because the future is unknown, the potential risks to humans at any given time are also unknown because unexpected situations can occur. An unexpected situation is one that the original developers of a particular safety strategy didn't envision. Humans are adept at finding new ways to get into predicaments, partly because we're both curious and creative. Finding a method to overcome the safety provided by an AI is in human nature because humans are inquisitive; we want to see what will happen if we try something — generally something stupid. Unpredictable situations aren't the only problem that an AI faces. Even if someone were to find every possible way in which a human could become unsafe, the processing power required to detect the event and determine a course of action would be astronomical. The AI would work so slowly that its response would always occur too late to make any difference. Consequently, developers of safety equipment that actually requires an AI to perform the required level of safety have to deal in probabilities and then protect against the situations that are most likely to happen.

Chapter **7**

Using AI to Address Medical Needs

M edicine is complicated. There is a reason it can take 15 or more years to train a doctor, depending on specialty (see https://work.chron.com/long-become-doctor-us-7921.html for details). By the time the school system packs a doctor with enough information to nearly burst, most other people have already been in the job force for 11 years (given that most will stop with an associate's or bachelor's degree). Meanwhile, the creation of new technologies, approaches, and so on all conspire to make the task even more complex. At some point, it becomes impossible for any one person to become proficient in even a narrow specialty. This is a prime reason that an irreplaceable human requires consistent, logical, and unbiased help in the form of an AI. The process begins by helping the doctor monitor patients (as described in the first section of this chapter) in ways that humans would simply find impossible. That's true because the number of checks is high, the need to perform them in a certain order and in a specific way is critical, and the potential for error is monumental.

Fortunately, people have more options today than ever before for doing many medical-related tasks on their own. For example, the use of games enables a patient to perform some therapy-related tasks alone, yet receive guidance from an application to help the person perform the task appropriately. Improved prosthetics and other medical aids also enable people to become more independent of professional human assistance. The second section of this chapter describes how AI can help assist people with their own medical needs.

Just as it proves difficult, if not impossible, to fix various devices without seeing the device in use in a specific environment, so humans sometimes defy the analysis needed to diagnose problems. Performing analysis in various ways can help a doctor find a specific problem and address it with greater ease. Today, a doctor can fit a patient with a monitoring device, perform remote monitoring, and then rely on an AI to perform the analysis required for diagnosis — all without the patient's spending more than one visit at the doctor's office (the one required to attach the monitoring device). In fact, in some cases, such as glucose monitors, the patient may even be able to buy the required device at the store so that the visit to the doctor's office becomes unnecessary as well. One of the more interesting additions to the health care arsenal during medical emergencies, such as pandemics, is the use of telepresence, which enables the doctor to interact with a patient without actually being in the same room. Even though the third section of this chapter doesn't go into the various analysis devices, you do get a good overview of their uses.

Of course, some interventions require the patient to undergo surgery or other procedures (as described in the fourth section of this chapter). A robotic solution can sometimes perform the task better than the doctor can. In some cases, a robot-assisted solution makes the doctor more efficient and helps focus the doctor's attention in areas that only a human can address. The use of various kinds of technology also makes diagnosis easier, faster, and more accurate. For example, using an AI can help a doctor identify the start of cancer far sooner than the doctor could perform the task alone.

Implementing Portable Patient Monitoring

A medical professional isn't always able to tell what is happening with a patient's health simply by listening to their heart, checking vitals, or performing a blood test. The body doesn't always send out useful signals that let a medical professional learn anything at all. In addition, some body functions, such as blood sugar, change over time, so constant monitoring becomes necessary. Going to the doctor's office every time you need one of these vitals checked would prove time consuming and possibly not all that useful. Older methods of determining some body characteristics required manual, external intervention on the part of the patient — an error-prone process in the best of times. For these reasons, and many more, an AI can help monitor a patient's statistics in a manner that is efficient, less error prone, and more consistent, as described in the following sections.

Wearing helpful monitors

All sorts of monitors fall into the helpful category. In fact, many of these monitors have nothing to do with the medical profession, yet produce positive results for your health. Consider the Moov monitor (https://welcome.moov.cc/), which monitors both heart rate and 3-D movement. The AI for this device tracks these statistics and provides advice on how to create a better workout. You actually get advice on, for example, how your feet are hitting the pavement during running and whether you need to lengthen your stride. The point of devices like these is to ensure that you get the sort of workout that will improve health without risking injury.

Mind you, if a watch-type monitoring device is too large, Oura (https://get.ouraring.com/overview) produces a ring that monitors about the same number of things that Moov does, but in a smaller package. This ring even tracks how you sleep to help you get a good night's rest. Rings do tend to come with an assortment of pros and cons. The article at https://www.wareable.com/smart-jewellery/best-smart-rings-1340 tells you more about these issues. Interestingly enough, many of the pictures on the site don't look anything like a fitness monitor, so you can have fashion and health all in one package.

Of course, if your only goal is to monitor your heart rate, you can get devices such as Apple Watch (https://support.apple.com/en-us/HT204666) that also provide some level of analysis using an AI. All these devices interact with your smartphone, so you can possibly link the data to still other applications or send it to your doctor as needed.

Relying on critical wearable monitors

A problem with some human conditions is that they change constantly, so checking intermittently doesn't really get the job done. Glucose, the statistic measured by diabetics, is one statistic that falls into this category. The more you monitor the rise and fall of glucose each day, the easier it becomes to change medications and lifestyle to keep diabetes under control. Devices such as the K'Watch (https://www.pkvitality.com/ktrack-glucose/) provide such constant monitoring, along with an app that a person can use to obtain helpful information on managing their diabetes. Of course, people have used intermittent monitoring for years; this device simply provides that extra level of monitoring that can help make having diabetes more of a nuisance than a life-altering issue. (The number of remote patient-monitoring devices produced by various companies is growing; see the article at https://tinyurl.com/c52uytse for details.)

WARNING

MEDICAL DEVICES AND SECURITY

A problem with medical technology of all sorts is the lack of security. Having an implanted device that anyone can hack is terrifying. The article at https://tinyurl.com/rjnathrw describes what could happen if someone hacked any medical device. Fortunately, according to many sources, no one has died yet.

However, imagine your insulin pump or implanted defibrillator malfunctioning as a result of hacking, and consider what damage it could cause. The Federal Drug Administration (FDA) has finally published guidance on medical-device security, as described in the article at https://tinyurl.com/w24cvfc7, but these guidelines apparently aren't enforced. In fact, this article goes on to say that the vendors are actively pursuing ways to avoid securing their devices.

The AI isn't responsible for the lack of security that these devices possess, but the AI could get the blame should a breach occur. The point is that you need to view all aspects of using AI, especially when it comes to devices that directly affect humans, such as implantable medical devices.

Some devices are truly critical, such as the Wearable Cardioverter Defibrillator (WCD), which senses your heart condition continuously and provides a shock should your heart stop working properly (see https://tinyurl.com/ybcew7h4 and https://tinyurl.com/jkzbv3x8 for details). This short-term solution can help a doctor decide whether you need the implanted version of the same device. There are pros and cons (https://tinyurl.com/8umynwjn) to wearing one, but then again, it's hard to place a value on having a shock available when needed to save a life. The biggest value of this device is the monitoring it provides. Some people don't actually need an implantable device, so monitoring is essential to prevent unnecessary surgery.

Using movable monitors

The number and variety of AI-enabled health monitors on the market today is staggering (see https://tinyurl.com/wt368ewk for some examples). For example, you can actually buy an AI-enabled toothbrush that will monitor your brushing habits and provide you with advice on better brushing technique (https://tinyurl.com/6ft7u37y). Oral B also has a number of toothbrushes that benefit from the use of AI: https://tinyurl.com/35xdarjj. When you think about it, creating a device like this presents a number of hurdles, not the least of which is keeping the monitoring circuitry happy inside the human mouth. Of course, some people may feel that the act of brushing their teeth really doesn't have much to do with good health, but it does (see https://tinyurl.com/6mfzc4hk).

Creating movable monitors generally means making them both smaller and less intrusive. Simplicity is also a requirement for devices designed for use by people with little or no medical knowledge. One device in this category is a wearable electrocardiogram (ECG). Having an ECG in a doctor's office means connecting wires from the patient to a semiportable device that performs the required monitoring. The QardioCore (https://tinyurl.com/3t4abkxb and https://store.getqardio.com/) provides the ECG without using wires, and someone with limited medical knowledge can easily use it. As with many devices, this one relies on your smartphone to provide needed analysis and make connections to outside sources as needed.

REMEMBER

Current medical devices work just fine, but they aren't portable. The point of creating AI-enabled apps and specialized devices is to obtain much needed data when a doctor actually needs it, rather than having to wait for that data. Even if you don't buy a toothbrush to monitor your technique or an ECG to monitor your heart, the fact that these devices are small, capable, and easy to use means that you may still benefit from them at some point.

Making Humans More Capable

Many of the current techniques for extending the healthy range of human life (the segment of life that contains no significant sickness), rather than just increasing the number of years of life depends on making humans more capable of improving their own health in various ways. You can find any number of articles that tell you 30, 40, or even 50 ways to extend this healthy range, but often it comes down to a combination of eating right, exercising enough and in the right way, and sleeping well. Of course, with all the advice out there, figuring out just which food, exercise, and sleep technique would work best for you could be nearly impossible. The following sections discuss ways in which an AI-enabled device might make the difference between having 60 good years and 80 or more good years. (In fact, it's no longer hard to find articles that discuss human life spans of 1,000 or more years in the future because of technological changes.)

Using games for therapy

A gaming console can serve as a powerful and fun physical therapy tool. Both Nintendo Wii and Xbox 360 see use in many different physical therapy venues (https://tinyurl.com/4dkp23k). The goal of these and other games is to get people moving in certain ways. The game automatically rewards proper patient movements, and a patient receives therapy in a fun way. Making the therapy fun means that the patient is more likely to do it and get better faster. You can now find very informative studies about the use of games and their combination with telehealth strategies at https://tinyurl.com/b6bt29r7 and https://letsplaytherapy.org/video-games-and-telehealth/.

BIAS, SYMPATHY, AND EMPATHY

Getting good care is the initial aim of anyone who enters any medical facility. The assumption is that the care is not only the best available but also fair. An AI can help in the medical field by ensuring that technical skills remain high and that no bias exists whatsoever — at least, not from the AI's perspective.

Humans will always exhibit bias because humans possess intrapersonal intelligence (as described in Chapter 1). Even the kindest, most altruistic person will exhibit some form of bias — generally unconsciously — creating a condition in which the caregiver sees one thing and the patient another (see the "Considering the Five Mistruths in Data" section in Chapter 2). However, the people being served will almost certainly notice, and their illness will likely amplify the unintended slight. Using an AI to ensure evenhandedness in dealing with patient issues is a way to avoid this issue. The AI can also help caregivers discover mistruths (unintended or otherwise) on the part of patients in relating their symptoms, thereby enhancing care.

The medical field can be problematic at times because technical skill often isn't enough. People frequently complain of the lack of a good bedside manner on the part of medical staff. The same people who want fair treatment also somehow want empathy from their caregivers (making the care unfair because it's now biased). Empathy differs from sympathy in context. People exhibit *empathy* when they are able to feel (almost) the same way the patient does and build a frame of reference with the patient. (It's important to note that no other person feels precisely the same way as you do because no other person has had precisely the same experiences that you've had.) Two exercises in the "Considering the software-based solutions" section, later in this chapter, help you understand how someone could build a frame of reference to create empathy. An AI could never build the required empathy because an AI lacks the required sense awareness and understanding to create a frame of reference, and the intrapersonal intelligence required to utilize such a frame of reference.

Unfortunately, empathy can blind a caregiver to true medical needs because the caregiver is now engaging in the mistruth of perspective by seeing only from the patient's point of view. So medical practitioners often employ *sympathy,* through which the caregiver looks in from the outside, understands how the patient might feel (rather than how the patient does feel), and doesn't build a frame of reference. Consequently, the medical practitioner can provide needed emotional support, but also see the need to perform tasks that the patient may not enjoy in the short term. An AI can't accomplish these tasks because an AI lacks intrapersonal intelligence and doesn't understand the concept of perspective well enough to apply it appropriately.

Of course, movement alone, even when working with the proper game, doesn't assure success. In fact, someone could develop a new injury when playing these games. The Jintronix add-on for the Xbox Kinect hardware standardizes the use of this game console for therapy (https://tinyurl.com/uzetv2tc and https://tinyurl.com/y42rmh4v), increasing the probability of a great outcome.

Considering the use of exoskeletons

One of the most complex undertakings for an AI is to provide support for an entire human body. That's what happens when someone wears an *exoskeleton* (essentially a wearable robot). An AI senses movements (or the need to move) and provides a powered response to the need. The military has excelled in the use of exoskeletons and is actively seeking more (see https://tinyurl.com/3sawszrb and https://tinyurl.com/tu525nuw for details). Imagine being able to run faster and carry significantly heavier loads as a result of wearing an exoskeleton. The video at https://tinyurl.com/p489dvj gives you just a glimpse of what's possible. The military continues to experiment, and those experiments often feed into civilian uses. The exoskeleton you eventually see (and you're almost guaranteed to see one at some point) will likely have its origins in the military.

Industry has also gotten in on the exoskeleton technology (see https://tinyurl.com/2j86w592 as an example). In fact, the use of exoskeletons is becoming ever more important as factory workers age (https://tinyurl.com/9h9j8sh9). Factory workers currently face a host of illnesses because of repetitive stress injuries. In addition, factory work is incredibly tiring. Wearing an exoskeleton not only reduces fatigue but also reduces errors and makes the workers more efficient. People who maintain their energy levels throughout the day can do more with far less chance of being injured, damaging products, or hurting someone else.

The exoskeletons in use in industry today reflect their military beginnings. Look for the capabilities and appearance of these devices to change in the future to look more like the exoskeletons shown in movies such as *Aliens* (https://tinyurl.com/krhh8b5k). The real-world examples of this technology (see the video and article at https://tinyurl.com/4wbsf7ea as an example) are a little less impressive but will continue to gain in functionality.

Exoskeletens can enhance people's physical abilities in downright amazing ways. For example, a Smithsonian article discusses using an exoskeleton to enable a child with cerebral palsy to walk (https://tinyurl.com/nyb5p3kd). Not all exoskeletons used in medical applications provide lifetime use, however. For example, an exoskeleton can help a person who experienced a stroke walk without impediment (https://tinyurl.com/439syr72). As the person regains skills, the exoskeleton provides less support until the wearer no longer needs it. Some users of the device have even coupled their exoskeleton with other products, such as Amazon's Alexa (see https://tinyurl.com/tp3kyxfk for details).

IMAGING THE DARK SIDE OF EXOSKELETONS

Despite an extensive search online, few nefarious uses for exoskeletons turned up, unless you consider the military applications negative. However, destroying is easier than creating. Somewhere along the way, someone will come up with negative uses for exoskeletons (and likely every other technology mentioned in this chapter). For example, imagine high-stakes thieves employing exoskeletons to obtain some sort of advantage during the theft of heavy objects (https://tinyurl.com/46tfte7c).

Even though this book is about clearing away the hype surrounding AI and presenting some positive uses for it, the fact remains that the smart individual does at least consider the dark side of any technology. This strategy becomes dangerous when people raise an alarm without any facts to support a given assertion. Yes, thieves could run amok with exoskeletons, which should provide incentive to properly secure them, but it also hasn't happened yet. Ethical considerations of potential uses, both positive and negative, always accompany creating a technology such as AI.

Throughout the book, you find various ethical and moral considerations in the positive use of AI to help society. It's definitely important to keep technology safe, but you also want to keep in mind that avoiding technology because of its negative potential is truly counterproductive.

REMEMBER

The overall purpose of wearing an exoskeleton isn't to make you into Iron Man. Rather, it's to cut down on repetitive stress injuries and help humans excel at tasks that currently prove too tiring or just beyond the limits of their body. From a medical perspective, using an exoskeleton is a win because it keeps people mobile longer, and mobility is essential to good health.

Addressing a Range of Physical Abilities

The creation of highly specialized prosthetics and other devices, many of them AI-enabled, has been a game changer for many people. For example, these days, some people can run a marathon or go rock climbing, even if they've experienced paralysis or the loss of a limb (https://tinyurl.com/ce958ms9). Then again, some people are using exoskeletons for an arguably less-than-productive use (https://tinyurl.com/tt9rvxdj).

THE GRIT AND PERSEVERANCE BEHIND THE AI DEVICE

The people you see online who are especially adept at having an amazing life with assistance from prosthetics or other devices have usually worked really hard to get where they are now. Using an AI-enabled device can get you a foot in the door, but to enter, you must be willing to do whatever it takes to make the device work for you, which usually requires hour upon hour of therapy. This chapter doesn't seek to make light of the incredible amount of work that these amazing people have put into making their lives better. Rather, it spotlights the technologies that help make their achievements possible. If you want to see something extraordinary, check out the ballerina at https://tinyurl.com/37vn8bfd. The article and its video makes plain the amount of work required to make these various technologies work.

REMEMBER

It's a fact of life that just about everyone has some challenge in terms of capabilities and skills. At the end of a long day, someone with 20-20 vision might benefit from magnifying software to make text or graphic elements larger. Color-translation software can help someone who sees the full spectrum of human color take in details that aren't normally visible. As people age, they tend to need assistance to hear, see, touch, or otherwise interact with common objects. Likewise, assistance with tasks such as walking could keep someone in their own home for their entire life. The point is that using various kinds of AI-enabled technologies can significantly help everyone to have a better life, as discussed in the sections that follow.

Considering the software-based solutions

Many people using computers today rely on some type of software-based solution to meet specific needs. One of the most famous of these solutions is a screen reader called Job Access With Speech (JAWS) (https://tinyurl.com/nwjn8jmb), which tells you about display content using sophisticated methods. As you might imagine, every technique that both data science and AI rely on to condition data, interpret it, and then provide a result likely occurs within the JAWS software, making it a good way for anyone to understand the capabilities and limits of software-based solutions. The best way for you to see how this works for you is to download and install the software, and then use it while blindfolded to perform specific tasks on your system. (Avoid anything that will terrify you, though, because you'll make mistakes.)

Accessibility software helps people who live with particular challenges perform incredible tasks. It can also help others understand what it would be like to maneuver through life with that specific challenge. A considerable number of such applications are available, but for one example, check out Vischeck at https://tinyurl.com/y6z7x8xs. This software lets you see graphics in the same way that people with specific color issues see them. (Note that the site may not work well with really large images or during times of high usage rates.) It's not that people with these conditions don't see color — in fact, they see it just fine. But a given color is simply shifted to a different color, so saying *color shifted* is likely a better term, and a term like *color blindness* doesn't apply.

Relying on hardware augmentation

Many kinds of human activity challenges require more than just software to address adequately. The "Considering the use of exoskeletons" section, earlier in this chapter, tells you about the various ways in which exoskeletons see use today in preventing injury, augmenting natural human capabilities, or addressing specific needs (such as enabling a person with paraplegia to walk). However, many other kinds of hardware augmentation address other needs, and the vast majority require some level of AI to work properly.

Consider, for example, the use of eye-gaze systems (https://eyegaze.com/). The early systems relied on a template mounted on top of the monitor. A person with quadriplegia could look at individual letters, and that action would be picked up by two cameras (one on each side of the monitor) and then typed into the computer. By typing commands this way, the person could perform basic tasks at the computer.

Some of the early eye-gaze systems connected to a robotic arm through the computer. The robotic arm could do extremely simple but important actions, such as help users get a drink or scratch their nose. Modern systems actually help connect a user's brain directly to the robotic arm, making it possible to perform tasks such as eating without help (see https://tinyurl.com/hyht79z9). In addition, even newer systems are doing things like restoring a person's sense of touch (https://tinyurl.com/ddfpkcze).

Seeing AI in prosthetics

You can find many examples of AI used in prosthetics. Yes, some passive examples exist, but most of the newer visions for prosthetics rely on dynamic approaches that require an AI to perform. One of the more amazing examples of AI-enabled prosthetics is the fully dynamic foot created by Hugh Herr (https://tinyurl.com/9v253u8c). This foot and ankle work so well that Hugh can perform tasks such as rock climbing. You can see a presentation that he gave at TED; go to https://tinyurl.com/ffpy5ff9.

WARNING

A moral dilemma that we might have to consider sometime in the future (thankfully not today) is when prosthetics actually allow their wearers to substantially surpass native human capability. For example, in the movie *Eon Flux*, the character Sithandra has hands for feet (https://tinyurl.com/k3eun74x). The hands are essentially a kind of prosthetic grafted to someone who used to have normal feet. The question arises as to whether this kind of prosthetic implementation is valid, useful, or even desirable. At some point, a group of people will need to sit down and ascertain where prosthetic use should end to maintain humans as humans (assuming that we decide to remain human and not evolve into some next phase).

Completing Analysis in New Ways

Using AI in a manner that best suits its capabilities maximizes the potential for medical specialists to use it in a meaningful way. Data analysis is one area in which AI excels. In fact, entire websites are devoted to the role that AI plays in modern medicine, such as the one at https://tinyurl.com/amanphxc.

Merely taking a picture of a potential tumor site and then viewing the result might seem to be all that a specialist needs to make a great diagnosis. However, most techniques for acquiring the required snapshot rely on going through tissue that isn't part of the tumor site, thereby obscuring the output. In addition, a physician wants to obtain the best information possible when viewing the tumor in its smallest stages.

Not only does using AI to help perform the diagnosis assist in identifying tumors when they're small and with greater accuracy, it also speeds up the analysis process immensely. Time is critical when dealing with many diseases. According to https://tinyurl.com/35umyv6k, the speed increase is monumental and the cost small for using this new approach.

As impressive as the detection and speed capabilities of AI are in this area, what really makes a difference is the capability to combine AI in various ways to perform Internet of Things (IoT) data compilations. When the AI detects a condition in a particular patient, it can automatically check the patient's records and display the relevant information onscreen with the diagnosed scans, as shown in the article at https://tinyurl.com/b5p8sdsr. Now the doctor has every last piece of pertinent information for a patient before making a diagnosis and considering a particular path. (To see other amazing uses of AI in medicine, check out the site at https://tinyurl.com/275mztss.)

Relying on Telepresence

In the future, you may be able to call on a doctor to help with a problem and not even go to the hospital or clinic to do it. For that matter, you may be able to call on just about any other professional the same way. The use of telepresence in all sorts of fields will likely increase as the availability of professionals in specific areas decreases due to continuing specialization. The following sections discuss telepresence and describe how it relies largely on AI in some respects.

Defining telepresence

The term *telepresence* simply means to be in one place and seem as though you're in another. The ScienceDirect article at https://tinyurl.com/xs2sb6sa talks about how telepresence and augmented reality walk side by side to provide special kinds of experiences. While augmented or virtual reality exist essentially in artificial worlds, telepresence exists in the real world. For example, using telepresence, you might be able to see the Grand Canyon more or less directly without actually being there. The thing that separates telepresence from simply using a camera is that, through the use of sensors, a person experiences telepresence through their own senses. It's almost, but not quite, the same as being there in person.

If the person is also able to interact with the other environment, perhaps through a robotic-like device, many people call it *teleoperation*. A gray area exists in this case because it's hard to tell precisely where telepresence ends and teleoperation begins in many cases. However, the central idea in both cases is that it feels as though you're actually there.

Considering examples of telepresence

One of the most common uses of telepresence today is to reduce costs in hospitals in various ways. For example, a robot could monitor a patient in ways that monitoring equipment can't, and then alert either a nurse or a doctor to changes in a patient's condition that the robot isn't designed to handle (https://tinyurl.com/ypzw52pt). Telepresence means being able to monitor patients from essentially anywhere, especially in their homes, making nursing home stays less likely (https://tinyurl.com/26tav7zv). In addition, telepresence allows a patient to visit with family when such visits wouldn't be possible for any of a number of reasons.

Telepresence is also making an appearance in factories and office buildings (https://tinyurl.com/4xsnjjtt). A security guard is safer in a secured room than walking the rounds. Using a telepresence robot allows the guard to patrol the premises without getting tired. In addition, it's possible to fit a robot with special vision to see things that a human guard can't see.

Enforced use of telepresence will likely increase its use and provide an incentive to improve the technology. During the Covid-19 pandemic, many doctors also began to rely on telepresence to maintain contact with their patients as described in articles like "Teleconsultations during a pandemic" at https://tinyurl.com/macuta3e. The National Institutes of Health (NIH) also recommended using telepresence for patient-based teaching as described at https://tinyurl.com/4j9zeb6j. Isolation during the pandemic was also a problem for many people, especially the older population, as described in the article at https://tinyurl.com/ykvadwxb. All of these pandemic-enhanced uses of telepresence will likely make the technology more common and potentially reduce its cost due to economies of scale.

TIP

The capabilities of the telepresence device determine its usefulness. The site at https://tinyurl.com/y7sm2ytr shows that the robotic form comes in all sorts of sizes and shapes to meet just about every need.

Understanding telepresence limitations

The problem with telepresence is that humans can quickly become too comfortable using it. For example, many people criticize a doctor who used telepresence, instead of a personal visit, to deliver devastating news to a family (see https://tinyurl.com/3azcb7w8). In some cases, personalized human touch and interaction is an essential component of life.

Telepresence also can't replace human presence in some situations requiring senses that these devices can't currently offer. For example, if the task requires the sense of smell, telepresence can't support the need at all. Given how often sense of smell becomes an essential part of performing a task, even in a hospital, overreliance on telepresence can be a recipe for disaster. The article at https://tinyurl.com/w8pbvx78 provides some additional insights as to when telepresence may simply be a bad idea.

Devising New Surgical Techniques

Robots and AI routinely participate in surgical procedures today. In fact, some surgeries would be nearly impossible without the use of robots and AI. However, the history of using this technology isn't very lengthy. The first surgical robot, Arthrobot, made its appearance in 1983 (see https://tinyurl.com/48bshu29 for details). Even so, the use of these life-saving technologies has reduced errors, improved results, decreased healing time, and generally made surgery less expensive over the long run. The following sections describe the use of robots and AI in various aspects of surgery.

Making surgical suggestions

You can view the whole idea of surgical suggestions in many different ways. For example, an AI could analyze all the data about a patient and provide the surgeon with suggestions about the best approaches to take based on that individual patient's record. The surgeon could perform this task, but it would take longer and might be subject to errors that the AI won't make. The AI doesn't get tired or overlook things; it consistently views all the data available in the same way every time.

Unfortunately, even with an AI assistant, surprises still happen during surgery, which is where the next level of suggestion comes into play (https://tinyurl.com/dw3f5m4e). According to the article at https://tinyurl.com/2zpuhywm, doctors can now have access to a device that works along the same lines as Alexa, Siri, Google Home, and Cortana (the AI in devices you may actually have in your own home). No, the device won't take the doctor's request for music to play during the surgery, but the surgeon can use the device to locate specific bits of information without having to stop. This means that the patient receives the benefit of what amounts to a second opinion to handle unforeseen complications during a surgery. Mind you, the device isn't actually doing anything more than making already existing research, which was created by other doctors, readily available in response to surgeon requests; no real thinking is involved.

Getting ready for surgery also means analyzing all those scans that doctors insist on having. Speed is an advantage that AI has over a radiologist. Products such as Enlitic (https://www.enlitic.com/), a deep-learning technology, can analyze radiological scans in milliseconds — up to 10,000 times faster than a radiologist. In addition, the system is 50 percent better at classifying tumors and has a lower false-negative rate (0 percent versus 7 percent) than humans. Another product in this category, Arterys (https://arterys.com/), can perform a cardiac scan in 6 to 10 minutes, rather than the usual hour. Patients don't have to spend time holding their breath, either. Amazingly, this system obtains several dimensions of data: 3-D heart anatomy, blood-flow rate, and blood-flow direction, in this short time.

Assisting a surgeon

Most robotic help for surgeons today assists, rather than replaces, the surgeon. The first robot surgeon, the PUMA system, appeared in 1986. It performed an extremely delicate neurosurgical biopsy, which is a nonlaparoscopic type of surgery. Laparoscopic surgery is minimally invasive, with one or more small holes serving to provide access to an organ, such as a gall bladder, for removal or repair. The first robots weren't adept enough to perform this task.

By 2000, the da Vinci Surgical System provided the ability to perform robotic laparoscopic surgery using a 3-D optical system. The surgeon directs the robot's movements, but the robot performs the actual surgery. The surgeon watches a high-definition display during the surgery and can actually see the operation better than being in the room performing the task personally. The da Vinci System also uses smaller holes than a surgeon can, reducing the risk of infection.

The most important aspect of the da Vinci Surgical System, though, is that the setup augments the surgeon's native capabilities. For example, if the surgeon shakes a bit during part of the process, the da Vinci Surgical System removes the shake — similarly to how anti-shake features work with a camera. The system also smoothes out external vibrations. The system's setup also enables the surgeon to perform extremely fine movements — finer than a human can natively perform, thereby making the surgery far more precise than the surgeon could accomplish alone.

TECHNICAL STUFF

The da Vinci Surgical System is a complex and extremely flexible device. The FDA has approved it for both pediatric and adult surgeries of the following types:

>> Urological surgeries

>> General laparoscopic surgeries

>> General noncardiovascular thoracoscopic surgeries

>> Thoracoscopically assisted cardiotomy procedures

The point behind including all this medical jargon is that the da Vinci Surgical System can perform many tasks without involving a surgeon directly. At some point, robot surgeons will become more autonomous, keeping humans even farther away from the patient during surgery. In the future, no one will actually enter the clean room with the patient, thereby reducing the chances of infection to nearly zero. You can read more about the da Vinci Surgical System at `https://tinyurl.com/4h44vtyy`.

Replacing the surgeon with monitoring

In *Star Wars*, you see robotic surgeons patching up humans all the time. In fact, you might wonder whether any human doctors are available. Theoretically, robots could take over some types of surgery in the future, but the possibility is still a long way off. Robots would need to advance quite a bit from the industrial sort of applications that you find today. The robots of today are hardly autonomous and require human intervention for setups.

However, the art of surgery for robots is making advances. For example, the Smart Tissue Autonomous Robot (STAR) outperformed human surgeons when sewing a pig intestine, as described at `https://tinyurl.com/aezx65u3`. Doctors supervised STAR during the surgery, but the robot actually performed the task on its own, which is a huge step forward in robotic surgery. The video at `https://tinyurl.com/p3dswzyx` is quite informative about where surgery is going. You can see a more technical video at `https://tinyurl.com/3dr4xbkk`.

Performing Tasks Using Automation

AI is great at automation. It never deviates from the procedure, never gets tired, and never makes mistakes as long as the initial procedure is correct. Unlike humans, AI never needs a vacation or a break, or even an eight-hour day (not that many in the medical profession have that luxury, either). Consequently, the same

AI that interacts with a patient for breakfast will do so for lunch and dinner as well. So at the outset, AI has some significant advantages if viewed solely on the bases of consistency, accuracy, and longevity (see the sidebar "Bias, sympathy, and empathy" for areas in which AI falls short). The following sections discuss various ways in which AI can help with automation through better access to resources, such as data.

Working with medical records

One major way in which an AI helps in medicine is with medical records. In the past, everyone used paper records to store patient data. Each patient might also have a blackboard that medical personnel use to record information daily during a hospital stay. Various charts contain patient data, and the doctor might also have notes. Having all these sources of information in so many different places made it hard to keep track of the patient in any significant way. Using an AI, along with a computer database, helps make information accessible, consistent, and reliable. Products such as DeepMind, now part of Google Health (https://tinyurl.com/yskwcm72 and https://health.google/) enable personnel to mine the patient's information to see patterns in data that aren't obvious.

Medicine is about a team approach, with many people of varying specialties working together. However, anyone who watches the process for a while soon realizes that the various specialists don't always communicate among themselves sufficiently because they're all quite busy treating patients. Products such as Cloud-MedX (https://cloudmedxhealth.com) take all the input from all the parties involved and perform risk analysis on it. The result is that the software can help locate potentially problematic areas that could reduce the likelihood of a good patient outcome. In other words, this product does some of the communicating that the various stakeholders would likely do if they weren't submerged in patient care.

Predicting the future

Some truly amazing predictive software based on medical records includes Autonomous Health, which uses algorithms to determine the likelihood of a patient's need for readmission to the hospital after a stay. By performing this task, hospital staff can review reasons for potential readmission and address them before the patient leaves the hospital, making readmission less likely. Along with this strategy, Zephyr Health (https://tinyurl.com/3782d8rp) helps doctors evaluate various therapies and choose those most likely to result in a positive outcome — again reducing the risk that a patient will require readmission to the hospital.

In some respects, your genetics form a map of what will happen to you in the future. Consequently, knowing about your genetics can increase your understanding of your strengths and weaknesses, helping you to live a better life. Deep Genomics (https://www.deepgenomics.com/) is discovering how mutations in your genetics affect you as a person. Mutations need not always produce a negative result; some mutations actually make people better, so knowing about mutations can be a positive experience, too. Check out the video at https://tinyurl.com/fjhs638b for more details.

Making procedures safer

Doctors need lots of data to make good decisions. However, with data being spread out all over the place, doctors who lack the ability to analyze that disparate data quickly often make imperfect decisions. To make procedures safer, a doctor needs not only access to the data but also some means of organizing and analyzing it in a manner reflecting the doctor's specialty. One such product is Oncora Medical (https://www.oncora.ai/), which collects and organizes medical records for radiation oncologists. As a result, these doctors can deliver the right amount of radiation to just the right locations to obtain a better result with a lower potential for unanticipated side effects.

Doctors also have trouble obtaining necessary information because the machines they use tend to be expensive and huge. An innovator named Jonathan Rothberg decided to change all that by using the Butterfly Network (https://www.butterflynetwork.com/). Imagine an iPhone-sized device that can perform both an MRI and an ultrasound. The picture on the website is nothing short of amazing.

Creating better medications

Everyone complains about the price of medications today. Yes, medications can do amazing things for people, but they cost so much that some people end up mortgaging homes to obtain them. Part of the problem is that testing takes a lot of time. Performing a tissue analysis to observe the effects of a new drug can take up to a year. Fortunately, products such as Strateos (https://strateos.com/) can greatly reduce the time required to obtain the same tissue analysis to as little as one day.

Of course, better still would be for the drug company to have a better idea of which drugs are likely to work and which aren't before investing any money in research. Atomwise (https://www.atomwise.com/) uses a huge database of molecular structures to perform analyses on which molecules will answer a particular need. In 2015, researchers used Atomwise to create medications that would make Ebola less likely to infect others. The analysis that would have taken human researchers months or possibly years to perform took Atomwise just one day to complete. This scenario also played out in the Covid-19 pandemic (see `https://tinyurl.com/ut2fh5fa`).

Drug companies also produce a huge number of drugs. The reason for this impressive productivity, besides profitability, is that every person is just a little different. A drug that performs well and produces no side effects on one person might not perform well at all for another person, and could even do harm. Turbine (`https://turbine.ai/`) enables drug companies to perform drug simulations so that the drug companies can locate the drugs most likely to work with a particular person's body. Turbine's current emphasis is on cancer treatments, but it's easy to see how this same approach could work in many other areas.

TIP

Medications can take many forms. Some people think they come only in pill or shot form, yet your body produces a wide range of medications in the form of microbiomes. Your body actually contains ten times as many microbes as it does human cells, and many of these microbes are essential for life; you'd quickly die without them. Pendulum Therapeutics (`https://pendulumlife.com/`) is using a variety of methods, including machine learning and various forms of data science (`https://tinyurl.com/387n554c`), to make these microbiomes work better for you so that you don't necessarily need a pill or a shot to cure something.

Some companies have yet to realize their potential, but they're likely to do so eventually. One such company is Recursion Pharmaceuticals (`https://www.recursion.com/`), which employs automation to explore ways to solve new problems using known drugs, bioactive drugs, and pharmaceuticals that didn't previously make the grade. The company has had some success in helping to solve rare genetic diseases, and it has a goal of curing 100 diseases in the long term (obviously, an extremely high goal to reach).

Combining Robots and Medical Professionals

Semi-autonomous robots with limited capabilities are starting to become integrated into society. Japan has used these robots for a while now (see `https://tinyurl.com/5x5u5va8`). The robots are also appearing in America in the form of RUDY (see `https://infrobotics.com/`). In most cases, these robots can perform simple tasks, such as reminding people to take medications and playing simple games, without much in the way of intervention. However, when needed, a doctor or other medical professional can take control of the robot from a remote location and perform more advanced tasks through the robot. Using this approach means that the person obtains instant help when necessary, reducing the potential for harm to the patient and keeping costs low.

REMEMBER

These sorts of robots are in their infancy now, but expect to see them improve with time. Although these robots are tools to assist medical personnel and can't actually replace a doctor or nurse for many specialized tasks, they do provide the constant surveillance that patients need, along with a comforting presence. In addition, the robots can reduce the need to hire humans to perform common, repetitive tasks (such as dispensing pills, providing reminders, and assisting with walking) that robots can perform quite well even now.

Chapter **8**

Relying on AI to Improve Human Interaction

eople interact with each other in myriad ways. In fact, few people realize just how many different ways communication occurs. When many people think about communication, they think about writing or talking. However, interaction can take many other forms, including eye contact, tonal quality, and even scent, as described in "The Truth about Pheromones" in the *Smithsonian Magazine*. An example of the computer version of enhanced human interaction is the electronic nose, which relies on a combination of electronics, biochemistry, and artificial intelligence to perform its task and has been applied to a wide range of industrial applications and research (see `https://tinyurl.com/488jfzut`). In fact, the electronic nose can even sniff out diseases (see `https://tinyurl.com/28cfcjek`). This chapter concentrates more along the lines of standard communication, however, including body language. You get a better understanding of how AI can enhance human communication through means that are less costly than building your own electronic nose.

AI can also enhance the manner in which people exchange ideas. In some cases, AI provides entirely new methods of communication, but in many cases, AI provides a subtle (or sometimes not so subtle) method of enhancing existing ways to exchange ideas. Humans rely on exchanging ideas to create new technologies, build on existing technologies, or learn about technologies needed to increase an individual's knowledge. Ideas are abstract, which makes exchanging them particularly difficult at times, so AI can provide a needed bridge between people.

At one time, if someone wanted to store their knowledge to share with someone else, they generally relied on writing. In some cases, they could also augment their communication by using graphics of various types. However, only some people can use these two forms of media to gain new knowledge; many people require more, which is why online sources such as YouTube have become so popular. Interestingly enough, you can augment the power of multimedia, which is already substantial, by using AI, and this chapter tells you how.

The final section of this chapter helps you understand how an AI can give you almost superhuman sensory perception. Perhaps you really want that electronic nose after all; it does provide significant advantages in detecting scents that are significantly less aromatic than humans can smell. Imagine being able to smell at the same level as a dog does (which uses 100 million aroma receptors, versus the 1 million aroma receptors that humans possess). It turns out there are two ways that let you achieve this goal: using monitors that a human accesses indirectly, and direct stimulation of human sensory perception.

Developing New Ways to Communicate

Communication involving a developed language initially took place between humans via the spoken versus written word. The only problem with spoken communication is that the two parties must appear near enough together to talk. Consequently, written communication is superior in many respects because it allows time-delayed communications that don't require the two parties to ever see each other. The three main methods of human nonverbal communication rely on

>> **Alphabets/Iconographs:** The abstraction of components of human words or symbols

>> **Language:** The stringing of words or symbols together to create sentences or convey ideas in written form

>> **Body language:** The augmentation of language with context

The first two methods are direct abstractions of the spoken word. They aren't always easy to implement, but people have been doing so for thousands of years. The body-language component is the hardest to implement because you're trying to create an abstraction of a physical process. Writing helps convey body language using specific terminology, such as that described at https://tinyurl.com/27newjbf. However, the written word falls short, so people augment it with symbols, such as emoticons and emojii (read about their differences at https://tinyurl.com/9jyc5n4n). The following sections discuss these issues in more detail.

Creating new alphabets

The introduction to this section discusses two new alphabets used in the computer age: emoticons and emojii (https://tinyurl.com/wjsw8te5 and https://emojipedia.org/). The sites where you find these two graphic alphabets online can list hundreds of them. For the most part, humans can interpret these iconic alphabets without too much trouble because they resemble facial expressions, but an application doesn't have the human sense of art, so computers often require an AI just to figure out what emotion a human is trying to convey with the little pictures. Fortunately, you can find standardized lists, such as the Unicode emoji chart at https://tinyurl.com/j4bdmm3m. Of course, a standardized list doesn't actually help with translation. The article "An Algortithm Trained on Emoji Knows When You're Being Sarcastic on Twitter" at MIT Technology Review.com provides more details on how someone can train an AI to interpret and react to emojii (and by extension, emoticons). You can actually see an example of this process at work at https://deepmoji.mit.edu/.

The emoticon is an older technology, and many people are trying their best to forget it (but likely won't succeed because emoticons are so easy to type). The emoji, however, is new and exciting enough to warrant a movie called *The Emoji Movie*. You can also rely on Google's AI to turn your selfies into emojii (see "Google's Allo Morphs Your Selfies into Custom Emojis" at CNET:). Many people have a hard time figuring some emojii out, so you can check Emojipedia (https://emojipedia.org/) to see what they mean.

REMEMBER

Humans have created new alphabets to meet specific needs since the beginning of the written word. Emoticons and emojii represent two of many alphabets that you can count on humans creating as the result of the Internet and the use of AI. In fact, it may actually require an AI to keep up with them all. However, it's equally important to remember that some characters are lost as time progresses. For example, check out the article "12 Characters that Didn't Make the Alphabet" at MentalFloss.com.

Working with emoji and other meaningful graphics

Many text references today are sprinkled with emojii and other iconographs. Most of the references you see online today deal with emojii and emoticons, either removing them or converting them to text, as explained in the article "Text Preprocessing: Handle Emoji and Emoticons" at Study Machine Learning.com.

It's not too uncommon to find bits and pieces of other languages sprinkled throughout a text, and these words or phrases need to be handled in a meaningful way. That's where articles like "Chinese Natural Language (Pre)processing: An Introduction" at Towards Data Science.com can come in very handy. The problem with translating some languages into a form where they can act as input to a Natural Language Processing (NLP) model is that the concept of the language differs from English. For example, when working with Chinese, you deal with ideas, rather than pronunciation as you do with English.

Some situations also require that you process meaningful graphics because part of the text meaning is in the graphic. This sort of translation need commonly arises in technical or medical texts. The article "How Image Analysis and Natural Language Processing can be combined to improve Precision Medicine" by Obi Igbokwe at Medium.com discusses how to accomplish this task.

REMEMBER

The point of these various translations of nontext into a textual form is that humans communicate in many ways, and AI can help make such communication easier and improve comprehension. In addition, using AI to perform NLP makes it possible to look for patterns, even in text that is heavily imbued with nontext elements.

Automating language translation

The world has always had a problem with the lack of a common language. Yes, English has become more or less universal — to some extent, but it's still not completely universal. Having someone translate between languages can be expensive, cumbersome, and error prone, so translators, although necessary in many situations, aren't necessarily a great answer either. For those who lack the assistance of a translator, dealing with other languages can be quite difficult, which is where applications such as Google Translate (see Figure 8-1) come into play.

One of the things you should note in Figure 8-1 is that Google Translate offers to automatically detect the language for you. What's interesting about this feature is that it works extremely well in most cases. Part of the responsibility for this feature is the Google Neural Machine Translation (GNMT) system. It can actually look at entire sentences to make sense of them and provide better translations than applications that use phrases or words as the basis for creating a translation (see https://tinyurl.com/8by975xx for details).

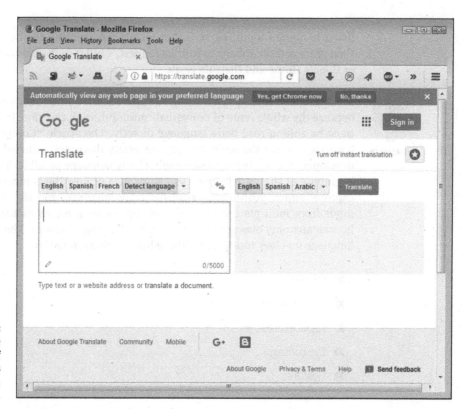

FIGURE 8-1:
Google Translate
is an example of
AI that performs
an essential,
everyday task.

TECHNICAL STUFF

What is even more impressive is that GNMT can translate between languages even when it doesn't have a specific translator, using an artificial language, an *interlingua* (see https://tinyurl.com/wcfk24jc). However, it's important to realize that an interlingua doesn't function as a universal translator; it's more of a universal bridge. Say that the GNMT doesn't know how to translate between Chinese and Spanish. However, it can translate between Chinese and English and between English and Spanish. By building a 3-D network representing these three languages (the interlingua), GNMT is able to create its own translation between Chinese and Spanish. Unfortunately, this system won't work for translating between Chinese and Martian because no method is available yet to understand and translate Martian in any other human language. Humans still need to create a base translation for GNMT to do its work.

Incorporating body language

A significant part of human communication occurs with body language, which is why the use of emoticons and emojii is important. However, people are becoming more used to working directly with cameras to create videos and other forms of communication that involve no writing. In this case, a computer could possibly listen to human input, parse it into tokens representing the human speech, and then process those tokens to fulfill a request, similar to the manner in which Alexa or Google Home and their ilk work.

REMEMBER

Unfortunately, merely translating the spoken word into tokens won't do the job because the whole issue of nonverbal communication remains. In this case, the AI must be able to read body language directly. The article "Computer Reads Body Language" from Carnegie Mellon University discusses some of the issues that developers must solve to make reading body language possible. The picture at the beginning of that article gives you some idea of how the computer camera must capture human positions to read the body language, and the AI often requires input from multiple cameras to make up for such issues as having part of the human anatomy obscured from the view of a single camera. The reading of body language involves interpreting these human characteristics:

>> Posture

>> Head motion

>> Facial expression

>> Eye contact

>> Gestures

Of course, there are other characteristics, but even if an AI can get these five areas down, it can go a long way to providing a correct body-language interpretation. In addition to body language, current AI implementations also take characteristics like tonal quality into consideration, which makes for an extremely complex AI that still doesn't come close to doing what the human brain does seemingly without effort.

TECHNICAL STUFF

After an AI can read body language, it must also provide a means to output it when interacting with humans. Given that reading body language (facial expressions, body position, placement of hands, and so on) is in its infancy, robotic or graphic presentation of body language is even less developed. The article "Robots Learn to Speak Body Language" at IEEE Spectrum.org points out that robots can currently interpret body language and then react appropriately in some few cases. Robots are currently unable to create good facial expressions, so according to the article "Realistic Robot Faces Aren't Enough" at The Conversation.com, the best-case scenario is to substitute posture, head motion, and gestures for body language. You can find yet more details in this ScienceDirect.com article, "Facially expressive humanoid robotic face." The result isn't all that impressive, yet.

Exchanging Ideas

An AI doesn't have ideas because it lacks both intrapersonal intelligence and the ability to understand. However, an AI can enable humans to exchange ideas in a manner that creates a whole that is greater than the sum of its parts. In many cases, the AI isn't performing any sort of exchange. The humans involved in the process perform the exchange by relying on the AI to augment the communication process. The following sections provide additional details about how this process occurs.

Creating connections

A human can exchange ideas with another human, but only as long as the two humans know about each other. The problem is that many experts in a particular field don't actually know each other — at least, not well enough to communicate. An AI can perform research based on the flow of ideas that a human provides and then create connections with other humans who have that same (or similar) flow of ideas.

One of the ways in which this communication creation occurs is in social media sites such as LinkedIn (`https://www.linkedin.com/`), where the idea is to create connections between people based on a number of criteria. A person's network becomes the means by which the AI deep inside LinkedIn suggests other potential connections. Ultimately, the purpose of these connections from the user's perspective is to gain access to new human resources, make business contacts, create a sale, or perform other tasks that LinkedIn enables using the various connections.

Augmenting communication

To exchange ideas successfully, two humans need to communicate well. The only problem is that humans sometimes don't communicate well, and sometimes they don't communicate at all. The issue isn't just one of translating words but also ideas. The societal and personal biases of individuals can preclude the communication because an idea for one group may not translate at all for another group. For example, the laws in one country could make someone think in one way, but the laws in another country could make the other human think in an entirely different manner.

Theoretically, an AI could help communication between disparate groups in numerous ways. Of course, language translation (assuming that the translation is accurate) is one of these methods. However, an AI could provide cues as to what is and isn't culturally acceptable by prescreening materials. Using categorization, an

AI could also suggest aids like alternative graphics and so on to help communication take place in a manner that helps both parties.

Defining trends

Humans often base ideas on trends. However, to visualize how the idea works, other parties in the exchange of ideas must also see those trends, and communicating using this sort of information is notoriously difficult. AI can perform various levels of data analysis and present the output graphically. The AI can analyze the data in more ways and faster than a human can so that the story the data tells is specifically the one you need it to tell. The data remains the same; the presentation and interpretation of the data change.

Studies show that humans relate better to graphical output than tabular output, and graphical output will definitely make trends easier to see. You generally use tabular data to present only specific information; graphics always work best for showing trends (see https://tinyurl.com/3hwsjwcy). Using AI-driven applications can also make creating the right sort of graphic output for a particular requirement easier. Not all humans see graphics in precisely the same way, so matching a graphic type to your audience is essential.

Using Multimedia

Most people learn by using multiple senses and multiple approaches. A doorway to learning that works for one person may leave another completely mystified. Consequently, the more ways in which a person can communicate concepts and ideas, the more likely it is that other people will understand what the person is trying to communicate. Multimedia normally consists of sound, graphics, text, and animation, but some multimedia does more.

AI can help with multimedia in numerous ways. One of the most important is in the creation, or authoring, of the multimedia. You find AI in applications that help with everything from media development to media presentation. For example, when translating the colors in an image, an AI may provide the benefit of helping you visualize the effects of those changes faster than trying one color combination at a time (the brute-force approach).

After using multimedia to present ideas in more than one form, those receiving the ideas must process the information. A secondary use of AI relies on the use of neural networks to process the information in various ways. Categorizing the multimedia is an essential use of the technology today. However, in the future you can look forward to using AI to help in 3-D reconstruction of scenes based on 2-D pictures. Imagine police being able to walk through a virtual crime scene with every detail faithfully captured.

MULTIMEDIA AND ADDRESSING PEOPLE'S FUNCTIONAL NEEDS

Most people have some particular functional need relating to how they take in and understand information. (If you're wondering about the use of the new accessibility terms in this book, please check out the resource at https://ncdj.org/style-guide/.) Considering such needs as part of people's use of multimedia is important. The whole intent of multimedia is to communicate ideas in as many ways as possible so that just about everyone can understand the ideas and concepts you want to present. Even when a presentation as a whole uses multimedia successfully, individual ideas can become lost when the presentation uses only one method to communicate them. For example, communicating a sound only aurally almost guarantees that only those with really good hearing will actually receive the idea. A subset of those with the required hearing still won't get the idea because it may appear as only so much noise to them, or they simply don't learn through the limited method offered in the presentation. Using as many methods as possible to communicate each idea is essential if you want to reach as many people as possible.

People used to speculate that various kinds of multimedia would appear in new forms. For example, imagine a newspaper that provides Harry Potter–like dynamic displays. Most of the technology pieces are actually available today, but the issue comes down to the market. For a technology to become successful, it must have a market — that is, a means for paying for itself.

Embellishing Human Sensory Perception

One way that AI truly excels at improving human interaction is by augmenting humans in one of two ways: by allowing them to use their native senses to work with augmented data, or by augmenting the native senses to do more. The following sections discuss both approaches to enhancing human sensing and therefore improve communication.

Shifting data spectrum

When performing various kinds of information gathering, humans often employ technologies that filter or shift the data spectrum with regard to color, sound, touch, or smell. The human still uses native capabilities, but some technology changes the input such that it works with that native capability. One of the most common examples of spectrum shifting is astronomy, in which shifting and filtering light enables people to see astronomical elements, such as nebula, in ways that the naked eye can't —thereby improving our understanding of the universe.

Teaching a robot to feel by touch is in its infancy as described at `https://tinyurl.com/ukjscsye` and `https://tinyurl.com/y998s2h8`. Most efforts today focus on helping the robot work better by using tactile responses as part of manipulating its machinery, such as the light touch needed to grasp an egg versus the heavier touch required to lift a barbell. When this technology moves far enough forward, it might become possible for various AIs to communicate with humans through direct touch or the description of various kinds of touch.

Shifting and filtering colors, sounds, touches, and smells manually can require a great deal of time, and the results can disappoint even when performed expertly, which is where AI comes into play. An AI can try various combinations far faster than a human, and can locate the potentially useful combinations with greater ease because an AI performs the task in a consistent manner.

The most intriguing technique for exploring our world, however, is completely different from what most people expect. What if you could smell a color or see a sound? The occurrence of *synesthesia*, which is the use of one sense to interpret input from a different sense, is well documented in humans (see `https://tinyurl.com/2s9tb284`; you can also find a range of related articles at `https://tinyurl.com/a8y44n2p`). People use AI to help study the effect, as described at `https://tinyurl.com/ec6mpbpa`. The interesting use of this technology, though, is to create a condition in which other people can actually use synesthesia as another means to see the world (see `https://www.fastcompany.com/3024927/this-app-aids-your-decision-making-by-mimicking-its-creators-synesthesia`).

Augmenting human senses

As an alternative to using an external application to shift data spectrum and somehow make that shifted data available for use by humans, you can augment human senses. In augmentation, a device, either external or implanted, enables a human to directly process sensory input in a new way. Many people view these new capabilities as the creation of cyborgs, as described at `https://tinyurl.com/xyvxcxbm`. The idea is an old one: Use tools to make humans ever more effective at performing an array of tasks. In this scenario, humans receive two forms of augmentation: physical and intellectual.

Physical augmentation of human senses already takes place in many ways, and it's guaranteed to increase as humans become more receptive to various kinds of implants. For example, night vision glasses currently allow humans to see at night, with high-end models providing color vision controlled by a specially designed processor. In the future, eye augmentation/replacement could allow people to see any part of the spectrum. This augmentation/replacement would be controlled by the person's thoughts, so that people would see only that part of the spectrum needed to perform a specific task.

Intelligence Augmentation requires more intrusive measures but also promises to allow humans to exercise far greater capabilities. Unlike AI, Intelligence Augmentation (IA) has a human actor at the center of the processing. The human provides the creativity and intent that AI currently lacks. You can read a discussion of the differences between AI and IA in "Intelligence Augmentation Vs. Artificial Intelligence" at the Planergy blog.

3

Working with Software-Based AI Applications

Chapter **9**

Performing Data Analysis for AI

A massing data isn't a modern phenomenon; people have amassed data for centuries. No matter whether the information appears in text or numeric form, people have always appreciated how data describes the surrounding world, and among other things, they use it to move civilization forward. Data has a value in itself. By using its content, humanity can learn, transmit critical information to descendants (no need to reinvent the wheel), and effectively act in the world.

People have recently learned that data contains more than surface information. If data is in an appropriate numerical form, you can apply special techniques devised by mathematicians and statisticians, called data analysis techniques, and extract even more knowledge from it. In addition, starting from simple data analysis, you can extract meaningful information and subject data to more advanced analytics using machine learning algorithms capable of predicting the future, classifying information, and effectively helping to make optimal decisions.

Data analysis and machine learning enable people to push data usage beyond previous limits to develop a smarter AI. This chapter introduces you to data analysis. It shows how to use data as a learning tool and starting point to solve challenging

AI problems, such as by suggesting the right product to a customer, understanding spoken language, translating English into German, automating car driving, and more.

Defining Data Analysis

The current era is called the Information Age not simply because we have become so data rich but also because society has reached a certain maturity in analyzing and extracting information from that data. Companies such as Alphabet (Google), Amazon, Apple, Facebook, and Microsoft, which have built their businesses on data, are ranked among the most valuable companies in the world. Such companies don't simply gather and keep stored data that's provided by their digital processes; they also know how to make it as valuable as oil by employing precise and elaborate data analysis. Google, for instance, records data from the web in general and from its own search engine, among other things, and in order to support its business, it has built a plurality of machine learning models that are continuously updated based on that data.

You may have encountered the "data is the new oil" mantra in the news, in magazines, or at conferences. The statement implies both that data can make a company rich and that it takes skill and hard work to make this happen. Though many have employed the concept and made it incredibly successful, it was Clive Humbly, a British mathematician, who first equated data to oil, given his experience with consumers' data in the retail sector. Humbly is known for being among the founders of Dunnhumby, a UK marketing company, and the mind behind Tesco's fidelity card program. In 2006, Humbly also emphasized that data is not just money that rains from the sky; it requires effort to make it useful. Just as you can't immediately use unrefined oil because it has to be changed into something else by chemical processes that turn it into gas, plastics, or other chemicals, so data must undergo significant transformations to acquire value.

The most basic data transformations are provided by *data analysis*, and you liken them to the basic chemical transformations that oil undergoes in a refinery before becoming valuable fuel or plastic products. Using just data analysis, you can lay down the foundation for more advanced data analysis processes that you can apply to data. Data analysis, depending on the context, refers to a large body of possible data operations, sometimes specific to certain industries or tasks. You can categorize all these transformations in four large and general families that provide an idea of what happens in data analysis:

» **Transforming:** Changes the data's structure. The term *transforming* refers to different processes, though the most common is putting data into ordered rows and columns in a *matrix format* (also called *flat-file transformation*). For instance, you can't effectively process data of goods bought in a supermarket until you've placed each customer in a single row and added products purchased to single columns within that row. You add those products as numeric entries that contain quantities or monetary value. Transforming can also involve specialized numeric transformations such as *scaling* and *shifting*, through which you change the *mean* (the average) and the *dispersion* (the way a numeric series is spread around its mean values) of the data. These processes make the data suitable for an algorithm.

» **Cleansing:** Fixes imperfect data. Depending on the means of acquiring the data, you may find different problems because of missing information, extremes in range, or simply wrong values. For instance, data in a supermarket may present errors when goods are labeled with incorrect prices. Some data is *adversarial*, which means that it has been created to spoil any conclusions. For instance, a product may have fake reviews on the Internet that change its rank. Cleansing helps to remove adversarial examples from data and to make conclusions reliable.

» **Inspecting:** Validates the data. Data analysis is mainly a human job, though software plays a big role. Humans can easily recognize patterns and spot strange data elements. For this reason, data analysis produces many data statistics and provides useful and insightful visualization, such as Health InfoScape by MIT Senseable Cities and General Electric, which helps grasp informative content at a glance. For example, you can see how diseases connect to one another based on data processed from 72 million records.

» **Modeling:** Grasps the relationship between the elements present in data. To perform this task, you need tools taken from statistics, such as correlations, chi-square tests, linear regression, and many others that can reveal whether some values truly are different from others or just related. For instance, when analyzing expenditures in a supermarket, you can determine that people buying diapers also tend to buy beer. Statistical analysis finds these two products associated many times in the same baskets. (This study is quite a legend in data analytics; see the short story in this *Forbes* article, "Birth of a legend.")

Data analysis isn't magic. You perform transformations, cleansing, inspecting, and modeling by using mass summation and multiplication based on matrix calculus (which is nothing more than the long sequences of summation and multiplication that many people learn in school). The data analysis arsenal also provides basic statistical tools, such as mean and variance, that describe data distribution, or sophisticated tools, such as correlation and linear regression analysis, that reveal whether you can relate events or phenomena to one another (like buying diapers and beer) based on the evidence. To discover more about such data techniques, both *Machine Learning For Dummies*, 2nd Edition, and *Python for Data Science For Dummies*, 2nd Edition, by John Paul Mueller and Luca Massaron (Wiley), offer a practical overview and explanation of each of them.

REMEMBER

What makes data analysis hard in the age of big data is the large volume of data that requires special computing tools, such as Hadoop (http://hadoop.apache.org/) and Apache Spark (https://spark.apache.org/), which are two software tools used to perform massive data operations. In spite of such advanced tools, it's still a matter of perspiration to manually prepare up to 80 percent of the data. The interesting *New York Times* interview in "For Big-Data Scientists, 'Janitor Work' Is Key Hurdle to Insights" with Monica Rogati, who is an expert in the field and an AI advisor to many companies, discusses this issue in more detail.

Understanding why analysis is important

Data analysis is essential to AI. In fact, no modern AI is possible without visualizing, cleansing, transforming, and modeling data before advanced algorithms enter the process and turn it into information of even higher value than before.

In the beginning, when AI consisted of purely algorithmic solutions and expert systems, scientists and experts carefully prepared the data to feed them. Therefore, for instance, if someone wanted an algorithm to process information, a data expert placed the correct data into *lists* (ordered sequences of data elements) or in other data structures that could appropriately contain the information and allow its desired manipulation. At such a time, data experts gathered and organized the data so that its content and form were exactly as expected, because it was created or selected for that specific purpose. Manipulating known data into a specific form posed a serious limitation because crafting data required a lot of time and energy; consequently, algorithms received less information than is available today.

Today, the attention has shifted from data production to data preparation by using data analysis. The idea is that various sources already produce data in such large quantities that you can find what you need without having to create special data for the task. For instance, imagine wanting an AI to control your pet door to let cats and dogs in but keep other animals out. Modern AI algorithms learn from task-specific data, which means processing a large number of images showing examples of dogs, cats, and other animals. Most likely, such a huge set of images will arrive from the Internet, maybe from social sites or image searches. Previously, accomplishing a similar task meant that algorithms would use just a few specific inputs about shapes, sizes, and distinctive characteristics of the animals, for example. The paucity of data meant that they could accomplish only a few limited tasks. In fact, no examples exist of an AI that can power a pet door using classic algorithms or expert systems.

Data analysis comes to the rescue of modern algorithms by providing information about the images retrieved from the Internet. Using data analysis enables AI to discover the image sizes, variety, number of colors, words used in the image titles, and so on. This is part of inspecting the data and, in this case, that's necessary to cleanse and transform it. For instance, data analysis can help you spot a photo of an animal erroneously labeled a cat (you don't want to confuse your AI) and help you transform the images to use the same color format (for example, shades of gray) and the same size.

Reconsidering the value of data

With the explosion of data availability on digital devices (as discussed in Chapter 2), data assumes new nuances of value and usefulness beyond its initial scope of instructing (teaching) and transmitting knowledge (transferring data). The abundance of data, when provided to data analysis, acquires new functions that distinguish it from the informative ones:

>> Data describes the world better by presenting a wide variety of facts, and in more detail by providing nuances for each fact. It has become so abundant that it covers every aspect of reality. You can use it to unveil how even apparently unrelated things and facts actually relate to each other.

>> Data shows how facts associate with events. You can derive general rules and learn how the world will change or transform, given enough data to dig out the rules you need.

In some respects, data provides us with new super-powers. Chris Anderson, *Wired*'s previous editor-in-chief, discusses how large amounts of data can help scientific discoveries outside the scientific method (see "The End of Theory: The Data Deluge Makes the Scientific Method Obsolete" at Wired.com). The author relies on the example of achievements of Google in the advertising and translation business sectors, in which Google achieved prominence not by using specific models or theories but rather by applying algorithms to learn directly from data.

DISCOVERING SMARTER AI DEPENDS ON DATA

More than simply powering AI, data makes AI possible. Some people would say that AI is the output of sophisticated algorithms of elevated mathematical complexity, and that's certainly true. Activities like vision and language understanding require algorithms that aren't easily explained in layman's terms and necessitate millions of computations to work. (Hardware plays a role here, too.)

Yet there's more to AI than algorithms. Dr. Alexander Wissner-Gross, an American research scientist, entrepreneur, and fellow at the Institute for Applied Computation Science at Harvard, provided his insights in an earlier interview at Edge.org ("Datasets Over Algorithms"). The interview reflects on why AI technology took so long to take off, and Wissner-Gross concludes that it might have been a matter of the quality and availability of data rather than algorithmic capabilities.

Wissner-Gross reviews the timing of most breakthrough AI achievements in preceding years, showing how data and algorithms contribute to the success of each breakthrough and highlighting how each of them was fresh at the time the milestone was reached. Wissner-Gross shows how data is relatively new and always updated, whereas algorithms aren't new discoveries, but rather rely on consolidation of older technology.

The conclusions of Wissner-Gross's reflections are that, on average, the algorithm is usually 15 years older than the data. He points out that data is pushing AI's achievements forward and leaves the reader wondering what could happen if feeding the presently available algorithms with better data in terms of quality and quantity were possible.

As in advertising, scientific data (such as from physics, chemistry or biology) can support innovation that allows scientists to approach problems without hypotheses, instead considering the variations found in large amounts of data and using discovery algorithms. In the past, scientists took uncountable observations and a multitude of experiments to gather enough deductions to describe the physics of the universe using the scientific method. This manual process allowed scientists to find many underlying laws of the world.

The ability to innovate using data alone is a major breakthrough in the scientific quest to understand the world. AI achievements such AlphaFold (described in "DeepMind solves 50-year-old 'grand challenge' with protein folding A.I." at CNBC.com) allow scientists to figure out how proteins fold in space and how they function without the need for long experimentation. For many other scientific tasks data analysis pairs observations expressed as inputs and outputs. This technique makes it possible to determine how things work and to define, thanks to machine learning, approximate rules (laws) of our world without having to resort to using manual observations and deductions. Many aspects of the scientific process are now faster and more automatic.

Defining Machine Learning

The pinnacle of data analysis is machine learning. You can successfully apply machine learning only after data analysis provides correctly prepared input. However, only machine learning can associate a series of outputs and inputs, as well as determine the working rules behind the output in an effective way. Data analysis concentrates on understanding and manipulating the data so that it can become more useful and provide insights on the world, whereas machine learning strictly focuses on taking inputs from data and elaborating a working, internal representation of the world that you can use for practical purposes. Machine learning enables people to perform such tasks as predicting the future, classifying things in a meaningful way, and making the best rational decision in a given context.

REMEMBER

The central idea behind machine learning is that you can represent reality by using a mathematical function that the algorithm doesn't know in advance, but which it can guess after seeing some data. You can express reality and all its challenging complexity in terms of unknown mathematical functions that machine learning algorithms find and make actionable. This concept is the core idea for all kinds of machine learning algorithms.

Learning in machine learning is purely mathematical, and it ends by associating certain inputs to certain outputs. It has nothing to do with understanding what the algorithm has learned (data analysis builds understanding to a certain extent), thus the learning process is often described as *training* because the algorithm is trained to match the correct answer (the output) to every question offered (the input). (*Machine Learning For Dummies*, 2nd Edition, by John Paul Mueller and Luca Massaron, describes in detail how this process works.)

In spite of lacking deliberate understanding and being simply a mathematical process, machine learning can prove useful in many tasks. It provides the AI application the power of doing the most rational thing given a certain context when learning occurs by using the right data. The following sections help describe how machine learning works in more detail, what benefits you can hope to obtain, and the limits of using machine learning within an application.

Understanding how machine learning works

Many people are used to the idea that applications start with a function, accept data as input, and then provide a result. For example, a programmer might create a function called Add( ) that accepts two values as input, such as 1 and 2, and provide the result, which is 3. The output of this process is a value. In the past, writing a program meant understanding the function used to manipulate data to create a given result with certain inputs. Machine learning turns this process around. In this case, you know that you have inputs, such as 1 and 2. You also know that the desired result is 3. However, you don't know what function to apply to create the desired result. Training provides a learner algorithm with all sorts of examples of the desired inputs and results expected from those inputs. The learner then uses this input to create a function. In other words, training is the process whereby the learner algorithm maps a flexible function to the data. The output is typically the probability of a certain class or a numeric value.

To give an idea of what happens in the training process, imagine a child learning to distinguish trees from other objects. Before the child can do so in an independent fashion, a teacher presents the child with a certain number of tree images, complete with all the facts that make a tree distinguishable from other objects of the world. Such facts could be features such as the tree's material (wood), its parts (trunk, branches, leaves or needles, roots), and location (planted into the soil). The child produces an idea of what a tree looks like by contrasting the display of tree features with the images of other, different objects, such as pieces of furniture that are made of wood but do not share other characteristics with a tree.

A machine learning classifier works the same. It builds its cognitive capabilities by creating a mathematical formulation that includes all the given features in a way that creates a function that can distinguish one class from another. Pretend that a mathematical formulation, also called *target function*, exists to express the characteristics of a tree. In such a case, a machine learning classifier can look for its representation as a replica or an approximation (a different function that works alike). Being able to express such mathematical formulation is the representation capability of the machine learning algorithm.

From a mathematical perspective, you can express the representation process in machine learning by using the equivalent term *mapping*. Mapping happens when you discover the construction of a function by observing its outputs. A successful mapping in machine learning is similar to a child internalizing the idea of an object. The child understands the abstract rules derived from the facts of the world in an effective way so that when the child sees a tree, for example, the child immediately recognizes it.

Such a representation (abstract rules derived from real-world facts) is possible because the learning algorithm has many internal parameters (consisting of vectors and matrices of values), which equate to the algorithm's memory for ideas that are suitable for its mapping activity that connects features to response classes. The dimensions and type of internal parameters delimit the kind of target functions that an algorithm can learn. An optimization engine in the algorithm changes parameters from their initial values during learning to represent the target's hidden function.

During optimization, the algorithm searches the possible variants of its parameter combinations to find one that allows correct mapping between features and classes during training. This process evaluates many potential candidate target functions from among those that the learning algorithm can guess. The set of all the potential functions that the learning algorithm can discover is the *hypothesis space*. You can call the resulting classifier with its set parameters a hypothesis, a way in machine learning to say that the algorithm has set parameters to replicate the target function and is now ready to define correct classifications (a fact demonstrated later).

The hypothesis space must contain all the parameter variants of all the machine learning algorithms that you want to try to map to an unknown function when solving a classification problem. Different algorithms can have different hypothesis spaces. What really matters is that the hypothesis space contains the target function (or its approximation, which is a different but similar function, because in the end all you need is something that works).

You can imagine this phase as the time when a child experiments with many different creative ideas by assembling knowledge and experiences (an analogy for the given features) in an effort to create a visualization of a tree. Naturally, the parents are involved in this phase, and they provide relevant environmental inputs. In machine learning, someone has to provide the right learning algorithms, supply some nonlearnable parameters (called hyperparameters), choose a set of examples to learn from, and select the features that accompany the examples. Just as a child can't always learn to distinguish between right and wrong if left alone in the world, so machine learning algorithms need guidance from human beings to learn successfully.

Understanding the benefits of machine learning

You find AI and machine learning used in a great many applications today. The only problem is that the technology works so well that you don't know that it even exists. In fact, you might be surprised to find that many devices in your home already make use of both technologies. Both technologies definitely appear in your car and the workplace. In fact, the uses for both AI and machine learning number in the millions — all safely out of sight even when they're quite dramatic in nature. Chapter 1 lists a few of the ways in which you might see AI used (fraud detection, resource scheduling, and others; see "Considering AI Uses" in that chapter), but that list doesn't even begin to scratch the surface. You can find AI used in many other ways. However, it's also useful to view uses of machine learning outside the normal realm that many consider the domain of AI. Here are a few uses for machine learning that you might not associate with an AI:

» **Access control:** In many cases, access control is a yes-or-no proposition. An employee smartcard grants access to a resource in much the same way that people have used keys for centuries. Some locks do offer the capability to set times and dates that access is allowed, but such coarse-grained control doesn't really answer every need. By using machine learning, you can determine whether an employee should gain access to a resource based on role and need. For example, an employee can gain access to a training room when the training reflects an employee role.

» **Animal protection:** The ocean might seem large enough to allow animals and ships to cohabitate without problem. Unfortunately, many animals get hit by ships each year. A machine learning algorithm could allow ships to avoid animals by learning the sounds and characteristics of both the animal and the ship.

» **Predicting wait times:** Most people don't like waiting when they have no idea how long the wait will be. Machine learning allows an application to determine waiting times based on staffing levels, staffing load, complexity of the problems the staff is trying to solve, availability of resources, and so on.

Being useful; being mundane

Even though the movies suggest that AI is sure to make a huge splash, and you do occasionally see incredible uses for AI in real life, most uses for AI are mundane and even boring. For example, Hilary Mason, general manager of machine learning at Cloudera, cites how machine learning is used in an international accounting firm to automatically fill in accounting questionnaires (see "Make AI Boring: The Road from Experimental to Practical" at InformationWeek.com). The act of performing this analysis is dull when compared to other sorts of AI activities, but the benefits are that the accounting firm saves money, and the results are better as well.

Specifying the limits of machine learning

Machine learning relies on algorithms to analyze huge datasets. Currently, machine learning can't provide the sort of AI that the movies present. Even the best algorithms can't think, feel, display any form of self-awareness, or exercise free will.

What machine learning can do is perform predictive analytics far faster than any human can. As a result, machine learning can help humans work more efficiently. The current state of AI, then, is one of performing analysis, but humans must still consider the implications of that analysis and make the required moral and ethical decisions. Essentially, machine learning provides just the learning part of AI, and that part is nowhere near ready to create an AI of the sort you see in films.

The main point of confusion between learning and intelligence is people's assumption that simply because a machine gets better at its job (learning), it's also aware (intelligence). Nothing supports this view of machine learning. The same phenomenon occurs when people assume that a computer is purposely causing problems for them. The computer can't assign emotions and therefore acts only upon the input provided and the instruction contained within an application to process that input. A true AI will eventually occur when computers can finally emulate the clever combination used by nature:

>> **Genetics:** Slow learning from one generation to the next

>> **Teaching:** Fast learning from organized sources

>> **Exploration:** Spontaneous learning through media and interactions with others

Apart from the fact that machine learning consists of mathematical functions optimized for a certain purpose, other weaknesses expose the limits of machine learning. You need to consider three important limits:

>> **Representation:** Representing some problems using mathematical functions isn't easy, especially with complex problems like mimicking a human brain. At the moment, machine learning can solve single, specific problems that answer simple questions, such as "What is this?" and "How much is it?" and "What comes next?"

>> **Overfitting:** Machine learning algorithms can seem to learn what you care about, but they actually often don't. Therefore, their internal functions mostly memorize the data without learning from the data. *Overfitting* occurs when your algorithm learns too much from your data, up to the point of creating functions and rules that don't exist in reality.

>> **Lack of effective generalization because of limited data:** The algorithm learns what you teach it. If you provide the algorithm with bad or weird data, it behaves in an unexpected way.

As for representation, a simple-learner algorithm can learn many different things, but not every algorithm is suited for certain tasks. Some algorithms are general enough that they can play chess, recognize faces on Facebook, and diagnose cancer in patients. An algorithm reduces the data inputs and the expected results of those inputs to a function in every case, but the function is specific to the kind of task you want the algorithm to perform.

The secret to machine learning is generalization. However, with generalization come the problems of overfitting and *biased data* (data that when viewed using various statistical measures is skewed in one direction or the other). The goal is to generalize the output function so that it works on data beyond the training examples. For example, consider a spam filter. Say that your dictionary contains 100,000 words (a small dictionary). A limited training dataset of 4,000 or 5,000 word combinations (as you would see them in a real sentence) must create a generalized function that can then find spam in the 2^100,000 combinations that the function will see when working with actual data. In such conditions, the algorithm will seem to learn the rules of the language, but in reality it won't do well. The algorithm may respond correctly to situations similar to those used to train it, but it will be clueless in completely new situations. Or, it can show biases in unexpected ways because of the kind of data used to train it.

For instance, Microsoft trained its AI, Tay, to chat with human beings on Twitter and learn from their answers. Unfortunately, the interactions went haywire because users exposed Tay to hate speech, raising concerns about the goodness of any AI powered by machine learning technology. (You can read some of the story at https://tinyurl.com/4bfakpac.) The problem was that the machine learning algorithm was fed bad, unfiltered data (Microsoft didn't use appropriate data analysis to clean and balance the input appropriately), which overfitted the result. The overfitting selected the wrong set of functions to represent the world in a general way as needed to avoid providing nonconforming output, such as hate speech. Of course, even if the output wasn't undesirable, it could still be nonconforming, such as giving wrong answers to straightforward questions. Other AI trained to chat with humans, such as the award-winning Kuki (https://www.kuki.ai/), aren't exposed to the same risks as Tay because their learning is strictly controlled and supervised by data analysis and human evaluation.

Considering How to Learn from Data

Everything in machine learning revolves around algorithms. An algorithm is a procedure or formula used to solve a problem. The problem domain affects the kind of algorithm needed, but the basic premise is always the same: to solve some sort of problem, such as driving a car or playing dominoes. In the first case, the problems are complex and many, but the ultimate problem is one of getting a passenger from one place to another without crashing the car. Likewise, the goal of playing dominoes is to win.

Learning comes in many different flavors, depending on the algorithm and its objectives. You can divide machine learning algorithms into three main groups, based on their purpose:

» Supervised learning

» Unsupervised learning

» Reinforcement learning

The following sections discuss what different kinds of algorithms are exploited by machine learning in more detail.

Supervised learning

Supervised learning occurs when an algorithm learns from example data and associated target responses that can consist of numeric values or string labels, such as classes or tags, in order to later predict the correct response when given new examples. The supervised approach is similar to human learning under the supervision of a teacher. The teacher provides good examples for the student to memorize, and the student then derives general rules from these specific examples.

You need to distinguish between *regression problems*, whose target is a numeric value, and *classification problems*, whose target is a qualitative variable, such as a class or a tag. A regression task could determine the average prices of houses in the Boston area, while an example of a classification task is distinguishing between kinds of iris flowers based on their sepal and petal measures. Here are some examples of supervised learning with important applications in AI described by their data input, their data output, and the real-world application they can solve:

Data Input (X)	Data Output (y)	Real-World Application
History of customers' purchases	A list of products that customers have never bought	Recommender system
Images	A list of boxes labeled with an object name	Image detection and recognition
English text in the form of questions	English text in the form of answers	Chatbot, a software application that can converse
English text	German text	Machine language translation
Audio	Text transcript	Speech recognition
Image, sensor data	Steering, braking, or accelerating	Behavioral planning for autonomous driving

Unsupervised learning

Unsupervised learning occurs when an algorithm learns from plain examples without any associated response, leaving the algorithm to determine the data patterns on its own. This type of algorithm tends to restructure the data into something else, such as new features that may represent a class or a new series of uncorrelated values. The resulting data are quite useful in providing humans with insights into the meaning of the original data and new useful inputs to supervised machine learning algorithms.

Unsupervised learning resembles methods used by humans to determine that certain objects or events are from the same class, such as observing the degree of similarity between objects. Some recommender systems that you find on the web in the form of marketing automation are based on this type of learning. The marketing automation algorithm derives its suggestions from what you've bought in the past. The recommendations are based on an estimation of what group of customers you resemble the most and then inferring your likely preferences based on that group.

Reinforcement learning

Reinforcement learning occurs when you present the algorithm with examples that lack labels, as in unsupervised learning. However, you can accompany an example with positive or negative feedback according to the consequences of the solution that the algorithm proposes.

Reinforcement learning is connected to applications for which the algorithm must make decisions (so the product is prescriptive, not just descriptive, as in unsupervised learning), and the decisions bear consequences. In the human world, it is just like learning by trial and error. Errors help you learn because they have a penalty added (cost, loss of time, regret, pain, and so on), teaching you that a certain course of action is less likely to succeed than others. An interesting example of reinforcement learning occurs when computers learn to play video games by themselves.

In this case, an application presents the algorithm with examples of specific situations, such as having the gamer stuck in a maze while avoiding an enemy. The application lets the algorithm know the outcome of actions it takes, and learning occurs while trying to avoid what it discovers to be dangerous and to pursue survival. You can see how Google DeepMind created a reinforcement learning program that plays old Atari video games on YouTube ("Google DeepMind's Deep Q-learning playing Atari Breakout"). When watching the video, notice how the program is initially clumsy and unskilled but steadily improves with training until it becomes a champion. The process is described as having strong and weak points by Raia Hadsell, a senior research scientist on the Deep Learning team at DeepMind, in an enlightening video from TEDx Talks, "Artificial intelligence, video games and the mysteries of the mind," on YouTube.

Chapter **10**

Employing Machine Learning in AI

Learning has been an important part of AI since the beginning because AI can mimic a human-like level of intelligence. Reaching a level of mimicry that effectively resembles learning took a long time and a variety of approaches. Today, machine learning can boast a quasi-human level of learning in specific tasks, such as image classification or sound processing, and it's striving to reach a similar level of learning in many other tasks.

Machine learning isn't completely automated. You can't tell a computer to read a book and expect it to understand anything. Automation implies that computers can learn how to program themselves to perform tasks instead of waiting for humans to program them. Currently, automation requires large amounts of human-selected data as well as data analysis and training (again, under human supervision). It's like taking a child by the hand for those first steps. Moreover, machine learning has other limits, which are dictated by how it learns from data.

Each family of algorithms has specific ways of accomplishing tasks, and this chapter describes those methods. The goal is to understand how AI makes decisions and predictions. Like discovering the man behind the curtain in the *Wizard of Oz*, you uncover the machinery and the operator behind AI in this chapter. Nevertheless, you still get to enjoy the amazing feeling of seeing the wondrous achievements that machine learning can provide.

Taking Many Different Roads to Learning

Just as human beings have different ways to learn from the world, so the scientists who approached the problem of AI learning took different routes. Each one believed in a particular recipe to mimic intelligence. Up to now, no single model has proven superior to any other. The *no free lunch* theorem, which states that each algorithm provides benefit only to specific problems, is in full effect. Each of these efforts has proven effective in solving particular problems, but not all at one time. Because the algorithms are equivalent in the abstract (see the "No free lunch" sidebar), no one algorithm is superior to the others unless proven in a specific, practical problem. The following sections provide additional information about this concept of using different methods to learn.

Discovering five main approaches to AI learning

An algorithm is a kind of container. It provides a box for storing a method to solve a particular kind of a problem. Algorithms process data through a series of well-defined states. The states need not be deterministic (in many algorithms finding the right solution is often a matter of chance), but the states are defined nonetheless. The sequence of states defines the range of mathematical solutions that the algorithm is able to grasp (technically referred to as the *space of hypothesis*). The goal is to create an output that solves a problem. In the supervised approach, the algorithm receives inputs that help define the output, but the focus is always on the output.

NO FREE LUNCH

A common theorem in mathematical folklore is the *no free lunch* theorem by David Wolpert and William Macready, which states that any two optimization algorithms are equivalent when their performance is averaged across all possible problems. Essentially, no matter which optimization algorithm you use, there won't be any advantage to using it across all possible problems. To gain an advantage, you must use it on those problems for which the algorithm excels. The paper "Simple explanation of the no free lunch theorem of optimization" by Yo-Chi Ho and David L. Pepyne, at ResearchGate. net, provides an accessible but rigorous explanation of the theorem. It's also a good idea to review the discussion at http://www.no-free-lunch.org/ for more details about no free lunch theorems; machine learning relies on two of them.

Algorithms must express the transitions between states using a well-defined and formal language that the computer can understand (usually, a computer language). In processing the data and solving the problem, the algorithm defines, refines, and applies a mathematical function. The function is always specific to the kind of problem being addressed by the algorithm.

As described in the "Avoiding AI Hype and Overestimation" section of Chapter 1, each of the five tribes has a different technique and strategy for solving problems that result in unique algorithms. Combining these algorithms should lead eventually to the master algorithm that will be able to solve any given problem. The following sections provide an overview of the five main algorithmic families.

Symbolic reasoning

One of the earliest tribes, the symbologists, believed that knowledge could be obtained by operating on symbols (signs that stand for a certain meaning or event) and deriving rules from them. By putting together complex systems of rules, you could attain a logic deduction of the result you wanted to know, thus the symbologists shaped their algorithms to produce rules from data. In symbolic reasoning, *deduction* expands the realm of human knowledge, while *induction* raises the level of human knowledge. Induction commonly opens new fields of exploration, while deduction explores those fields.

Connections modeled on the brain's neurons

The connectionists are perhaps the most famous of the five tribes. This tribe strives to reproduce the brain's functions by using silicon instead of biological neurons. Essentially, each of the algorithmic neurons (created as an algorithm that models the real-world counterpart) solves a small piece of the problem, and using many neurons in parallel solves the problem as a whole.

The use of *backpropagation*, or backward propagation of errors, seeks to determine the conditions under which errors are removed from networks built to resemble human neurons by changing the *weights* (how much a particular input figures into the result) and *biases* (how features are selected) of the network. The goal is to continue changing the weights and biases until such time as the actual output matches the target output. At this point, the artificial neuron fires and passes its solution along to the next neuron in line. The solution created by just one neuron is only part of the whole solution. Each neuron passes information to the next neuron in line until the group of neurons creates a final output. Such a method proved the most effective in human-like tasks such as recognizing objects, understanding written and spoken language, and chatting with humans.

Evolutionary algorithms that test variation

The evolutionaries rely on the principles of evolution to solve problems. In other words, this strategy is based on the survival of the fittest (removing any solutions that don't match the desired output). A fitness function determines the viability of each function in solving a problem. Using a tree structure, the solution method looks for the best solution based on function output. The winner of each level of evolution gets to build the next-level functions. The idea is that the next level will get closer to solving the problem but may not solve it completely, which means that another level is needed. This particular tribe relies heavily on recursion and languages that strongly support recursion to solve problems. An interesting output of this strategy has been algorithms that evolve: One generation of algorithms actually builds the next generation.

Bayesian inference

A group of scientists called Bayesians perceived that uncertainty was the key aspect to keep an eye on, and that learning wasn't assured but rather took place as a continuous updating of previous beliefs that grew more and more accurate. This perception led the Bayesians to adopt statistical methods and, in particular, derivations from Bayes' theorem, which helps you calculate probabilities under specific conditions (for instance, the chance of seeing a card of a certain *seed*, the starting value for a pseudo-random sequence, drawn from a deck after three other cards of the same seed have been drawn).

Systems that learn by analogy

The analogyzers use kernel machines to recognize patterns in data. By recognizing the pattern of one set of inputs and comparing it to the pattern of a known output, you can create a problem solution. The goal is to use similarity to determine the best solution to a problem. It's the kind of reasoning that determines that using a particular solution worked in a given circumstance at some previous time; therefore, using that solution for a similar set of circumstances should also work. One of the most recognizable outputs from this tribe is recommender systems. For example, when you buy a product on Amazon, the recommender system comes up with other, related products that you might also want to buy.

The ultimate goal of machine learning is to combine the technologies and strategies embraced by the five tribes to create a single algorithm (the master algorithm) that can learn anything. Of course, achieving that goal is a long way off. Even so, scientists such as Pedro Domingos (https://homes.cs.washington.edu/~pedrod/) are currently working toward that goal.

Delving into the three most promising AI learning approaches

Later sections in this chapter explore the nuts and bolts of the core algorithms chosen by the Bayesians, symbologists, and connectionists. These tribes represent the present and future frontier of learning from data because any progress toward a human-like AI derives from them, at least until a new breakthrough with new and more incredible and powerful learning algorithms occurs. The machine learning scenery is certainly much larger than these three algorithms, but the focus for this chapter is on these three tribes because of their current role in AI. Here's a synopsis of the approaches in this chapter:

>> **Naïve Bayes:** This algorithm can be more accurate than a doctor in diagnosing certain diseases. In addition, the same algorithm can detect spam and predict sentiment from text. It's also widely used in the Internet industry to easily treat large amounts of data.

>> **Bayesian networks (graph form):** This graph offers a representation of the complexity of the world in terms of probability.

>> **Decision trees:** The decision tree type of algorithm represents the symbologists best. The decision tree has a long history and indicates how an AI can make decisions because it resembles a series of nested decisions, which you can draw as a tree (hence the name).

The next chapter, "Improving AI with Deep Learning," introduces neural networks, an exemplary type of algorithm proposed by the connectionists and the real engine behind the AI renaissance. Chapter 11 first discusses how a neural network works and then explains deep learning and why it's so effective in learning.

REMEMBER

All these sections discuss types of algorithms. These algorithm types are further divided into subcategories. For example, decision trees come categorized as regression trees, classification trees, boosted trees, bootstrap aggregated, and rotation forest. You can even drill down into subtypes of the subcategories. A Random Forest classifier is a kind of bootstrap aggregating, and there are even more levels from there. After you get past the levels, you begin to see the actual algorithms, which number into the thousands. In short, this book is giving you an overview of an infinitely more complex topic that could require many volumes to cover in any detail. The takeaway is to grasp the type of algorithm and not to get mired in detail.

Awaiting the next breakthrough

In the 1980s, as expert systems ruled the AI scenery, most scientists and practitioners deemed machine learning to be a minor branch of AI that was focused on learning how to best answer simple predictions from the environment (represented by data) using optimization. Today, machine learning has the upper hand in AI, outweighing expert systems in many applications and research developments, and powering AI applications that scientists previously regarded as impossible at such a level of accuracy and performance. Neural networks, the solution proposed by the connectionists, made the breakthrough possible in the last few years by using a mix of increased hardware capacity, more suitable data, and the efforts of scientists such as Geoffrey Hinton, Yann LeCun, Yoshua Bengio, and many others.

The capabilities offered by neural network algorithms (newly branded deep learning because of increased complexity) are increasing daily. Frequent news reports recount the fresh achievements in audio understanding, image and video recognition, language translation, and even lip reading. (Even though deep learning lacks HAL9000 performance, it's approaching human performance; see "Lip-Reading AI is Under Development, Under Watchful Eyes" at aitrends.com, which talks about Speech Recognition App for the Voice Impaired, SRAVI, a product that may be certified by the time you read this book.) The improvements are the result of intensive funding from large and small companies to engage researchers and of the availability of powerful software, such as Google's TensorFlow (https://www.tensorflow.org/) and PyTorch, an open source machine learning library primarily developed by Facebook's AI Research lab (FAIR) (see https://pytorch.org/). These types of powerful software give both scientists and practitioners access to the technology.

Look for even more sensational AI innovations in the near future. Of course, researchers could always hit a wall again, as happened in the previous AI winters. No one can know whether AI will reach the human level using the present technology or someone will discover a master algorithm, as Pedro Domingos predicted (see his TEDx talk "The Quest for the Master Algorithm" at YouTube.com), that will solve all AI problems (some of which we have yet to imagine). Nevertheless, machine learning is certainly not a fad driven by hype; it's here to stay, either in its present, improved form, or in the form of new algorithms to come.

Exploring the Truth in Probabilities

Some websites would have you believe that statistics and machine learning are two completely different approaches. For example, when you read a blog post called "Statistics vs. Machine Learning, fight!" by Brendan O'Connor (http://

brenocon.com/blog/2008/12/statistics-vs-machine-learning-fight/), you get the idea that the two methodologies are not only different but also downright hostile toward each other. Statistics, contrary to machine learning, were born in an age of limited computational power (you had to solve calculations by hand at that time). Thus, statistics rely more on simplistic mathematical assumptions that render computations easier. Although statistics show a more theoretical approach to problems, whereas machine learning is purely based on data, statistics and machine learning have a lot in common. Also, statistics represents one of the five tribes (schools of thought) that make machine learning feasible.

Statistics often resort to probabilities — which are a way to express uncertainty regarding world events — and so do machine learning and AI (to a larger extent than pure statistics). Not all problems are like the games of chess or Go, which let you take a large but limited number of actions when you decide to take them. If you want to learn how to move a robot in a corridor crowded with people, or have a self-driving car successfully engage in a crossing, you have to consider that plans (such as for moving from point A to point B) don't always have a single outcome and that many results are possible, each one with a different likelihood. In a sense, probability supports AI systems in their reasoning, providing decision-making support and making what seem to be the best, most rational choices despite uncertainty. Uncertainty can exist for various reasons, and AI should be made aware of the level of uncertainty by an effective use of probability:

1. Some situations can't offer certainty because they're random in nature. Similar situations are inherently stochastic. For instance, in card games, you can't be sure what hand you'll have after the dealer shuffles and deals the cards.

2. Even if a situation isn't random, not observing all its aspects (incomplete observation) creates uncertainty over how things will turn out. For instance, a robot walking down a corridor crowded with people can't know the intended direction of each person (it can't read their minds), but it can formulate a guess based on a partial observation of their behavior. As with any guess, the robot has a chance of being right and of being wrong.

3. Limits in the hardware that records world data (called sensors) and approximations in data processing can render results produced from such data uncertain. Measuring is often subject to errors because of the tools used and how the measuring is done. In addition, humans are often subject to cognitive biases and easily fall prey to illusions or blind spots. Similarly, AI is limited by the quality of the data it receives. Approximations and errors introduce uncertainty into every algorithm.

Determining what probabilities can do

Probability tells you the likelihood of an event, and you express it as a number. For instance, if you throw a coin in the air, you don't know whether it will land as heads or tails, but you can tell the probability of both outcomes. The probability of an event is measured in the range from 0 (no probability that an event occurs) to 1 (certainty that an event occurs). Intermediate values, such as 0.25, 0.5, and 0.75, say that the event will happen with a certain frequency when tried enough times. If you multiply the probability by an integer number representing the number of trials you're going to try, you get an estimate of how many times an event should happen on average if all the trials are tried. For instance, if you have an event occurring with probability $p = 0.25$ and you try 100 times, you're likely to witness that event happen $0.25 * 100 = 25$ times.

As it happens, the outcome of $p = 0.25$ is the probability of picking a certain suit when choosing a card randomly from a deck of cards. French playing cards make a classic example of explaining probabilities. The deck contains 52 cards equally divided into four suits: clubs and spades, which are black, and diamonds and hearts, which are red. So if you want to determine the probability of picking an ace, you must consider that there are four aces of different suits. The answer in terms of probability is $p = 4/52 = 0.077$.

Probabilities are between 0 and 1; no probability can exceed such boundaries. You define probabilities empirically from observations. Simply count the number of times a specific event happens with respect to all the events that interest you. For example, say that you want to calculate the probability of how many times fraud happens when doing banking transactions, or how many times people get a certain disease in a particular country. After witnessing the event, you can estimate the probability associated with it by counting the number of times the event occurs and dividing by the total number of events.

You can count the number of times the fraud or the disease happens by using recorded data (mostly taken from records in databases or from direct observation) and then divide that figure by the total number of generic events or observations available. Therefore, you divide the number of frauds by the number of transactions in a year, or you count the number of people who fell ill during the year with respect to the population of a certain area. The result is a number ranging from 0 to 1, which you can use as your baseline probability for a certain event given certain circumstances.

Counting all the occurrences of an event is not always possible, so you need to know about sampling. By sampling, which is an act based on certain probability expectations, you can observe a small part of a larger set of events or objects, yet be able to infer correct probabilities for an event, as well as exact measures such as quantitative measurements or qualitative classes related to a set of objects. For instance, if you want to track the sales of cars in the United States for the past month, you don't need to track every sale in the country. By using a sample comprising the sales from a few car sellers around the country, you can determine quantitative measures, such as the average price of a car sold, or qualitative measures, such as the car model sold most often.

Considering prior knowledge

Probability makes sense in terms of time and space, but some other conditions also influence the probability you measure. The context is important. When you estimate the probability of an event, you may (sometimes wrongly) tend to believe that you can apply the probability that you calculated to each possible situation. The term to express this belief is *a priori probability*, meaning the general probability of an event.

For example, when you toss a coin, if the coin is fair, the a priori probability of a head is about 50 percent (when you also assume the existence of a tiny likelihood of the coin's landing on its edge). No matter how many times you toss the coin, when faced with a new toss, the probability for heads is still about 50 percent. However, in some other situations, if you change the context, the a priori probability is not valid anymore because something subtle happened and changed it. In this case, you can express this belief as an *a posteriori probability*, which is the a priori probability after something happened to modify the count.

REMEMBER

The Latin terms *a priori* and *a posteriori* derive from the treatise Elements by the Greek mathematician Euclid (`https://mathcs.clarku.edu/~djoyce/java/elements/toc.html`). It describes a priori as what comes before and a posteriori as what comes after.

For instance, the a priori probability of a rainy day in the place you live during springtime could be roughly about 20 percent (it depends on where you live on Earth; elsewhere probabilities may be different). However, such probability may differ drastically if you consider only specific temperature and pressure ranges. For instance, when you notice that air pressure is turning low but the temperature is steadily high, the probability of rain drastically increases, and you have a high probability of experiencing a thunderstorm. Therefore, given a different context, the a posteriori probability is different from the expected a priori one. The following sections help you understand the usefulness of probability in more detail.

Conditional probability and Naïve Bayes

You can view cases such as the weather-related ones mentioned in the previous section as *conditional probability*, and express it as p(y|x), which you read as the probability of event y happening given that x has happened. Conditional probabilities are a very powerful tool for machine learning and AI. In fact, when the a priori probability changes greatly because of certain circumstances, knowing the possible circumstances can boost your chances of correctly predicting an event by observing examples — which is exactly what machine learning is intended to do. For example, as previously mentioned, the expectation of a rainy day could be low in your location depending on the current season. However, if you observe temperature, humidity, and atmospheric pressure, you find that certain combinations lead to an increased probability of rain. If the percentage of rainy days is very high when certain conditions are met, contrary to the a priori probability, a machine learning algorithm, called Naïve Bayes, can provide a probability estimation from knowing meteorological measurements.

In fact, the Naïve Bayes algorithm takes advantage of boosting the chance of a correct prediction by knowing the circumstances surrounding the prediction. Everything starts with the Reverend Bayes and his revolutionary theorem of probabilities. In fact, as noted elsewhere, in the book one of the machine learning tribes is named after him (the Bayesians). Bayesians use various statistical methods to solve problems, all based on observing probabilities of the desired outcome in the right context, before and after observing the outcome itself. Based on these observations, they solve the sunrise problem (estimating the likelihood that the sun will rise tomorrow) by chaining repeated observations and continuously updating their estimate of the probability of the sun rising again proportionally to the number of times they have witnessed a long series of dawns before. You can read about Bayesian reasoning applied to a newborn baby observing the sun by reading this article that appeared in the *Economist* at https://www. economist.com/science-and-technology/2000/09/28/in-praise-of-bayes (you may have to supply an email address to obtain a free subscription).

Data scientists have great expectations for the development of advanced algorithms based on Bayesian probability. The article "Can Bayesian Networks provide answers when Machine Learning comes up short?" at diginiomica.com describes why Bayes theorem is so important. Yet, the foundations of Bayes' theorem (the premises used) aren't all that complicated (although they may be a bit counterintuitive if you normally consider, as most people do, only the a priori probabilities without considering a posteriori ones).

Considering Bayes' theorem

Apart from being a Presbyterian minister, the Reverend Thomas Bayes was also a statistician and philosopher who formulated his theorem during the first half of the eighteenth century. The theorem was never published while he was alive. Its publication revolutionized the theory of probability by introducing the idea of conditional probability mentioned in the previous section. Thanks to Bayes' theorem, predicting the probability of an outcome like having a rainy day given certain conditions becomes easier when you apply his formula. Here's the formula used by Thomas Bayes:

```
P(B|E) = P(E|B)*P(B) / P(E)
```

REMEMBER

The Reverend Bayes didn't devise Naïve Bayes; he only formulated the theorem. In truth, there is no sure attribution of the algorithm. It first appeared in a textbook in 1973 without any reference to its creator and passed unobserved for more than a decade until, in 1990, researchers noticed how it performed incredibly accurate predictions if fed with enough accurate data. Reading the formula using the previous example as input can provide a better understanding of an otherwise counter-intuitive formula:

>> **P(B|E):** The probability of a belief (B) given a set of evidence (E) (posterior probability). Read *belief* as an alternative way to express a hypothesis. In this case, the hypothesis is that it rains, and the evidence is a low measure of atmospheric pressure. Knowing the probability of such a belief given evidence can help to predict the weather with some confidence.

>> **P(E|B):** The probability of having low atmospheric pressure when it rains. This term refers to the probability of the evidence in the subgroup, which is itself a conditional probability. In this case, the figure is 90 percent, which translates to a value of 0.9 in the formula (prior probability).

>> **P(B):** The general probability of having a rainy day; that is, the a priori probability of the belief. In this case, the probability is 20 percent, or a value of 0.2 (likelihood).

>> **P(E):** The general probability of measuring low atmospheric pressure. Here it is another a priori probability, this time related to the observed evidence. In this formula, it is a 25 percent probability, which is a value of 0.25 (evidence).

If you solve the previous problem using the Bayes formula and the values you have singled out, the result is $0.9 * 0.2 / 0.25 = 0.72$. That's a high percentage of likelihood, which leads you to affirm that given such evidence (low atmospheric pressure), there is a good probability that it will rain soon.

Another common example, which can raise some eyebrows and is routinely found in textbooks and scientific magazines, is that of the positive medical test. It is quite interesting for a better understanding of how prior and posterior probabilities may indeed change a lot under different circumstances.

Say that you're worried that you have a rare disease experienced by 1 percent of the population. You take the test and the results are positive. Medical tests are never perfectly accurate, and the laboratory tells you that when you are ill, the test is positive in 99 percent of the cases, whereas when you are healthy, the test will be negative in 99 percent of the cases. Now, using these figures, you immediately believe that you're ill, given the high percentage of positive tests when a person is ill (99 percent). However, the reality is quite different. In this case, the figures to plug into the Bayes' theorem are as follows:

```
P(B|E) = P(E|B)*P(B) / P(E)
```

>> 0.99 as P(E|B)

>> 0.01 as P(B)

>> 0.01 * 0.99 + 0.99 *0.01 = 0.0198 as P(E)

The calculations are then $0.99 * 0.01 / 0.0198 = 0.5$, which corresponds to just a 50 percent probability that you're ill. In the end, your chances of not being ill are more than you expected. This kind of result is called a *false positive paradox*, where the indicators seem to point to a positive result, but the math says otherwise. You may wonder how this is possible. The fact is that the number of people seeing a positive response from the test is as follows:

>> **Who is ill and gets the correct answer from the test:** This group is the true positives, and it amounts to 99 percent of the 1 percent of the population who gets the illness.

>> **Who isn't ill and gets the wrong answer from the test:** This group is the 1 percent of the 99 percent of the population who gets a positive response even though they aren't ill. Again, this is a multiplication of 99 percent and 1 percent. This group corresponds to the false positives.

If you look at the problem using this perspective, it becomes evident why. When limiting the context to people who get a positive response to the test, the probability of being in the group of the true positives is the same as that of being in the false positives.

Envisioning the world as a graph

Bayes' theorem can help you deduce how likely something is to happen in a certain context, based on the general probabilities of the fact itself and the evidence you examine, and combined with the probability of the evidence given the fact. Seldom will a single piece of evidence diminish doubts and provide enough certainty in a prediction to ensure that it will happen. As a true detective, to reach certainty, you have to collect more evidence and make the individual pieces work together in your investigation. Noticing how atmospheric pressure has decreased isn't enough to determine whether it is going to rain. Adding data about humidity, season, and location could help increase confidence.

The Naïve Bayes algorithm helps you arrange all the evidence you gather and reach a more solid prediction with a higher likelihood of being correct. Gathered evidence considered separately couldn't save you from the risk of predicting incorrectly, but all evidence summed together can reach a more definitive resolution. The following example shows how things work in a Naïve Bayes classification. This is an old, renowned problem, but it represents the kind of capability that you can expect from an AI. The dataset is from the paper "Induction of Decision Trees" by John Ross Quinlan at dl.acm.org. Quinlan is a computer scientist who contributed to the development of another machine learning algorithm, decision trees, in a fundamental way, but his example works well with any kind of learning algorithm. The problem requires that the AI guess the best conditions to play tennis given the weather conditions. The set of features described by Quinlan is as follows:

>> **Outlook:** Sunny, overcast, or rainy

>> **Temperature:** Cool, mild, or hot

>> **Humidity:** High or normal

>> **Windy:** True or false

The following table contains the database entries used for the example:

Outlook	Temperature	Humidity	Windy	Play Tennis
Sunny	Hot	High	False	No
Sunny	Hot	High	True	No
Overcast	Hot	High	False	Yes
Rainy	Mild	High	False	Yes
Rainy	Cool	Normal	False	Yes
Rainy	Cool	Normal	True	No
Overcast	Cool	Normal	True	Yes
Sunny	Mild	High	False	No
Sunny	Cool	Normal	False	Yes
Rainy	Mild	Normal	False	Yes
Sunny	Mild	Normal	True	Yes

Outlook	Temperature	Humidity	Windy	Play Tennis
Overcast	Mild	High	True	Yes
Overcast	Hot	Normal	False	Yes
Rainy	Mild	High	True	No

The option of playing tennis depends on the four arguments shown in Figure 10-1.

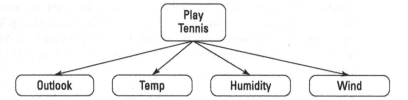

The result of this AI learning example is a decision as to whether to play tennis, given the weather conditions (the evidence). Using just the outlook (sunny, overcast, or rainy) won't be enough, because the temperature and humidity could be too high or the wind might be strong. These arguments represent real conditions that have multiple causes, or causes that are interconnected. The Naïve Bayes algorithm is skilled at guessing correctly when multiple causes exist.

The algorithm computes a score, based on the probability of making a particular decision and multiplied by the probabilities of the evidence connected to that decision. For instance, to determine whether to play tennis when the outlook is sunny but the wind is strong, the algorithm computes the score for a positive answer by multiplying the general probability of playing (9 played games out of 14 occurrences) by the probability of the day's being sunny (2 out of 9 played games) and of having windy conditions when playing tennis (3 out of 9 played games). The same rules apply for the negative case (which has different probabilities for not playing given certain conditions):

```
likelihood of playing: 9/14 * 2/9 * 3/9 = 0.05
likelihood of not playing: 5/14 * 3/5 * 3/5 = 0.13
```

Because the score for the likelihood of not playing is higher, the algorithm decides that it's safer not to play under such conditions. It computes such likelihood by summing the two scores and dividing both scores by their sum:

```
probability of playing : 0.05 / (0.05 + 0.13) = 0.278
probability of not playing : 0.13 / (0.05 + 0.13) = 0.722
```

You can further extend Naïve Bayes to represent relationships that are more complex than a series of factors that hint at the likelihood of an outcome using a *Bayesian network*, which consists of graphs showing how events affect each other. Bayesian graphs have nodes that represent the events and arcs showing which events affect others, accompanied by a table of conditional probabilities that show how the relationship works in terms of probability. Figure 10-2 shows a famous example of a Bayesian network taken from a 1988 academic paper, "Local computations with probabilities on graphical structures and their application to expert systems," by Lauritzen, Steffen L. and David J. Spiegelhalter, published by the *Journal of the Royal Statistical Society* (find it on the Wiley Online Library).

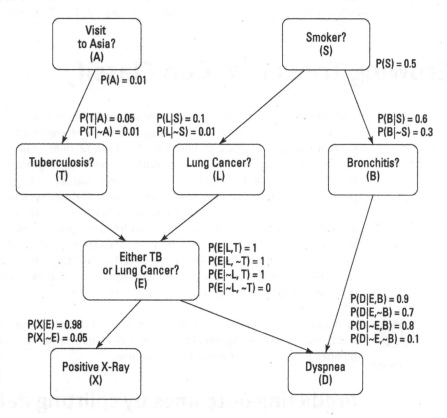

FIGURE 10-2:
A Bayesian network can support a medical decision.

The depicted network is called *Asia*. It shows possible patient conditions and what causes what. For instance, if a patient has dyspnea, it could be an effect of tuberculosis, lung cancer, or bronchitis. Knowing whether the patient smokes, has been to Asia, or has anomalous x-ray results (thus giving certainty to specific pieces of evidence, a priori in Bayesian language) helps infer the real (posterior) probabilities of having any of the pathologies in the graph.

Bayesian networks, though intuitive, have complex math behind them, and they're more powerful than a simple Naïve Bayes algorithm because they mimic the world as a sequence of causes and effects based on probability. Bayesian networks are so effective that you can use them to represent any situation. They have varied applications, such as medical diagnoses, the fusing of uncertain data arriving from multiple sensors, economic modeling, and the monitoring of complex systems such as a car. For instance, because driving in highway traffic may involve complex situations with many vehicles, the Analysis of MassIve Data STreams (AMIDST) consortium, in collaboration with the automaker Daimler, devised a Bayesian network that can recognize maneuvers by other vehicles and increase driving safety. You can read more about this project and see the complex Bayesian network in "Analysis of MassIve Data STreams - AMIDST" at vbn.auu.dk.

Growing Trees that Can Classify

A decision tree is another type of key algorithm in machine learning that contributes to AI implementation and learning. Decision tree algorithms aren't new, but they do have a long history. The first algorithm of their kind dates back to the 1970s (with many ensuing variants). When you consider experiments and original research, the use of decision trees goes back even earlier — they are as old as the perceptron, the forerunner of neural networks. As the core symbologist algorithm, decision trees have enjoyed a long popularity because they're an intuitive type of algorithm. It's easy to translate the output into rules and therefore make the output easily understood by humans. Decision trees are also extremely easy to use. All these characteristics make them an effective and appealing no-brainer with respect to models that require complex input data matrix transformations or extremely accurate tuning of hyperparameters.

Symbolism is the AI approach based on logic statements and extensive use of deduction. *Deduction* expands knowledge from what we know, and *induction* formulates general rules starting from evidence.

Predicting outcomes by splitting data

If you have a group of measures and want to describe them using a single number, you use an arithmetic *mean* (summing all the measures and dividing by the number of measures). In a similar fashion, if you have a group of classes or qualities (for instance, you have a dataset containing records of many breeds of dogs or types of products), you can use the most frequent class in the group to represent them all, which is called the *mode*. The mode is another statistical measure like mean, but it contains the value (a measure or a class) that appears most often. Both the mean and the mode strive to report a number or class that provides you with the most confidence in guessing the next group element, because they produce the fewest mistakes. In a sense, they're predictors that learn the most probable answer from existing data. Decision trees leverage means and modes as predictors by splitting the dataset into smaller sets whose means or modes are the best possible predictors for the problem at hand.

TIP

Dividing a problem in order to arrive at a solution easily is also a common strategy in many *divide-and-conquer* algorithms. As with an enemy army in battle, if you can split your foe and fight it singularly, you can attain an easier victory.

Using a sample of observations as a starting point, the algorithm retraces the rules that generated the output classes (or the numeric values when working through a regression problem) by dividing the input matrix into smaller and smaller partitions until the process triggers a rule for stopping. Such retracing from particular toward general rules is typical of human inverse deduction, as treated by logic and philosophy.

REMEMBER

In a machine learning context, such inverse reasoning is achieved by applying a search among all the possible ways to split the training data (the *in-sample* when discussed in statistics) and decide, regardless of what could happen in the following steps, to use the split that maximizes statistical measurements on the resulting partitions.

The division occurs to enforce a simple principle: Each partition of the initial data must make predicting the target outcome easier, which is characterized by a different and more favorable distribution of classes (or values) than the original sample. The algorithm creates partitions by splitting the data. It determines the data splits by first evaluating the features. Then it evaluates the values in the features that could bring the maximum improvement of a special statistical measure — that is, the measure that plays the role of the cost function in a decision tree.

A number of statistical measurements determine how to make the splits in a decision tree. All abide by the idea that a split must improve on the original sample, or another possible split, when it makes prediction safer. Among the most used measurements are Gini impurity, information gain, and variance reduction (for regression problems). These measurements operate similarly, so this chapter focuses on information gain because it's the most intuitive measurement and conveys how a decision tree can detect an increased predictive ability (or a reduced risk) in the easiest way for a certain split. Ross Quinlan created a decision tree algorithm based on information gain (ID3) in the 1970s, and it's still quite popular thanks to its recently upgraded version to C4.5. Information gain relies on the formula for informative entropy (devised by Claude Shannon, an American mathematician and engineer known as the father of information theory), a generalized formulation that describes the expected value from the information contained in a message:

```
Shannon Entropy E = -Σ(p(i)@@tslog2(p(i)))
```

In the formula, you consider all the classes one at a time, and you sum together the multiplication result of each of them. In the multiplication each class has to take, p(i) is the probability for that class (expressed in the range of 0 to 1) and log2 is the base 2 logarithm. Starting with a sample in which you want to classify two classes having the same probability (a 50/50 distribution), the maximum possible entropy is Entropy = -0.5*log2(0.5) -0.5*log2(0.5) = 1.0. However, when the decision tree algorithm detects a feature that can split the dataset into two partitions, where the distribution of the two classes is 40/60, the average informative entropy diminishes:

```
Entropy = -0.4*log2(0.4) -0.6*log2(0.6) = 0.97
```

Note the entropy sum for all the classes. Using the 40/60 split, the sum is less than the theoretical maximum of 1 (diminishing the entropy). Think of the entropy as a measure of the mess in data: The less mess, the more order, and the easier it is to guess the right class. After a first split, the algorithm tries to split the obtained partitions further using the same logic of reducing entropy. It progressively splits any successive data partition until no more splits are possible because the subsample is a single example or because it has met a stopping rule.

Stopping rules are limits to the expansion of a tree. These rules work by considering three aspects of a partition: initial partition size, resulting partition size, and information gain achievable by the split. Stopping rules are important because decision tree algorithms approximate a large number of functions; however, noise and data errors can easily influence this algorithm. Consequently, depending on the sample, the instability and variance of the resulting estimates affect decision tree predictions.

Making decisions based on trees

As an example of decision tree use, this section uses the same Ross Quinlan dataset discussed in the "Envisioning the world as a graph" section, earlier in the chapter. Using this dataset lets us present and describe the ID3 algorithm, a special kind of decision tree found in the paper "Induction of Decision Trees," mentioned previously in this chapter. The dataset is quite simple, consisting of only 14 observations relative to the weather conditions, with results that say whether playing tennis is appropriate.

The example contains four features: outlook, temperature, humidity, and wind, all expressed using qualitative classes instead of measurements (you could express temperature, humidity, and wind strength numerically) to convey a more intuitive understanding of how the weather features relate to the outcome. After these features are processed by the algorithm, you can represent the dataset using a tree-like schema, as shown in Figure 10-3. As the figure shows, you can inspect and read a set of rules by splitting the dataset to create parts in which the predictions are easier by looking at the most frequent class (in this case, the outcome, which is whether to play tennis).

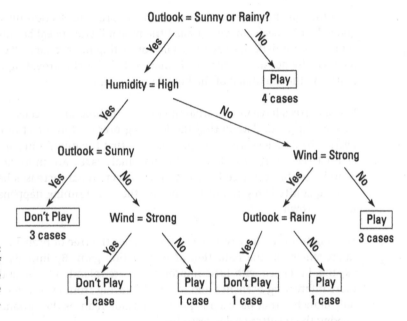

FIGURE 10-3: A visualization of the decision tree built from the play-tennis data.

To read the nodes of the tree, just start from the topmost node, which corresponds to the original training data; next, start reading the rules. Note that each node has two derivations: The left branch means that the upper rule is true (stated as yes in a box), and the right one means that it is false (stated as no in a box).

On the right of the first rule, you see an important terminal rule (a terminal leaf), in a circle, stating a positive result, Yes, that you can read as play tennis=True. According to this node, when the outlook isn't sunny (Sun) or rainy (Rain), it's possible to play. (The numbers under the terminal leaf show four examples affirming this rule and zero denying it.) Note that you could understand the rule better if the output simply stated that when the outlook is overcast, play is possible. Frequently, decision tree rules aren't immediately usable, and you need to interpret them before use. However, they are clearly intelligible (and much better than a coefficient vector of values).

On the left, the tree proceeds with other rules related to Humidity. Again, on the left, when humidity is high and outlook is sunny, most terminal leaves are negative, except when the wind isn't strong. When you explore the branches on the right, you see that the tree reveals that play is always possible when the wind isn't strong, or when the wind is strong but it doesn't rain.

Pruning overgrown trees

Even though the play tennis dataset in the previous section illustrates the nuts and bolts of a decision tree, it has little probabilistic appeal because it proposes a set of deterministic actions (it has no conflicting instructions). Training with real data usually doesn't feature such sharp rules, thereby providing room for ambiguity and the likelihood of the hoped for outcome.

Decision trees have more variability in their estimations because of the noise that they obtain from data during the learning process (an effect of overfitting). To overfit the data less, the example specifies that the minimum split has to involve at least five examples. Because the terminal leaves are numerically larger, the confidence that the tree is picking the correct signal increases because the evidence quantity is higher. Also, it prunes the tree. Pruning happens when the tree is fully grown.

Starting from the leaves, the example prunes the tree of branches, showing little improvement in the reduction of information gain. By initially letting the tree expand, branches with little improvement are tolerated because they can unlock more interesting branches and leaves. Retracing from leaves to root and keeping only branches that have some predictive value reduces the variance of the model, making the resulting rules restrained.

TIP

For a decision tree, pruning is just like brainstorming. First, the algorithm generates all possible ramifications of the tree (as you do with ideas in a brainstorming session). Second, when the brainstorming concludes, only feasible ideas are retained, and the algorithm keeps only what really works.

IN THIS CHAPTER

» **Beginning with the limited perceptron**

» **Getting the building blocks of neural networks and backpropagation**

» **Perceiving and detecting objects in images using convolutions**

» **Using sequences and catching them with RNNs**

» **Discovering the creative side of AI thanks to GANs**

Chapter **11**

Improving AI with Deep Learning

Newspapers, business magazines, social networks, and nontechnical websites are all saying the same thing: AI is cool stuff that's going to revolutionize the world because of deep learning. Actually, AI is a far larger field than machine learning, and deep learning is just a small part of machine learning.

It's important to distinguish hype used to lure investors and show what this technology can actually do, which is the overall purpose of this chapter. The article at https://tinyurl.com/2n2w4ktv contains a useful comparison of the roles of the three methods of manipulating data into useful output (AI, machine learning, and deep learning), which this chapter describes in detail.

This chapter helps you understand deep learning from a practical and technical point of view, and understand what deep learning can achieve in the near term by exploring its possibilities and limitations. The chapter begins with the history and basics of neural networks. It then presents the state-of-the-art results from convolutional neural networks, recurrent neural networks (both for supervised learning), and generative adversarial networks (a kind of unsupervised learning).

Shaping Neural Networks Similar to the Human Brain

The following sections present a family of learning algorithms that derive inspiration from how the brain works. They're neural networks, the core algorithm of the connectionists' tribe that best mimics neurons inside human brains at a smaller scale. (See Chapter 1 for an overview of the five tribes of machine learning employed by various scientists.)

REMEMBER

Connectionism is the machine learning approach based on neuroscience, as well as the example of biologically interconnected networks.

Introducing the neuron

Human brains have billions of neurons, which are cells that receive, process, and transmit electric and chemical signals. Each neuron possesses a nucleus with filaments that act as inputs; *dendrites* that receive signals from other neurons; and a single output filament, the *axon*, that terminates with synapses devoted to outside communication. Neurons connect to other neurons and transmit information between them using chemicals, whereas information inside the neuron itself is electrically processed. You can read more about neuronal structure in "What's the Basic Structure of Nerves?" at Dummies.com (or in *Neuroscience For Dummies*, 2nd Edition, by Frank Amthor (Wiley).

Reverse-engineering how a brain processes signals helps the connectionists define neural networks based on biological analogies and their components. Connectionists thus use an abundance of brain terms such as neurons, activation, and connections as names for mathematical operations. Yet, in spite of the biological terms, neural networks resemble nothing more than a series of multiplications and summations when you check their math formulations. These algorithms are extraordinarily effective at solving complex problems such as image and sound recognition or machine language translation; using specialized hardware, they can execute prediction computations quickly.

Starting with the miraculous perceptron

The core of a neural network algorithm is the neuron (also called a unit). Many neurons arranged in an interconnected structure make up a neural network, with each neuron linking to the inputs and outputs of other neurons. Thus, a neuron can input data from examples or transmit the results of other neurons, depending on its location in the neural network.

SEEING DEEP LEARNING AS AUGMENTATION

Chapter 10 discusses Bayesian networks and includes an example of how such networks can provide diagnostic hints to a doctor. To do this, the Bayesian network requires well-prepared probability data. Deep learning can create a bridge between the capability of algorithms to make the best decision possible using all the required data and the data that is actually available, which is never in the best format for machine learning algorithms to understand. Photos, images, sound recording, web data (especially from social networks), and company records all require data analysis to make the data suitable for machine learning purposes.

In contrast to Bayesian networks, deep learning algorithms need very few instructions about the data they are working on. A deep learning algorithm could help doctors by matching extensive knowledge in medicine (using all available sources, including books, white papers, and the latest research from the National Institutes of Health) and patient information. The patient information, in turn, could come from previous diagnoses and medicine prescriptions, or even from social media evidence (so that doctors don't need to ask whether the patient has been in Asia, for example; the AI will detect it from its photos on Instagram or Facebook). This scenario may sound like sci-fi, but creating such a system is nearly possible today; for instance, a deep learning AI can now detect pneumonia from x-rays at a level exceeding practicing radiologists, thanks to the Stanford Machine Learning Group (https://tinyurl.com/2kzrrjhb).

Deep learning also appears in many applications. You find it in social networks in which images and content are automatically classified; in search engines when queries are retrieved; in online advertising when consumers are targeted; in mobile phones and digital assistants for speech, language understanding, or translation tasks; in self-driving cars for vision detection; and in a Go game by AlphaGo against a champion. In less widely known applications, deep learning can also power robotics and earthquake predictions. You might also find applications such as TinEye (https://tineye.com/) helpful. In this case, you supply an image, and TinEye finds it for you on the Internet.

Frank Rosenblatt at the Cornell Aeronautical Laboratory created the first example of a neuron of this kind, the perceptron, a few decades ago. He devised the perceptron in 1957 under the sponsorship of the United States Naval Research Laboratory (NRL). Rosenblatt was a psychologist as well as a pioneer in the field of artificial intelligence. Proficient in cognitive science, his idea was to create a computer that could learn by trial and error, just as a human does.

The perceptron was just a smart way to trace a separating line in a simple space made by the input data, as shown in Figure 11-1, in which you have two features (in this case, the size and level of domestication of an animal) to use to distinguish two classes (dogs and cats in this example). The perceptron formulation produces a line in a Cartesian space where the examples divide more or less perfectly into groups. The approach is similar to Naïve Bayes, described in Chapter 10, which sums conditional probabilities multiplied by general ones in order to classify data.

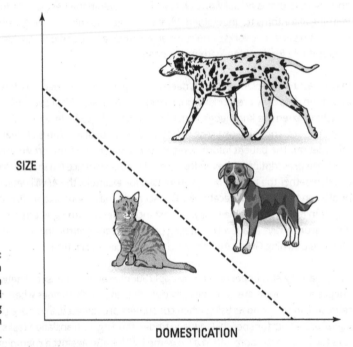

FIGURE 11-1: Example of a perceptron in simple and challenging classification tasks.

The perceptron didn't realize the full expectations of its creator or financial supporters. It soon displayed a limited capacity, even in its image-recognition specialization. The general disappointment ignited the first AI winter and abandonment of connectionism until the 1980s. Yet, some research continued despite the loss of funding. (Dr. Nils J. Nilsson, now retired but formerly a Stanford AI professor, tells more about progress during this time in the article at https://tinyurl.com/47h9j8v2.)

However, the ideas prompted by the perceptron were here to stay. Later on, experts tried to create a more advanced perceptron, and they succeeded. Neurons in a neural network are a further evolution of the perceptron: They are many, they connect to each other, and they imitate our neurons when they activate under a certain stimulus. In observing human brain functionalities, scientists noticed that neurons receive signals but don't always release a signal of their own. Releasing a signal depends on the amount of signal received. When a neuron acquires enough stimuli, it fires an answer; otherwise, it remains silent. In a similar fashion, algorithmic neurons, after receiving data, sum it and use an activation function to evaluate the result. If the input they receive achieves a certain threshold, the neuron transforms and transmits the input value; otherwise, it simply dies.

TIP

Neural networks use special functions called *activation functions* to fire a result. All you need to know is that they are a key neural network component because they allow the network to solve complex problems. They are like doors, letting the signal pass or stop. They don't simply let the signal pass, however; they transform it in a useful way. Deep learning, for instance, isn't possible without efficient activation functions such as the Rectified Linear Unit (ReLU), and thus activation functions are an important aspect of the story.

Mimicking the Learning Brain

In a neural network, you must consider the architecture first, which is the arrangement of the neural network components. The following sections discuss neural network architectural considerations.

Considering simple neural networks

Contrary to other algorithms, which have a fixed pipeline that determines how algorithms receive and process data, neural networks require that you decide how information flows by fixing the number of units (the neurons) and their distribution in layers called the *neural network architecture*, as shown in Figure 11-2.

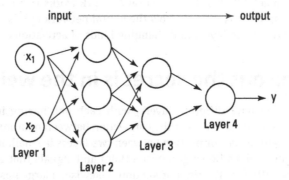

FIGURE 11-2:
A neural network
architecture, from
input to output.

The figure shows a simple neural network architecture. Note how the layers filter and process information in a progressive way. This is a *feed-forward input* because data feeds one direction into the network. Connections exclusively link units in one layer with units in the following layer (information flows from left to right). No connections exist between units in the same layer or with units outside the next layer. Moreover, the information pushes forward (from the left to the right). Processed data never returns to previous neuron layers.

REMEMBER

In more advanced neural network applications, you also have to decide on the layer types you need and the large number of parameters that will influence the layers' behavior. Neural networks are extremely flexible, and that aspect is a double-edged sword: You increase the power of the machine learning tool as complexity skyrockets.

Using a neural network is like using a stratified filtering system for water: You pour the water from above, and the water is filtered at the bottom. The water has no way to go back up; it just goes forward and straight down, and never laterally. In the same way, neural networks force data features to flow through the network and mix with each other as dictated by the network's architecture. By using the best architecture to mix features, the neural network creates newly composed features at every layer and helps achieve better predictions. Unfortunately, in spite of the efforts of academics to discover a theoretical rule, you have no way to determine the best architecture without empirically trying different solutions and testing whether output data helps predict your target values after flowing through the network. This need for manual configuration illustrates the *no-free-lunch theorem* (which you can read about in Chapter 10) in action. The gist of it is that an architecture that works the best on one task won't necessarily perform successfully on other problems.

TIP

Sometimes concepts can be understood better if directly tested in reality. Google offers a Neural Network Playground (`http://playground.tensorflow.org`) in which you can actually test how a neural network works in an intuitive manner, as shown in Figure 11-3. You see how the neural network builds a neural network by adding or removing layers and changing kinds of activations.

Figuring out the secret is in the weights

Neural networks have different layers, with each one having its own weights. *Weights* represent the strength of the connection between neurons in the network. When the weight of the connection between two layers is small, it means that the network dumps values flowing between them and signals that taking this route isn't likely to influence the final prediction. Likewise, a large positive or negative value affects the values that the next layer receives, thus determining certain predictions. This approach is analogous to brain cells, which don't stand alone but connect with other cells. As someone grows in experience, connections between neurons tend to weaken or strengthen to activate or deactivate certain brain network cell regions, causing other processing or an activity (a reaction to a danger, for instance, if the processed information signals a life-threatening situation).

FIGURE 11-3:
The Neural Network Playground lets you see how modifying a neural network changes how it works.

Each successive layer of neural network units progressively processes values taken from features, as in a conveyor belt. As the network transmits data, it arrives at each unit as a summated value produced by the values present in the previous layer and weighted by connections in the present layer. When the data received from other neurons exceeds a certain threshold, the activation function opportunely increases or modifies the value stored in the unit; otherwise, it extinguishes the signal by reducing or cancelling it. After activation function processing, the result is ready to push forward to the next layer's connection. These steps repeat for each layer until the values reach the end, and you have a result.

The weights of the connections provide a way to combine the inputs in a new way, creating new features by mixing processed inputs in a creative way because of weights and activation functions. The activation, because of the transformation it applies, also renders nonlinear the resulting recombination of the inputs received by the connections. Both of these neural network components enable the algorithm to learn complex target functions that represent the relationship between the input features and the target outcome.

Understanding the role of backpropagation

Learning occurs in a human brain because of the formation and modification of synapses between neurons, based on stimuli received by trial-and-error experience. Neural networks provide a way to replicate this process as a mathematical formulation called *backpropagation*. Here's how this architecture of interconnected computing units can solve problems: The units receive an example, and if they don't guess correctly, they retrace the problem in the system of existing weights using backpropagation and fix it by changing some values. This process goes on for many iterations before a neural network can learn. Iterations in a neural network are called *epochs*, a name that fits perfectly because a neural network may need days or weeks of training to learn complex tasks.

TECHNICAL STUFF

Backpropagation math is quite advanced and requires knowledge of concepts such as derivatives. You can read a detailed but accessible math description in *Machine Learning For Dummies*, 2nd Edition, by John Paul Mueller and Luca Massaron (Wiley) and get an overview of the necessary calculations. Backpropagation as a concept is intuitive enough to grasp and convey because it resembles what people do when performing a task using iterated approximate trial and error. Since the appearance of the backpropagation algorithm in the 1970s, developers have fixed it many times and are currently discussing whether to rethink it. (You can read the opinion of Geoffrey Hinton, one of the coauthors of the method, at https:// tinyurl.com/rrea42wz.) Backpropagation is at the core of the present AI renaissance. In the past, each neural network learning process improvement resulted in new applications and a renewed interest in the technique. Also, the current deep learning revolution, which involves a revival of neural networks (abandoned at the beginning of the 1990s), resulted from key advances in the way neural networks learn from their errors.

Introducing Deep Learning

After backpropagation, the next improvement in neural networks led to deep learning. Research continued in spite of the AI winter, and neural networks overcame technical problems, such as the *vanishing gradient,* which limits the dimensionality of neural networks. Developers needed larger neural networks to solve certain problems, so large that creating such a large neural network was not feasible in the 1980s. Moreover, researchers started taking advantage of the computational developments in CPUs and GPUs (the graphic processing units better known for their application in gaming).

TECHNICAL STUFF

The vanishing gradient is when you try to transmit a signal through a neural network and the signal quickly fades to near-zero values; after that, it can't get through the activation functions anymore. This happens because neural networks are chained multiplications. Each near-zero multiplication decreases the values rapidly, and activation functions need large enough values to let the signal pass. The farther neuron layers are from the output, the higher the likelihood that they'll get locked out of updates because the signals are too small and the activation functions will stop them. Consequently, your network stops learning as a whole, or it learns at an incredibly slow pace.

New solutions help avoid the problem of the vanishing gradient and many other technical problems, allowing larger *deep networks* in contrast to the simpler *shallow networks* of the past. Deep networks are possible thanks to the studies of scholars from the University of Toronto in Canada, such as Geoffrey Hinton (https://tinyurl.com/2nwjwzay), who insisted on working on neural networks, even when they seemed to most people to be an old-fashioned machine learning approach.

GPUs are powerful matrix and vector calculation computing units necessary for backpropagation. These technologies make training neural networks achievable in a shorter time and accessible to more people. Research also opened a world of new applications. Neural networks can learn from huge amounts of data and take advantage of big data (images, text, transactions, and social media data), creating models that continuously perform better, depending on the flow of data you feed them.

Big players such as Google, Facebook, Microsoft, and IBM spotted the new trend and have, since 2012, started acquiring companies and hiring experts (Hinton now works with Google; LeCun, the creator of Convolutional Neural Networks, leads Facebook AI research) in the new fields of deep learning. The Google Brain project, run by Andrew Ng and Jeff Dean, put together 16,000 computers to calculate a deep learning network with more than a billion weights, thus enabling unsupervised learning from YouTube videos. The computer network could even determine what a cat is by itself, without any human intervention (as you can read in this article from *Wired* at https://tinyurl.com/u4ssuh6j).

UNDERSTANDING DEEP LEARNING ISSUES

As things stand now, people have an unrealistic idea of how deep learning can help society as a whole. You see a deep learning application beat someone at chess or Go and think that if it can do that really amazing thing, what other amazing things can it do? The problem is that even its proponents don't understand deep learning very well. In technical papers about deep learning, the author often describes layers of nebulous processing organized into a network without any sort of discourse as to what really happens in each of those boxes. Recent advances point out that deep learning networks are basically a way to memorize data and then retrieve relevant bits of it using similarity between the actual problem and the memorized one. (You can read an amazing scientific paper on the topic by Pedro Domingos here: https://tinyurl.com/46wfu3mr.) The essential point to remember is that deep learning doesn't actually understand anything. It uses a massive number of examples to derive statistically based pattern matching using mathematical principles. When an AI wins a game involving a maze, it doesn't understand the concept of a maze; it simply knows that certain inputs manipulated in specific ways create certain winning outputs.

In contrast to humans, deep learning must rely on a huge number of examples to discover specific relationships between inputs and outputs. If you tell a child that everyone between a certain age is a *tween* — neither a child nor a teen — the child will be able to recognize anyone fitting the category of a tween with a high percentage of accuracy, even when the other person is a complete unknown. Deep learning would require special training to accomplish the same task, and it would be easy to fool because examples outside its experience wouldn't register.

Humans can also create hierarchies of knowledge without any sort of training. We know, for example, without much effort that dogs and cats are both animals. In addition, in knowing that dogs and cats are animals, a human can easily make the leap to see other animals as animals, even without specific training. Deep learning would require separate training for each thing that is an animal. In short, deep learning can't transfer what it knows to other situations as humans can.

Even with these limitations, deep learning is an amazing tool, but it shouldn't be the only tool in the AI toolbox. Using deep learning to see patterns where humans can't is the perfect way to apply this technology. Patterns are an essential part of discovering new things. For example, human testing of compounds to battle cancer or fight a coronavirus pandemic could take an immense amount of time. By seeing patterns where humans can't, deep learning could make serious inroads toward a solution with a lot less effort than humans would require.

Explaining the differences between deep learning and other forms of neural networks

Deep learning may seem to be just a larger neural network that runs on more computers — in other words, just a mathematics and computational power technology breakthrough that makes larger networks available. However, something inherently qualitative changed in deep learning as compared to shallow neural networks. It's more than the paradigm shift of brilliant techs at work. Deep learning shifts the paradigm in machine learning from feature creation (features that make learning easier and that you have to create using data analysis) to feature learning (complex features automatically created based on the actual data). Such an aspect couldn't be spotted otherwise when using smaller networks but becomes evident when you use many neural network layers and lots of data.

When you look inside deep learning, you may be surprised to find a lot of old technology, but amazingly, everything works as it never had before. Because researchers finally figured out how to make some simple, good-ol' solutions work together, big data can automatically filter, process, and transform data. For instance, new activations like ReLU aren't all that new; they've been known since the perceptron. Also, the image-recognition abilities that initially made deep learning so popular aren't new. Initially, deep learning achieved great momentum thanks to Convolutional Neural Networks (CNN). Discovered in the 1980s by the French scientist Yann LeCun (whose personal home page is at `http://yann.lecun.com/`), such networks now bring about astonishing results because they use many neural layers and lots of data. The same goes for technology that allows a machine to understand human speech or translate from one language to another; it's decades-old technology that a researcher revisited and got to work in the new deep learning paradigm.

Of course, part of the difference is also provided by data (more about this later), the increased usage of GPUs, and computer networking. Together with *parallelism* (more computers put in clusters and operating in parallel), GPUs allow you to create larger networks and successfully train them on more data. In fact, a GPU is estimated to perform certain operations 70 times faster than any CPU, allowing a cut in training times for neural networks from weeks to days or even hours.

TECHNICAL STUFF

For more information about how much a GPU can empower machine learning through the use of a neural network, peruse this technical paper on the topic: `https://icml.cc/2009/papers/218.pdf`.

TIP

GPUs aren't the only option for building effective deep learning solutions promptly. Special application-specific integrated circuits (ASIC) have made an appearance, and the designers have demonstrated that those circuits perform even better than GPUs. For instance, Google started developing the Tensor Processing Unit (TPU) in 2015. In 2018, Google made TPUs available in its cloud centers. A TPU is a blazing-fast, application-specific integrated circuit to accelerate the calculations involved in deep learning when using Google's specialized computational library, TensorFlow. See the "Working with Deep Learning Processors (DLPs)" section of Chapter 4 for details on other alternatives.

Finding even smarter solutions

Deep learning influences AI's effectiveness in solving problems in image recognition, machine translation, and speech recognition that were initially tackled by classic AI and machine learning. In addition, it presents new and advantageous solutions:

» Continuous learning using *online learning*

» Reusable solutions using *transfer learning*

» More democratization of AI using open source frameworks

» Simple straightforward solutions using *end-to-end learning*

The following sections describe these four new approaches.

Using online learning

Neural networks are more flexible than other machine learning algorithms, and they can continue to train as they work on producing predictions and classifications. This capability comes from optimization algorithms that allow neural networks to learn, which can work repeatedly on small samples of examples (called *batch learning*) or even on one example at a time (called *online learning*). Deep learning networks can build their knowledge step by step and be receptive to new information that may arrive (like a baby's mind, which is always open to new stimuli and to learning experiences). For instance, a deep learning application on a social media website can be trained on cat images. As people post photos of cats, the application recognizes them and tags them with an appropriate label. When people start posting photos of dogs on the social network, the neural network doesn't need to restart training; it can continue by learning images of dogs as well. This capability is particularly useful for coping with the variability of Internet data. A deep learning network can be open to novelty and adapt its weights to deal with it.

Using transfer learning

Flexibility is handy even when a network completes its training, but you must reuse it for purposes different from the initial learning. Networks that distinguish objects and correctly classify them require a long time and a lot of computational capacity to learn what to do. Extending a network's capability to new kinds of images that weren't part of the previous learning means transferring the knowledge to this new problem (*transfer learning*).

For instance, you can transfer a network that's capable of distinguishing between dogs and cats to perform a job that involves spotting dishes of macaroni and cheese. You use the majority of the layers of the network as they are (you freeze them) and then work on the final, output layers (*fine-tuning*). In a short time, and with fewer examples, the network will apply what it learned in distinguishing dogs and cats to macaroni and cheese. It will perform even better than a neural network trained only to recognize macaroni and cheese.

Transfer learning is something new to most machine learning algorithms and opens up a possible market for transferring knowledge from one application to another, from one company to another. Google is already doing that, actually sharing its immense data repository by making public the networks it built on it (as detailed in this post: https://tinyurl.com/448hkhpa). This is a step in democratizing deep learning by allowing everyone to access its potentiality. To make things even better, there is now a lite version of the TensorFlow Object Recognition API for mobile devices, which is described at https://tinyurl.com/yuyznrh9.

Democratization by using open source frameworks

Today, networks can be accessible to everyone, including access to tools for creating deep learning networks. It's not just a matter of publicly divulging scientific papers explaining how deep learning works; it's a matter of programming. In the early days of deep learning, you had to build every network from scratch as an application developed in a language such as C++, which limited access to a few well-trained specialists. Scripting capabilities today (for instance, using Python; go to https://www.python.org/) are better because of a large array of open source deep learning frameworks, such as TensorFlow by Google (https://www.tensorflow.org/) or PyTorch by Facebook (https://pytorch.org/). These frameworks allow the replication of the most recent advances in deep learning using straightforward commands.

Along with many lights come some shadows. Neural networks need huge amounts of data to work, and data isn't accessible to everybody because larger organizations hold it. Transfer learning can mitigate the lack of data, but only partially, because certain applications do require actual data. Consequently, the democratization of AI is limited. Moreover, deep learning systems are so complex that their outputs are both hard to explain (allowing bias and discrimination to flourish) and frail because tricks can fool those systems (see https://tinyurl.com/5ua5jw42 for details). Any neural network can be sensitive to *adversarial attacks,* which are input manipulations devised to deceive the system into giving a wrong response.

Using end-to-end learning

Finally, deep learning allows *end-to-end learning,* which means that it solves problems in an easier and more straightforward way than previous deep learning solutions and might therefore have more impact when solving problems. Say that you wanted to solve a difficult problem, such as having AI recognize known faces or drive a car. Using the classical AI approach, you would have to split the problem into more manageable sub-problems to achieve an acceptable result in a feasible time. For instance, if you wanted to recognize faces in a photo, previous AI systems arranged the problem into these parts:

1. Find the faces in the photo.

2. Crop the faces from the photo.

3. Process the cropped faces to have a pose similar to an ID card photo.

4. Feed the processed cropped faces as learning examples to a neural network for image recognition.

Today, you can feed the photo to a deep learning architecture and guide it to learn to find faces in the images and then classify them. You can use the same approach for language translation, speech recognition, or even self-driving cars (as discussed in Chapter 14). In all cases, you simply pass the input to a deep learning system and obtain the wanted result.

Detecting Edges and Shapes from Images

Convolutional Neural Networks (also known as ConvNet or CNN) have fueled the recent deep learning renaissance. Practitioners and academics are persuaded that deep learning is a feasible technique because of its results in image-recognition tasks. This success has produced a sort of gold rush, with many people trying to apply the same technology to other problems. The following sections discuss how CNNs help detect image edges and shapes for tasks such as deciphering handwritten text.

Starting with character recognition

CNNs aren't a new idea. They appeared at the end of the 1980s as the work of Yann LeCun (now director of AI at Facebook) when he worked at AT&T Labs-Research, together with Yoshua Bengio, Leon Bottou, and Patrick Haffner on a network named LeNet5. You can see the network at http://yann.lecun.com/exdb/lenet/ or in this video, in which a younger LeCun himself demonstrates the network: https://tinyurl.com/3rnwr6de. At that time, having a machine able to decipher handwritten numbers was quite a feat, one that assisted the postal service in automating zip code detection and sorting incoming and outgoing mail.

Developers achieved some results earlier by connecting a number of images to a detection neural network. Each image pixel connected to a node in the network. The problem of using this approach is that the network can't achieve translation invariance, which is the capability to decipher the number under different conditions of size, distortion, or position in the image, as exemplified in Figure 11-4. A similar neural network could detect only similar numbers — those that it has seen before. Also, it made many mistakes. Transforming the image before feeding it to the neural network partially solved the problem by resizing, moving, cleaning the pixels, and creating special chunks of information for better network processing. This technique, called *feature creation*, requires both expertise on the necessary image transformations as well as many computations in terms of data analysis. Image-recognition tasks at that time were more the work of an artisan than a scientist.

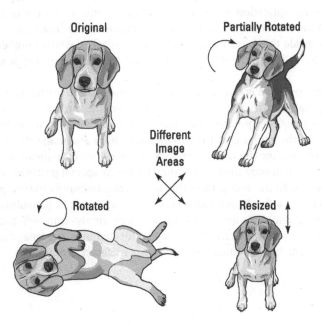

FIGURE 11-4: Using translation invariance, a neural network spots the dog and its variations.

Convolutions easily solved the problem of translation invariance because they offer a different image-processing approach inside the neural network. Convolutions are the foundation of LeNet5 and provide the basic building blocks for all actual CNNs performing the following:

>> **Image classification:** Determining what object appears in an image

>> **Image detection:** Finding where an object is in an image

>> **Image segmentation:** Separating the areas of an image based on their content; for example, in an image of a road, separating the road itself from the cars on it and the pedestrians

Explaining how convolutions work

To understand how convolutions work, you start from the input, which is an image composed of one or more pixel layers, called channels, using values from 0 (the pixel is fully switched on) to 255 (the pixel is switched off). For instance, RGB images have individual channels for red, green, and blue colors. Mixing these channels generates the palette of colors as you see them on the screen.

The input data receives simple transformations to rescale the pixel values (for instance, to set the range from zero to one) and then pass on those values. Transforming the data makes the convolutions' work easier because convolutions are simply multiplication and summation operations, as shown in Figure 11-5. The convolution neural layer takes small portions of the image, multiplies the pixel values inside the portion by a grid of particularly devised numbers, sums everything derived from the multiplication, and projects it into the next neural layer.

Such an operation is flexible because backpropagation forms the basis for numeric multiplication inside the convolution (see the article at `https://tinyurl.com/2e2293b9` for precisely how the convolution step works, including an animation), and the values that the convolution filters are image characteristics, which are important for the neural network to achieve its classification task. Some convolutions catch only lines, some only curves or special patterns, no matter where they appear in the image (and this is the translation invariance property of convolutions). As the image data passes through various convolutions, it's transformed, assembled, and rendered in increasingly complex patterns until the convolution produces reference images (for instance, the image of an average cat or dog), which the trained CNN later uses to detect new images.

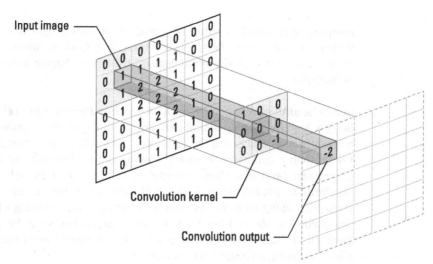

Input image

Convolution kernel

Convolution output

TECHNICAL
STUFF

If you want to know more about convolutions, you can check out a visualization created by some Google researchers from Research and Google Brain. The visualization is of the inner workings of a 22-layer network developed by scientists at Google called GoogleLeNet (see the paper at https://tinyurl.com/6x8zuk5c). In the appendix (https://tinyurl.com/3d77zthf), they show examples from the layers assigned to detect first edges, then textures, then full patterns, then parts, and finally entire objects.

Interestingly, setting basic ConvNet architectures isn't hard. Just imagine that the more layers you have, the better (up to a certain limit, however). You set the number of convolution layers and some convolution behavior characteristics, like how the grid is made (*filter*, *kernel*, or *feature detector* values), how the grid slides in the image (*stride*), and how it behaves around the image borders (*padding*).

REMEMBER

Looking at how convolutions work hints that going deep in deep learning means that data goes into deeper transformations than it does under any machine learning algorithm or a shallow neural network. The more layers, the more transformations an image undergoes, and the deeper it becomes.

Advancing using image challenges

CNNs are a smart idea. AT&T actually implemented LeNet5 into ATM check readers. However, another AI winter started in the mid 1990s, with many researchers and investors losing faith that neural networks could revolutionize AI. In addition, the data lacked complexity at the time. Researchers were able to achieve results comparable to LeNet5's using new machine learning algorithms called Support Vector Machines (from the Analogiers tribe) and Random Forests, a sophistication of decision trees from the symbologists' tribe (see Chapter 10 for an explanation of that tribe).

Only a handful of researchers, such as Geoffrey Hinton, Yann LeCun, and Yoshua Bengio, kept developing neural network technologies until a new dataset offered a breakthrough and ended the AI winter. Meanwhile, 2006 saw an effort by Fei-Fei Li, then a computer science professor at the University of Illinois Urbana-Champaign (and now chief scientist at Google Cloud as well as professor at Stanford) to provide more real-world datasets to better test algorithms. She started amassing an incredible number of images, representing a large number of object classes. She and her team achieved such a huge task by using Amazon's Mechanical Turk, a service that you use to ask people to do microtasks for you (like classifying an image) for a small fee.

The resulting dataset, completed in 2009, was called ImageNet and contained 3.2 million labeled images, arranged into 5,247 hierarchically organized categories. You can explore it at https://image-net.org/ or read the original paper that presents the dataset at https://tinyurl.com/yy98efcj. ImageNet soon appeared at a 2010 competition in which neural networks proved their capability to correctly classify images arranged into 1,000 classes.

In seven years of competition (the challenge closed definitely in 2017), the winning algorithms raised the accuracy in predicting the images from 71.8 percent to 97.3 percent, which surpasses human capabilities (yes, humans make mistakes in classifying objects). At the beginning, researchers noticed that their algorithms started working better with more data (there was nothing like ImageNet at that time), and then they started testing new ideas and improved neural network architectures. That brought about a host of innovations in the way to process data, to build layers, and to connect them all together. Striving to achieve better results on the ImageNet competition had favorable impacts on all related fields of deep learning research.

Although the ImageNet competitions don't take place anymore, researchers are even today developing more CNN architectures, enhancing accuracy or detection capabilities as well as robustness. In fact, many deep learning solutions are still experimental and not yet applied to critical applications, such as banking or security, not just because of difficulties in their interpretability but also because of possible vulnerabilities.

WARNING

Vulnerabilities come in all forms. Researchers have found that by adding specially devised noise or changing a single pixel in an image, a CNN can radically change its answers, in *nontargeted* (you just need to fool the CNN) or *targeted* (you want the CNN to provide a specific answer) attacks. You can investigate more about this matter in the OpenAI tutorial at https://tinyurl.com/amp8w5c. OpenAI is a nonprofit AI research company. The paper entitled "One pixel attack for fooling deep neural networks" (https://tinyurl.com/4std9cc8) is also helpful. The point is that CNNs aren't a safe technology yet. You can't simply use them in place of your eyes; you have to use great care with them.

Learning to Imitate Art and Life

CNNs didn't impact just computer vision tasks (such as vision in self-driving cars) but are important for many other applications as well (for example, they're necessary for virtual assistant AI technology such as Alexa, Siri, or Google Assistant). CNNs persuaded many researchers to invest time and effort in the deep learning revolution. The consequent research and development sprouted new ideas. Subsequent testing finally brought innovation to AI by helping computers learn to understand spoken language, translate written foreign languages, and create both text and modified images, thus demonstrating how complex computations about statistical distributions can be translated into a kind of artistry, creativity, and imagination. If you talk of deep learning and its possible applications, you also have to mention Recurrent Neural Networks (RNN) and Generative Adversarial Networks (GAN) or you won't have a clear picture of what deep learning can do for AI.

Memorizing sequences that matter

One of the weaknesses of CNNs is the lack of memory. They do well with understanding a single picture, but trying to understand a picture in a context, like a frame in a video, translates into an inability to get the right answer to difficult AI challenges. Technically, a CNN can recognize a set of patterns, but without much distinction of how they are spatially arranged (hence their property of translation invariance). Instead, when the sequence in which patterns appear does matter, CNNs don't offer any particular advantage. Many important problems are sequences. If you want to understand a book, you read it page by page. The sequences are nested. Within a page is a sequence of words, and within a word is a sequence of letters. To understand the book, you must understand the sequence of letters, words, and pages. An RNN is the answer because it processes new inputs while tracking past inputs. The input in the network doesn't just proceed forward as usual in a neural network, but also loops inside it. It's as if the network hears an echo of itself.

If you feed an RNN a sequence of words, the network will learn that when it sees a word, preceded by certain other words, it can determine how to complete the phrase. RNNs aren't simply a technology that can automate input compilation (as when a browser automatically completes search terms as you type words). In addition, RNNs can feed sequences and provide a translation as output, such as the overall meaning of a phrase (so now, AI can disambiguate phrases where wording is important) or translate text into another language (again, translation works in a context). This even works with sounds, because it's possible to interpret certain sound modulations as words. RNNs allow computers and mobile phones to understand, with great precision, not only what you said (it's the same technology that automatically subtitles) but also what you meant to say, opening the door to computer programs that chat with you and to digital assistants such as Siri, Cortana, and Alexa.

Discovering the magic of AI conversations

A *chatbot* is software that can converse with you through two methods: auditory (you speak with it and listen to answers) or textual (you type what you want to say and read the answers). You may have heard of it under other names (conversational agent, chatterbot, talkbot, and others), but the point is that you may already use one on your smartphone, computer, or a special device. Siri, Cortana, and Alexa are all well-known examples. You may also exchange words with a chatbot when you contact a firm's customer service by web or phone, or through an app on your mobile phone when using Twitter, Slack, Skype, or other applications for conversation.

Chatbots are big business because they help companies save money on customer service operators — maintaining constant customer contact and serving those customers — but the idea isn't new. Even if the name is recent (devised in 1994 by Michael Mauldin, the inventor of the Lycos search engine), chatbots are considered the pinnacle of AI. According to Alan Turing's vision, detecting a strong AI by talking with it shouldn't be possible. Turing devised a famous conversation-based test to determine whether an AI has acquired intelligence equivalent to a human being.

You have a weak AI when the AI shows intelligent behavior but isn't conscious like a human being. A strong AI occurs when the AI can really think as a human.

The Turing test requires a human judge to interact with two subjects through a computer terminal: one human and one machine. The judge evaluates which one is an AI based on the conversation. Turing asserted that if an AI can trick a human being into thinking that the conversation is with another human being, it's possible to believe that the AI is at the human level of AI. The problem is hard because it's not just a matter of answering properly and in a grammatically correct way, but also a matter of incorporating the context (place, time, and characteristics of the person the AI is talking with) and displaying a consistent personality (the AI should be like a real persona, both in background and attitude).

Since the 1960s, challenging the Turing test has proved to be motivation for developing chatbots, which are based on the idea of *retrieval-based models*. That is, a Natural Language Processing (NLP) algorithm parses language that is input by the human interrogator. Certain words or sets of words recall preset answers and feedback from chatbot memory storage.

TIP

NLP is data analysis focused on text. The algorithm splits text into tokens (elements of a phrase such as nouns, verbs, and adjectives) and removes any less useful or confounding information. The tokenized text is processed using statistical operations or machine learning. For instance, NLP can help you tag parts of speech and identify words and their meaning, or determine whether one text is similar to another.

Joseph Weizenbaum built the first chatbot of this kind, ELIZA, in 1966 as a form of computer psychological therapist. ELIZA was made of simple heuristics, which are base phrases to adapt to the context and keywords that triggered ELIZA to recall an appropriate response from a fixed set of answers. You can try an online version of ELIZA at https://tinyurl.com/3cfrj53y. You might be surprised to read meaningful conversations such as the one produced by ELIZA with its creator: https://tinyurl.com/j3zw42fj.

Retrieval-based models work fine when interrogated using preset topics because they incorporate human knowledge, just as an expert system does (as discussed in Chapter 3), thus they can answer with relevant, grammatically correct phrases. Problems arise when confronted with off-topic questions. The chatbot can try to fend off these questions by bouncing them back in another form (as ELIZA did) and be spotted as an artificial speaker. A solution is to create new phrases, for instance, based on statistical models, machine learning, or even a pretrained RNN, which could be built on neutral speech or could even reflect the personality of a specific person. This approach is called *generative-based models* and is the frontier of chatbots today because generating language on the fly isn't easy.

Generative-based models don't always answer with pertinent and correct phrases, but many researchers have made advances recently, especially in RNNs. As noted in previous sections, the secret is in the sequence: You provide an input sequence in one language and an output sequence in another language, as in a machine translation problem. In this case, you provide both input sequence and output sequence in the same language. The input is a part of a conversation, and the output is the following reaction.

Given the actual state of the art in chatbot building, RNNs work great for short exchanges, although obtaining perfect results for longer or more articulated phrases is more difficult. As with retrieval-based models, RNNs recall information they acquire, but not in an organized way. If the scope of the discourse is limited, these systems can provide good answers, but they degrade when the context is open and general because they would need knowledge comparable to what a human acquires during a lifetime. (Humans are good conversationalists based on experience and knowledge.)

Data for training an RNN is really the key. For instance, Google Smart Reply, a chatbot by Google, offers quick answers to emails. The story at https://tinyurl.com/2d43528f tells more about how this system is supposed to work. In the real world, it tended to answer most conversations with "I love you" because it was trained using biased examples. Something similar happened to Microsoft's Twitter chatbot Tay, whose ability to learn from interactions with users led it astray because conversations were biased and malicious (https://tinyurl.com/55v6dxuh).

TIP

If you want to know the state of the art in the chatbot world, you can keep updated about yearly chatbot competitions in which Turing tests are applied to the current technology. For instance, the Lobner prize is the most famous one (https://tinyurl.com/cwb2zr8c) and the right place to start. Though still unable to pass the Turing test, the most recent winner of the Lobner prize at the time of the writing of this book was Mitsuku (for the fourth time in a row), a program that can reason about specific objects proposed during the discourse; it can also play games and even perform magic tricks (https://tinyurl.com/uvmh8cnk).

Going for the state of the pretrained art

RNNs have come a long way in recent years. When researchers and practitioners experienced how much more useful RNNs are than the previous statistical approach of analyzing text as a pool of words (the commonly used technical term is *bag of words*), they started using them in mass and, as they tested more and more applications, they also discovered limitations that they tried to overcome.

As initially devised, RNNs had limits. In particular, they needed too much data to learn from and they couldn't really remember information that appeared earlier in a phrase. Moreover, many researchers reported that RNNs were just a look-back algorithm (also called backjumping; scroll down to Chapter 6 at https://tinyurl.com/2snz8rep for more details) when processing text and that sometimes you need to look further into a phrase in order to make sense of what has been said before. Thus, in order to cope with the memory limitations of the RNNs and the multiple relations of words in a phrase, researchers devised the Long Short-Term Memory (LSTM) and the Gated Recurrent Unit (GRU) neural units, which can both remember and forget previous words in a smarter way. The researchers also made all these neural units read text bi-directionally, so they can pick a word from both the start and the end of the phrase and make sense of everything.

REMEMBER

Sepp Hochreiter, a computer scientist who made many contributions to the fields of machine learning, deep learning, and bioinformatics, and Jürgen Schmidhuber, a pioneer in the field of artificial intelligence, invented LSTMs. See: "Long Short-Term Memory" in the MIT Press journal *Neural Computation*. The GRU first appeared in the paper called "Learning Phrase Representations using RNN Encoder-Decoder for Statistical Machine Translation" (https://arxiv.org/pdf/1406.1078.pdf).

Working with word embeddings

Researchers found creating pretrained models useful for dealing with data quantity limitations. Pretrained models for word embeddings are similar to image pretrained models in that they process large amounts of publicly available textual data to provide a means to score a word in a phrase in a meaningful way. The idea is to change words into numbers. The numbers aren't randomly chosen, but relate to each other in the same way as words relate by meaning. For example, you can transform the names of different foods into columns of numeric values (a matrix) in such a way that the words that show fruits can have a similar score on a particular column. On the same column, vegetables can get different values, but not too far from those of fruit. Finally, the names of meat dishes can be far away in value from fruits and vegetables. The values are similar when the words are synonymous or refer to a similar concept called *semantic similarity*, with *semantic* referring to the meaning of words.

These pretrained models are called *embeddings*. Embeddings aren't new; they have a long history. The concept of embeddings appeared in statistical multivariate analysis under the name of *multivariate correspondence analysis.* Since the 1970s, Jean-Paul Benzécri, a French statistician and linguist, along with many other French researchers from the French School of Data Analysis, discovered how to map a limited set of words into low-dimensional spaces (usually 2-D representations, such as a topographic map). This process turns words into meaningful numbers and projections, a discovery that brought about many applications in linguistics and the social sciences and paved the way for the recent advancements in language processing using deep learning.

REMEMBER

The word *embedding* refers to nothing more than a mapping function that transforms words into numeric sequences that are meaningful for a deep learning algorithm. Popular word embeddings are Google's Word2Vec, Stanford's Global Vectors (GloVe), and Facebook's fastText.

Finding out the limits of BERT and GPT-3

Word embeddings such as Word2Vec and others aren't the only advanced technique that you can use to make deep learning solutions shine with unstructured text. Recently, a series of pretrained networks appeared that make modeling language problems even easier. For instance, one of the most promising is the Google Bidirectional Encoder Representations from Transformers (BERT). Here's a link to the Google AI blog post describing the technique: https://tinyurl.com/b7vhn8d6. The interesting part of BERT is that it produces even more useful embeddings because it can map words into numbers differently based on the other words that appear with it in the phrase. Even if embeddings are just numbers, recent developments show an approach similar to how humans understand the meaning of words based on their context.

Based on the same philosophy, the GPT-3 neural network, created by OpenAI, a San Francisco–based artificial intelligence research laboratory, can achieve even more competitive results than the BERT. A GPT-3 can answer questions, write and summarize essays, generate adventure games (just try AI Dungeon to get an idea: https://play.aidungeon.io/), translate languages, and even write computer code, as described here: https://tinyurl.com/3w5y53wf. Yet, it's important to realize that technology is still far from a real AI. When faced with interacting with a human, deep learning networks such as GPT-3 and BERT, or other, even more complex ones (such as the gigantic one that Google recently trained: https://tinyurl.com/2cnppm3n) really can't understand the discourse. They can only process the phrases in order to achieve a particular, pre-ordered result.

Making one AI compete against another AI

RNNs and transformers can make a computer converse with you, and if you have no idea that the neural network is reactivating sequences of words that it has previously learned, you get the idea that something related to intelligence is going on behind the scenes. In reality, no thought or reasoning goes on behind it, although the technology doesn't simply recall preset phrases but is fairly articulated.

Generative Adversarial Networks (GANs) represent another kind of deep learning technology that can give you an even stronger illusion that the AI can display creativity. Again, this technology relies on recalling previous examples and the machine's understanding that the examples contain rules — rules that the machine can play with as a child plays with toy bricks (technically, the rules are the statistical distributions underlying the examples). Nevertheless, a GAN is an incredible type of technology that has displayed promise for a fairly large number of future applications, in addition to the uses today (see https://tinyurl.com/na74p3uz as an example).

GANs originated from the work of a few researchers at the Departement d'informatique et de recherche operationnelle at Montreal University in 2014, and the most notable among them is Ian Goodfellow (see the white paper at https://tinyurl.com/4r65ca6e). The proposed new deep learning approach immediately raised interest and now is one of the most researched technologies, with constant developments and improvements. Yann LeCun found Generative Adversarial Networks to be "the most interesting idea in the last ten years in machine learning" (https://tinyurl.com/y4j7ch6b). In an interview at MIT Technology Review, Ian Goodfellow explains that level of enthusiasm with this intriguing statement: "You can think of generative models as giving artificial intelligence a form of imagination" (https://tinyurl.com/zpzrsdpp).

To see a basic GAN in action (there are now many sophisticated variants, and more are being developed), you need a reference dataset, usually consisting of real-world data, whose examples you would like to use to teach the GAN. For instance, if you have a dog image dataset, you expect the GAN to learn how a dog looks from the dataset. After learning about dogs, the GAN can propose plausible, realistic images of dogs that are different from those in the initial dataset. (They'll be new images; simply replicating existing images is considered an error from a GAN.)

The dataset is the starting point. You also need two neural networks, each one specializing in a different task and both in competition with each other. One network is called the *generator*; it takes an arbitrary input (for instance, a sequence of random numbers) and generates an output (for instance, a dog's image), which is an *artifact* because it's artificially created using the generator network. The second network is the *discriminator*, which must correctly distinguish the products of the generator, the artifacts, from the examples in the training dataset.

When a GAN starts training, both the networks try to improve by using backpropagation (explained in the "Understanding the role of backpropagation" section, earlier in this chapter), based on the results of the discriminator. The errors the discriminator makes in distinguishing a real image from an artifact propagate to the discriminator (as with a classification neural network). The correct discriminator answers propagate as errors to the generator (because it was unable to make artifacts similar to the images in the dataset, and the discriminator spotted them). Figure 11-6 shows this relationship.

The original images chosen by Goodfellow to explain how a GAN works are that of the art faker and the investigator. The investigator gets skilled in detecting forged art, but the faker also improves in order to avoid detection by the investigator.

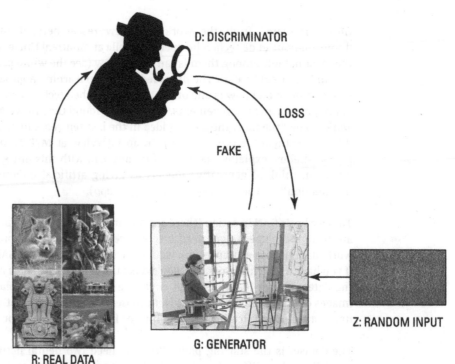

FIGURE 11-6: How a GAN network works, oscillating between generator and discriminator.

D: DISCRIMINATOR

LOSS

FAKE

Z: RANDOM INPUT

G: GENERATOR

R: REAL DATA

Photos courtesy of (montage, clockwise from bottom left): Lileephoto/Shutterstock; Menno Schaefer/Shutterstock; iofoto/Shutterstock; vilainecrevette/iStockphoto; Middle: Rana Faure/Corbis/VCG/Getty Images

You may wonder how the generator learns to create the right artifacts if it never sees an original. Only the discriminator sees the original dataset when it tries to distinguish real art from the generator artifacts. Even if the generator never examines anything from the original dataset, it receives hints through the work of the discriminator. They're slight hints, guided by many failed attempts at the beginning from the generator. It's like learning to paint the Mona Lisa without having seen it and with only the help of a friend telling you how well you've guessed. The situation is reminiscent of the theorem called the infinite army of monkeys, with some differences. In this theorem, you expect the monkeys to write Shakespeare's poems by mere luck (see `https://tinyurl.com/2t8v5bbr`). In this case, the generator uses randomness only at the start, and then it's slowly guided by feedback from the discriminator. With some modifications of this basic idea, GANs have become capable of the following:

>> Creating photo-realistic images of objects such as fashion items, as well as interior or industrial design based on a word description (you ask for a yellow and white flower and you get it, as described in this paper: `https://tinyurl.com/wu2n8nxn`)

>> Modifying existing images by applying higher resolution, adding special patterns (for instance, transforming a horse into a zebra: https://tinyurl.com/mbf5rwex), and filling in missing parts (for example, you want to remove a person from a photo, and a GAN replaces the gap with some plausible background, as in this image-completion neural architecture: https://tinyurl.com/3ryvpzy2)

>> Many frontier applications, such as ones for generating movement from static photos; creating complex objects such as complete texts (which is called *structured prediction* because the output is not simply an answer, but rather a set of answers that relate to each other); creating data for supervised machine learning; or even generating powerful cryptography (https://tinyurl.com/yzwhsa8c)

TIP

GANs are a deep learning frontier technology, and there are many open and new areas of research for its application in AI. If AI will have an imaginative and creative power, it will probably derive from technologies like GANs. You can get an idea of what's going on with this technology by reading the pages on GANs from OpenAI, a nonprofit AI research company founded by Greg Brockman, Ilya Sutskever, Elon Musk (PayPal, SpaceX, and Tesla founder), and Sam Altman (https://openai.com/blog/generative-models/).

Pondering reinforcement learning

Deep learning isn't limited to supervised learning predictions. You also use deep learning for unsupervised learning and reinforcement learning (RL). Unsupervised learning supports a number of established techniques, such as autoencoders and self-organizing maps (SOMs), which can help you to segment your data into homogeneous groups or to detect anomalies in your variables. Even though scientists are still researching and developing unsupervised learning, reinforcement learning has recently taken the lion's share of attention in both the academic papers and popularity among practitioners. RL achieves smarter solutions for problems such as parking a car, learning to drive in as little as 20 minutes (as this paper illustrates: https://tinyurl.com/nr5wzvwx), controlling an industrial robot, and more. (This article by Yuxi Li provides a complete list of reinforcement learning applications as of 2019: https://tinyurl.com/e4t2887v.)

RL provides a compact way of learning without gathering large masses of data, but it also involves complex interaction with the external world. Because RL begins without any data, interacting with the external world and receiving feedback defines the method used to obtain the data it requires. You could use this approach for a robot, moving in the physical world, or for a bot, wandering in the digital one.

In RL, you have an agent (which could be a robot in the real world or a bot in the digital one) interacting with an environment that could include a virtual or other sort of world with its own rules. The agent can receive information from the environment (called the state) and can act on it, sometimes changing it. More important, the agent can receive an input from the environment, a positive or negative one, based on its sequence of actions or inactions. The input is a reward even when negative. The purpose of RL is to have the agent learn how to behave to maximize the total sum of rewards received during its experience inside the environment.

Understanding how reinforcement learning works

You can determine the relationship between the agent and the environment from Figure 11-7. Note the time subscripts. If you consider the present instant in time as t, the previous instant is t−1. At time t−1, the agent acts and then receives both a state and a reward from the environment. Based on the sets of values relative to the action at time t, state at time t−1, and reward at time t, an RL algorithm can learn the action to obtain a certain environmental state.

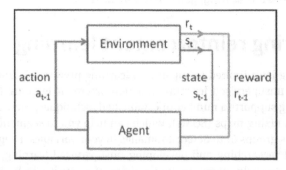

FIGURE 11-7:
A schema of how an agent and an environment interact in RL.

Ian Goodfellow, the AI research scientist behind the creation of GANs, believes that better integration between RL and deep learning is among the top priorities for further deep learning advances. Better integration leads to smarter robots. Integration is now a hot topic, but until recently, RL typically had stronger bonds to statistics and algorithms than to neural networks, at least until the Google deep learning research team proved the contrary.

Progressing with Google AI and DeepMind discoveries

At Google DeepMind, a research center in London owned by Google, they took a well-known RL technique called Q-learning and made it work with deep learning rather than the classical computation algorithm. The new variant, named Deep Q-Learning, uses both convolutions and regular dense layers to obtain problem input and process it. At Google, they used this solution to create a Deep Q-Network (DQN) which has been successfully used to play vintage Atari 2600 games at expert human level and win (see https://tinyurl.com/t2u3dhf8). The algorithm learned to play in a relatively short time and found clever strategies that only the most skilled game players use.

REMEMBER

The idea behind Deep Q-Learning is to approximately determine the reward of an agent after taking a certain action, given the present state of the agent and the environment. In a human sense, the algorithm simply associates state and actions with expected rewards, which is done using a mathematical function. The algorithm, therefore, can't understand whether it's playing a particular game; its understanding of the environment is limited to the knowledge of the reported state deriving from taken actions.

In the recent years, the DeepMind team has continued exploring other possible RL solutions for playing Atari games. In particular, the team has tried to understand whether learning a model of the environment (in this case, the rules and characteristics of a specific Atari game) by image inputs could help the RL achieve even better results. In collaboration with Google AI and the University of Toronto, they finally introduced DreamerV2 (you can read more about it here: https://tinyurl.com/3jjkdwne), an RL agent-based application that achieves human-level performance on Atari games by means of creating a world model of the game itself through images of the game. In simple words, the DreamerV2 takes hints from provided images of the game and, on its own, figures out game object positions, trajectory, effects and so on. Whereas DQN mapped actions and rewards, this RL agent goes beyond those tasks and re-creates an internal representation of the game in order to understand it even better. This is similar to what humans do when they develop internal images and ideas of the external world.

The dream of scientists is to create a general RL agent that can approach different problems and solve them, in the same spontaneous way as humans do. Recently, though, the most astonishing results have again occurred with task-specific problems that don't transfer easily to other situations.

Clear examples are the AI built to beat humans at games such as chess or Go. Chess and Go are both popular board games that share characteristics, such as being played by two players who move in turns and lack a random element (no dice are thrown, as in backgammon). Apart from that, they have different game rules and complexity. In chess, each player has 16 pieces to move on the board according to type, and the game ends when the king piece is stalemated or checkmated — unable to move further. Experts calculate that about 10^{123} different chess games are possible, which is a large number when you consider that scientists estimate the number of atoms in the known universe at about 10^{80}. Yet, computers can master a single game of chess by determining the future possible moves far enough ahead to have an advantage against any human opponent. In 1997, Deep Blue, an IBM supercomputer designed for playing chess, defeated Garry Kasparov, the world chess champion.

REMEMBER

A computer cannot prefigure a complete game of chess using brute force (calculating every possible move from the beginning to the end of the game). It uses some heuristics and its ability to look into a certain number of future moves. Deep Blue was a computer with high computational performance that could anticipate more future moves in the game than any previous computer.

In Go, you have a 19-x-19 grid of lines containing 361 spots on which each player places a stone (usually black or white in color) each time a player takes a turn. The purpose of the game is to enclose in stones a larger portion of the board than one's opponent's. Considering that, on average, each player has about 250 possible moves at each turn, and that a game consists of about 150 moves, a computer would need enough memory to hold 250^{150} games, which is on the order of 10^{360} boards. From a resource perspective, Go is more complex than chess, and experts used to believe that no computer software would be able to beat a human Go master within the next decade using the same approach as Deep Blue. Yet, a computer system called AlphaGo accomplished it using RL techniques.

DeepMind developed AlphaGo in 2016, which featured Go playing skills never attained before by any hardware and software solution. After setting up the system, DeepMind had AlphaGo test itself against the strongest Go champion living in Europe, Fan Gui, who had been the European Go champion three times. DeepMind challenged him in a closed-door match, and AlphaGo won all the games, leaving Fan Gui amazed by the game style displayed by the computer.

Then, after Fan Gui helped refine the AlphaGo skills, the DeepMind team, led by their CEO Demis Hassabis and chief scientist David Silver, challenged Lee Sedol, a South Korean professional Go player ranked at the ninth dan, the highest level a master can attain. AlphaGo won a series of four games against Lee Sedol and lost only one. Apart from the match it lost because of an unexpected move from the champion, it actually led the other games and amazed the champion by playing unexpected, impactful moves. In fact, both players, Fan Gui and Lee Sedol, felt that playing against AlphaGo was like playing against a contestant coming from another reality: AlphaGo moves resembled nothing they had seen before.

TIP

The story behind AlphaGo is so fascinating that someone made a film out of it named *AlphaGo*. It's well worth seeing: https://tinyurl.com/58hvfs79.

The DeepMind team that created AlphaGo didn't stop after the success of its solution; it soon retired AlphaGo and created even more incredible systems. First, the team built up AlphaGo Zero, which is AlphaGo trained by playing against itself. Then it created Alpha Zero, which is a general program that can learn to play chess and shogi, the Japanese chess game, by itself. If AlphaGo demonstrated how to solve a problem deemed impossible for computers, AlphaGo Zero demonstrated that computers can attain super-capabilities using self-learning (which is RL in its essence). In the end, its results were even better than with those starting from human experience: AlphaGo Zero has challenged the retired AlphaGo and won 100 matches without losing one. Finally, the DeepMind team even perfected Alpha Zero by further developing it into MuZero (see `https://tinyurl.com/bephn4e8`), an AI algorithm matching Alpha Zero's results in chess and shogi, but improving it in Go (thus setting a new world standard) and even Atari games.

REMEMBER

Alpha Zero managed to reach the pinnacle of performance starting with zero data. This capability goes beyond the idea that data is needed to achieve every AI target (as Alon Halevy, Peter Norvig, and Fernando Pereira stated just a few years ago in the white paper at `https://tinyurl.com/4et9hktx`). Alpha Zero is possible because we know the generative processes used by Go game players, and DeepMind researchers were able to re-create a perfect Go environment.

4

Working with AI in Hardware Applications

IN THIS PART . . .

Engaging in robotic mayhem.

Fly everywhere with drones.

Let an AI do the driving for you.

Chapter **12**

Developing Robots

People often mistake robotics for AI, but robotics are different from AI. Artificial intelligence aims to find solutions to some difficult problems related to human abilities (such as recognizing objects, or understanding speech or text); robotics aims to use machines to perform tasks in the physical world in a partially or completely automated way. It helps to think of AI as the software used to solve problems, and of robotics as the hardware for making these solutions a reality.

Robotic hardware may or may not run using AI software. Humans remotely control some robots, as with the da Vinci robot discussed in the "Assisting a surgeon" section of Chapter 7. In many cases, AI does provide augmentation, but the human is still in control. Between these extremes of human control are robots that take more or less detailed instructions by humans (such as going from point A to point B on a map, or picking up an object) and rely on AI to execute the orders. Other robots autonomously perform assigned tasks without any human intervention. Integrating AI into a robot makes the robot smarter and more useful in performing tasks, but robots don't always need AI to function properly. Human imagination has made the two overlap as a result of sci-fi films and novels.

This chapter explores how this overlap happened and distinguishes between the current realities of robots and how the extensive use of AI solutions could transform them. Robots have existed in production since 1960s. This chapter also explores how people are employing robots more and more in industrial work, scientific discovery, medical care, and war. Some AI discoveries are accelerating this process because they solve difficult problems in robots, such as recognizing objects in the world, predicting human behavior, understanding voice commands, speaking correctly, learning to walk upright and, yes, doing backflips, as you can read in this article on recent robotic milestones: https://tinyurl.com/6smshpfk. Note that things have progressed since this first backflip with a backflipping cheetah (https://tinyurl.com/2av7r6be).

Defining Robot Roles

Robots are a relatively recent idea. The word comes from the Czech word *robota*, which means "forced labor." The term first appeared in the 1920 play *Rossum's Universal Robots*, written by Czech author Karel Čapek. However, humanity has long dreamed of mechanical beings. Ancient Greeks developed a myth of a bronze mechanical man, Talus, built by the god of metallurgy, Hephaestus, at the request of Zeus, the father of the gods. The Greek myths also contain references to Hephaestus building other automata, apart from Talus. *Automata* are self-operated machines that executed specific and predetermined sequences of tasks (in contrast to robots, which have the flexibility to perform a wide range of tasks). The Greeks actually built water-hydraulic automata that worked the same as an algorithm executed in the physical world. As algorithms, automata incorporate the intelligence of their creator, thus providing the illusion of being self-aware, reasoning machines.

REMEMBER

Differentiating automata from other human-like animations is important. Nowadays we have holograms, which are not automata (although AI can also power them) — they are just light projections with no mechanical parts. As another example of some myths not fitting in as automata, but inspiring robotic thoughts, the Golem (https://tinyurl.com/4m33pw7x) is a mix of clay and magic. No machinery is involved; therefore, it isn't akin to any device as discussed in this chapter. Like holograms, it doesn't qualify as automata.

You find examples of automata in Europe throughout the Greek civilization, the Middle Ages, the Renaissance, and modern times. Many designs by mathematician and inventor Al-Jazari appear in the Middle East (see https://tinyurl.com/e7yjh557 for details). China and Japan have their own versions of automata. Some automata are complex mechanical designs, but others are complete hoaxes, such as the Mechanical Turk, an eighteenth-century machine that was said to be able to play chess but hid a man inside.

The robots described by Čapek were not exactly mechanical automata, but rather living beings engineered and assembled as if they were automata. His robots possessed a human-like shape and performed specific roles in society meant to replace human workers. Reminiscent of Mary Shelley's Frankenstein, Čapek's robots were something that people view as *androids* today: bioengineered artificial beings, as described in Philip K. Dick's novel *Do Androids Dream of Electric Sheep?* (the inspiration for the film *Blade Runner*). Yet, the name *robot* also describes autonomous mechanical devices not made to amaze and delight, but rather to produce goods and services. In addition, robots became a central idea in sci-fi, both in books and movies, further contributing to a collective imagination of the robot as a human-shaped AI, designed to serve humans — not too dissimilar from Čapek's original idea of a servant. Slowly, the idea transitioned from art to science and technology and became an inspiration for scientists and engineers.

REMEMBER

Čapek created both the idea of robots and that of a robot apocalypse, like the AI takeover you see in sci-fi movies and that, given AI's recent progress, is feared by notable figures such as the founder of Microsoft, Bill Gates, physicist Stephen Hawking, and the inventor and business entrepreneur Elon Musk. Čapek's robotic slaves rebel against the humans who created them at the end of *Rossum's Universal Robots* by eliminating almost all of humanity. However, cooler heads are debunking such extreme thinking, such as the Scientific American article at `https://tinyurl.com/4zbjcesu`.

Overcoming the sci-fi view of robots

The first commercialized robot, the Unimate (`https://tinyurl.com/442x33mw`), appeared in 1961. It was simply a robotic arm — a programmable mechanical arm made of metal links and joints — with an end that could grip, spin, or weld manipulated objects according to instructions set by human operators. It was sold to General Motors to use in the production of automobiles. The Unimate had to pick up die castings from the assembly line and weld them together, a physically dangerous task for human workers. To get an idea of the capabilities of such a machine, check out this video: `https://tinyurl.com/jzt5w2hh`. The following sections describe the realities of robots today.

Considering robotic laws

Before the appearance of Unimate, and long before the introduction of many other robot arms employed in industry that started working with human workers in assembly lines, people already knew how robots should look, act, and even think. Isaac Asimov, an American writer renowned for his works in science fiction and popular science, produced a series of novels in the 1950s that suggested a completely different concept of robots from those used in industrial settings.

REMEMBER

Asimov coined the term *robotics* and used it in the same sense as people use the term *mechanics*. His powerful imagination still sets the standard today for people's expectations of robots. Asimov set robots in an age of space exploration, having them use their positronic brains to help humans daily to perform both ordinary and extraordinary tasks. A *positronic brain* is a fictional device that makes robots in Asimov's novels act autonomously and be capable of assisting or replacing humans in many tasks. Apart from providing human-like capabilities in understanding and acting (a clear display of a strong AI), the positronic brain works under the three laws of robotics as part of the hardware, controlling the behavior of robots in a moral way:

1. A robot may not injure a human being or, through inaction, allow a human being to come to harm.

2. A robot must obey the orders given it by human beings except where such orders would conflict with the First Law.

3. A robot must protect its own existence as long as such protection does not conflict with the First or Second Laws.

Later the author added a zeroth rule, with higher priority over the others in order to assure that a robot acted to favor the safety of the many:

0. A robot may not harm humanity, or, by inaction, allow humanity to come to harm.

Central to all Asimov's stories on robots, the three laws allow robots to work with humans without any risk of rebellion or AI apocalypse. Impossible to bypass or modify, the three laws execute in priority order and appear as mathematical formulations in the positronic brain functions. Unfortunately, the laws have loophole and ambiguity problems, from which arise the plots of most of his novels. The three laws come from a fictional *Handbook of Robotics*, 56th Edition, 2058 A.D. and rely on principles of harmlessness, obedience, and self-survival.

Asimov imagined a universe in which you can reduce the moral world to a few simple principles, with some risks that drive many of his story plots. In reality, Asimov believed that robots are tools to serve humankind and that the three laws could work even in the real world to control their proper use (read this 1981 interview in *Compute!* magazine for details: https://tinyurl.com/227352ff). Defying Asimov's optimistic view, however, current robots don't have the capability to

>> Understand the three laws of robotics

>> Select actions according to the three laws

>> Sense and acknowledge a possible violation of the three laws

Some may think that today's robots really aren't very smart because they lack these capabilities, and they'd be right. However, the Engineering and Physical Sciences Research Council (EPSRC), which is the UK's main agency for funding research in engineering and the physical sciences, promoted revisiting Asimov's laws of robotics in 2010 for use with real robots, given the technology of the time. The result is much different from the original Asimov statements (see `https://tinyurl.com/5cmr7bdr`). The conversation is ongoing, as described in the article at `https://tinyurl.com/ztnwk4jk`. These revised principles admit that robots may even kill (for national security reasons) exactly because they are a tool. As with all the other tools, complying with the law and existing morals is up to the human user, not the machine, with the robot perceived as an executor. In addition, someone (a human being) should always be accountable for the results of a robot's actions.

TIP

The EPSRC's principles offer a more realistic point of view on robots and morality, considering the weak AI technology in use now, but they could also provide a partial solution in advanced technology scenarios. Chapter 14 discusses problems related to using self-driving cars, a kind of mobile robot that drives for you. For example, in the exploration of the *trolley problem* in that chapter, you face possible but unlikely moral problems that challenge the reliance on automated machines when it's time to make certain choices.

Defining actual robot capabilities

Not only are existing robot capabilities still far from the human-like robots found in Asimov's works, they're also of different categories. The kind of biped robot imagined by Asimov is currently the rarest and least advanced.

The most frequent category of robots is the robot arm, such as the previously described Unimate. Robots in this category are also called *manipulators*. You can find them in factories, working as industrial robots, where they assemble and weld at a speed and precision unmatched by human workers. Some manipulators also appear in hospitals to assist in surgical operations. Manipulators have a limited range of motion because they integrate into their location (they might be able to move a little, but not a lot because they lack motors that would allow movement or require an electrical hookup), so they require help from specialized technicians to move to a new location. In addition, manipulators used for production tend to be completely automated (in contrast to surgical devices, which are remote controlled, relying on the surgeon to make medical operation decisions). More than 2.7 million manipulators appeared in factories throughout the world as of September 2020, 42 percent of them located in Japan or China according to `https://tinyurl.com/s99cj96n`. (These statistics don't account for other kinds of robots.)

The second largest, and growing, category of robots is that of *mobile robots*. Their specialty, contrary to that of manipulators, is to move around by using wheels, rotors, wings, or even legs. The major use of these robots is in industry as described in "Mobile robotics applications" at Robotnik.eu. Mobile robots are mostly unmanned (no one travels with them) and remotely controlled, but autonomy is increasing, and you can expect to see more independent robots in this category. Two special kinds of mobile robots are flying robots, called *drones* (see Chapter 13), and self-driving cars (discussed in Chapter 14).

The last kind of robots is the *mobile manipulator,* which can move (as do mobile robots) and manipulate (as do robot arms). The pinnacle of this category doesn't just consist of a robot that moves and has a mechanical arm but also imitates human shape and behavior. The *humanoid robot* is a biped (has two legs) that has a human-like torso and communicates with humans through voice and expressions. This kind of robot is what sci-fi dreamed of, but it's not easy to obtain. The Covid-19 pandemic has spawned greater use of humanoid robots like Sophia (see https://tinyurl.com/2ve3479k).

Being humanoid can be hard

Human-like robots are hard to develop, and scientists are still at work on them. Not only does a humanoid robot require enhanced AI capabilities to make it autonomous, it also needs to move as humans do. The biggest hurdle, though, is getting humans to accept a machine that looks like humans. The following sections look at various aspects of creating a humanoid robot.

Creating a robot that walks

Consider the problem of having a robot walking on two legs (*a bipedal robot*). This is something that humans learn to do adeptly and without conscious thought, but it's very problematic for a robot. Four-legged robots balance easily, and they don't consume much energy doing so. Humans, however, do consume energy simply by standing up, as well as by balancing and walking. Humanoid robots, like humans, have to continuously balance themselves, and do it in an effective and economic way. Otherwise, the robot needs a large battery pack, which is heavy and cumbersome, making the problem of balance even more difficult.

A video provided by IEEE Spectrum gives you a better idea of just how challenging the simple act of walking can be. The video shows robots involved in the DARPA Robotics Challenge (DRC), a challenge held by the U.S. Defense Advanced Research Projects Agency from 2012 to 2015: https://tinyurl.com/xsatxdfp. The purpose of the DRC is to explore robotic advances that could improve disaster and humanitarian operations in environments that are dangerous to humans (https://tinyurl.com/p2ndh952). For this reason, you see robots walking in different terrains, opening doors, grasping tools such as an electric drill, or trying to operate a valve wheel. A robot called Atlas, from Boston Dynamics, shows promise, as described in this article: https://tinyurl.com/6smshpfk. The Atlas robot truly is exceptional but still has a long way to go. The challenge is ongoing, as described at https://tinyurl.com/kwhdhkkj.

SEE SPOT DANCE! THE ROBOTS OF BOSTON DYNAMICS

Boston Dynamics, a company that dates to 1992, has gained fame and reputation as the pioneer of agile robots inspired by humans and animals. Alphabet X's division purchased the company in 2013, and then sold it in 2017 to the Japanese company Softbank, which controlled it until Hyundai recently acquired an 80-percent stake in it. The South Korean industrial conglomerate intends to leverage the company's capabilities for autonomous vehicles and smart factories. Boston Dynamics' most renowned robots are Spot (https://www.bostondynamics.com/spot), a four-legged canine robot, and Atlas (https://www.bostondynamics.com/atlas), a bipedal humanoid robot, which represents the most human-like robot on the market at the moment. Atlas has been developed under the supervision of Defense Advanced Research Projects Agency (DARPA; https://www.darpa.mil/) and it participated in two DARPA Robotics Challenges, placing second in 2015. It was revamped in 2016 (with a new, less menacing look). You see the newer version in most of the video you find online (just like the one in which the Atlas robot dances together with all other Boston Dynamics creations: https://tinyurl.com/2sckhjmk). The new Atlas version is designed to easily operate both outdoors and inside thanks to its advanced sensors and hydraulic actuators. In spite of the public fears that the robot may be used for warfare, in 2013 DARPA confirmed its intentions to employ the Atlas robot exclusively for emergency search-and-rescue operations in environments dangerous to human beings.

REMEMBER

A robot with wheels can move easily on roads, but in certain situations, you need a human-shaped robot to meet specific needs. Most of the world's infrastructures are made for a person to navigate. The presence of obstacles, such as the passage size, or the presence of doors or stairs, makes using differently shaped robots difficult. For instance, during an emergency, a robot may need to enter a nuclear power station and close a valve. The human shape enables the robot to walk around, descend stairs, and turn the valve wheel.

Overcoming human reluctance: The uncanny valley

Humans have a problem with humanoid robots that look a little too human. In 1970, a professor at the Tokyo Institute of Technology, Masahiro Mori, studied the impact of robots on Japanese society. He coined the term *Bukimi no Tani Genshō*, which translates to *uncanny valley*. Mori realized that the more realistic robots look, the greater affinity humans feel toward them. This increase in affinity remains true until the robot reaches a certain degree of realism, at which point, we start disliking them strongly (even feeling revulsion). The revulsion increases until the robot reaches the level of realism that makes them a copy of a human being. You can find this progression depicted in Figure 12-1 and described in Mori's original paper at: `https://tinyurl.com/5zxepyux`.

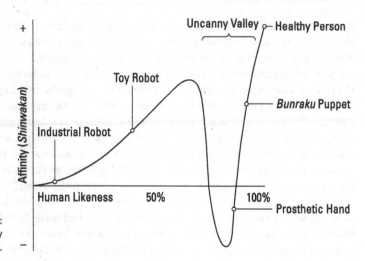

Various hypotheses have been formulated about the reasons for the revulsion that humans experience when dealing with a robot that is almost, but not completely, human. Cues that humans use to detect robots are the tone of the robotic voice, the rigidity of movement, and the artificial texture of the robot's skin. Some scientists attribute the uncanny valley to cultural reasons, others to psychological or biological ones. One experiment with monkeys found that primates might undergo a similar experience when exposed to more or less realistically processed photos of monkeys rendered by 3-D Computer-Generated Imagery (CGI) technology (see the story here: `https://tinyurl.com/c69vbhzt`). Monkeys participating in the experiment displayed a slight aversion to realistic photos, hinting at a common biological reason for the uncanny valley. An explanation could therefore relate to a self-protective reaction against beings negatively perceived as unnatural-looking because they're ill or even possibly dead. The research is ongoing as described in the article at `https://tinyurl.com/ye9dshs4`.

The interesting point about the uncanny valley is that if we need humanoid robots because we want them to assist humans, we must also consider their level of realism and key aesthetic details in order to achieve a positive emotional response that will allow users to accept robotic help. Some observations show that even robots with little human resemblance generate attachment and create bonds with their users. For instance, many U.S. soldiers report feeling a loss when their small tactical robots for explosive detection and handling are destroyed in action. (You can read an article about this on the MIT Technological Review: `https://tinyurl.com/6chj2m3a`.) At the other extreme, some robots have been cancelled because people thought they were too creepy, such as the New York police dog Spot (`https://tinyurl.com/79dkb8vt`). Even though Spot doesn't look much like a dog, the headless aspect of the robot seemed to make people feel uneasy. Perhaps it would have received a better reception if it had had a head of some sort.

An interesting experiment to overcome the uncanny valley is SEER, the Simulative Emotional Expression Robot, a humanoid robotic head developed as an artistic work by the Japanese artist Takayuki Todo. (You can see the robotic head in action on the artist's website: `http://www.takayukitodo.com/`.) To overcome the uncanny valley, Todo has worked on the child-like aspect of the robotic head and on its gaze. Because the SEER's head has a camera that can record the reactions of a human counterpart, the robot can reciprocate reactions by imitating human expressions thanks to the movement of its metallic eyebrows or just uninterrupted eye contact.

Working with robots

Different types of robots have different applications. As humans developed and improved the three classes of robots (manipulator, mobile, and humanoid), new fields of application opened to robotics. It's now impossible to enumerate exhaustively all the existing uses for robots, but the following sections touch on some of the most promising and revolutionary uses.

Enhancing economic output

Manipulators, or industrial robots, still account for the largest percentage of operating robots in the world. However, you see them used more in some countries than in others. The article "Robot Race: The World's Top 10 automated countries" at IFR.org is enlightening because robot use has increased even faster than predicted, but where they have increased (mostly in Asia) is as important as the fact that usage has increased. In fact, factories (as an entity) will use robots to become smarter, a concept dubbed *Industry 4.0*. Thanks to widespread use of the Internet, sensors, data, and robots, Industry 4.0 solutions allow easier customization and higher quality of products in less time than they can achieve without robots. No matter what, robots already operate in dangerous environments, and for tasks such as welding, assembling, painting, and packaging, they operate faster, with higher accuracy, and at lower costs than human workers can.

Taking care of you

Since 1983, robots have assisted surgeons in difficult operations by providing precise and accurate cuts that only robotic arms can provide. Apart from offering remote control of operations (keeping the surgeon out of the operating room to create a more sterile environment), an increase in automated operations are steadily opening the possibility of completely automated surgical operations in the near future, as speculated in this article: https://tinyurl.com/c2j4cabm. You might also want to check out the Society of Robotic Surgery (SRS) page at https://tinyurl.com/4vwcjrab to discover more about the human end of this revolution.

Providing services

Robots provide other care services, both in private and public spaces. The most famous indoor robot is the Roomba vacuum cleaner, a robot that will vacuum the floor of your house by itself (it's a robotic bestseller, having exceeded 30 million units sold according to https://tinyurl.com/3hyp8kkd), but there are other service robots to consider as well.

The definition of a service robot is changing almost daily because of a combination of worldwide events like the Covid-19 pandemic, the overall aging of the population, and the ability of technology to meet certain needs. The article at https://tinyurl.com/2cjzune7 provides some insights into how people view service robots today, but it's guaranteed that the definitions will change in the future.

TIP

Many service robots today are specifically targeted at home use (rather than a combination of industrial, institutional, and home use), like the Roomba, but you can use them in many different areas, as described in the articles at https://tinyurl.com/2a8j2wby and https://tinyurl.com/6dxnhfbt. There is also the use of robots for elder care, as described at https://tinyurl.com/aj2zxwc6, with an eye toward keeping elderly people in their homes as long as possible.

Venturing into dangerous environments

Robots go where people can't, or would be at great risk if they did. Some robots have been sent into space (with the NASA Mars rover Perseverance, https://tinyurl.com/5f8aj2cv, being one of the most notable attempts), and more will support future space exploration. (Chapter 16 discusses robots in space.) Many other robots stay on earth and are employed in underground tasks, such as transporting ore in mines or generating maps of tunnels in caves. Underground robots are even exploring sewer systems, as Luigi (a name inspired from the brother of a famous plumber in videogames) does. Luigi is a sewer-trawling robot developed by MIT's Senseable City Lab to investigate public health in a place where humans can't go unharmed because of high concentrations of chemicals, bacteria, and viruses (see https://tinyurl.com/da4hwucw). There are now armies of these sewer crawling robots who get rid of *fatbergs*, nasty conglomerations of non-biodegradeable substances like wet wipes (see the story at https://tinyurl.com/9pu9bwzc).

Robots are even employed where humans will definitely die, such as in nuclear disasters like Three Mile Island, Chernobyl, and Fukushima. These robots remove radioactive materials and make the area safer. High-dose radiation even affects robots because radiation causes electronic noise and signal spikes that damage circuits over time. In addition, unless the circuitry is hardened, radiation can do physical damage to the robot. Only *radiation hardened electronic components* allow robots to resist the effects of radiation enough to carry out their job, such as the Little Sunfish, an underwater robot that operates in one of Fukushima's flooded reactors where the meltdown happened (as described in this article at `https://tinyurl.com/yes4duwd`).

In addition, warfare or criminal scenes represent life-threatening situations in which robots see frequent use for transporting weapons or defusing bombs. These robots can also investigate packages that could include a lot of harmful things other than bombs. Robot models such as iRobot's PackBot (from the same company that manufactures Rumba, the house cleaner) or QinetiQ North America's Talon handle dangerous explosives by remote control, meaning that an expert in explosives controls their actions at a distance. Some robots can even act in place of soldiers or police in reconnaissance tasks or direct interventions (for instance, police in Dallas used a robot to take out a shooter `https://tinyurl.com/fk85wpsb`). Of course, there are lots of questions being asked about this practice, as detailed at `https://tinyurl.com/56xk4pzw`.

REMEMBER

People expect the military to increasingly use robots in the future. Beyond the ethical considerations of these new weapons, it's a matter of the old guns-versus-butter model (see `https://tinyurl.com/8jsws3c8` and `https://tinyurl.com/pta7ufdr`), meaning that a nation can exchange economic power for military power. Robots seem a perfect fit for that model, moreso than traditional weaponry that needs trained personnel to operate. Using robots means that a country can translate its productive output into an immediately effective army of robots at any time, something that the *Star Wars* prequels demonstrate all too well.

Understanding the role of specialty robots

Specialty robots include drones and SD cars. Drones are controversial because of their usage in warfare, but unmanned aerial vehicles (UAVs) are also used for monitoring, agriculture, and many less menacing activities, as discussed in Chapter 13.

People have long fantasized about cars that can drive by themselves. Most car producers have realized that being able to produce and commercialize SD cars could change the actual economic balance in the world. At one point, it seemed as if the world were on the cusp of seeing SD cars, as described in this article at the WashingtonPost.com: `https://tinyurl.com/dnh7k48y`). However, for a whole lot of reasons today, SD car technology has stalled, as described at The Guardian. com (https://tinyurl.com/4sfju66h). Chapter 14 discusses SD cars, their technology, and their implications in more detail.

Assembling a Basic Robot

An overview of robots isn't complete without discussing how to build one, given the state of the art, and considering how AI can improve its functioning. The following sections discuss robot basics.

Considering the components

A mobile robot's purpose is to act in the world, so it needs *effectors*, which are moving legs or wheels that provide the *locomotion capability*. It also needs arms and pincers to grip, rotate, translate (modify the orientation outside of rotation), and thus provide *manipulating capabilities.* When talking about the capability of the robot to do something, you may also hear the term *actuator* used interchangeably with effectors. An actuator is one of the mechanisms that compose the effectors, allowing a single movement. Thus, a robot leg has different actuators, such as electric motors or hydraulic cylinders that perform movements like orienting the feet or bending the knee.

Acting in the world requires determining the composition of the world and understanding where the robot resides in the world. *Sensors* provide input that reports what's happening outside the robot. Devices like cameras, lasers, sonars, and pressure sensors measure the environment and report to the robot what's going on as well as hint at the robot's location. The robot therefore consists mainly of an organized bundle of sensors and effectors. Everything is designed to work together using an architecture, which is exactly what makes up a robot. (Sensors and effectors are actually mechanical and electronic parts that you can use as stand-alone components in different applications.)

The common internal architecture is made of parallel processes gathered into layers that specialize in solving one kind of problem. Parallelism is important. As human beings, we perceive a single flow of consciousness and attention; we don't need to think about basic functions such as breathing, heartbeat, and food digestion because these processes go on by themselves in parallel to conscious thought. Often we can even perform one action, such as walking or driving, while talking or doing something else (although it may prove dangerous in some situations). The same goes for robots. For instance, in the three-layer architecture, a robot has many processes gathered into three layers, each one characterized by a different response time and complexity of answer:

>> **Reactive:** Takes immediate data from the sensors, the channels for the robot's perception of the world, and reacts immediately to sudden problems (for instance, turning immediately after a corner because the robot is going to crash into an unknown wall).

>> **Executive:** Processes sensor input data, determines where the robot is in the world (an important function called localization), and decides what action to execute given the requirements of the previous layer, the reactive one, and the following one, the deliberative.

>> **Deliberative:** Makes plans on how to perform tasks, such as planning how to go from one point to another and deciding what sequence of actions to perform to pick up an object. This layer translates into a series of requirements for the robot that the executive layer carries out.

Another popular architecture is the pipeline architecture, commonly found in SD cars, which simply divides the robot's parallel processes into separate phases such as sensing, perception (which implies understanding what you sense), planning, and control.

Sensing the world

Chapter 14 discusses sensors in detail and presents practical applications to help explain SD cars. Many kinds of sensors exist, with some focusing on the external world and others on the robot itself. For example, a robotic arm needs to know how much its arm extended or whether it reached its extension limit. Furthermore, some sensors are active (they actively look for information based on a decision of the robot), while others are passive (they receive the information constantly). Each sensor provides an electronic input that the robot can immediately use or process in order to gain a perception.

Perception involves building a local map of real-world objects and determining the location of the robot in a more general map of the known world. Combining data from all sensors, a process called *sensor fusion*, creates a list of basic facts for the robot to use. Machine learning helps in this case by providing vision algorithms using deep learning to recognize objects and segment images (as discussed in Chapter 11). It also puts all the data together into a meaningful representation using unsupervised machine learning algorithms. This is a task called *low-dimensional embedding*, which means translating complex data from all sensors into a simple flat map or other representation. Determining a robot's location is called *simultaneous localization and mapping (SLAM)*, and it is just like when you look at a map to understand where you are in a city.

Controlling a robot

After sensing provides all the needed information, planning provides the robot with the list of the right actions to take to achieve its objectives. Planning is done programmatically (by using an expert system, for example, as described in Chapter 3) or by using a machine learning algorithm, such as Bayesian networks, as described in Chapter 10. The technology that appears to hold the most promise today, though, is reinforcement learning, as described at `https://tinyurl.com/346x9tut`. This advance is only recently possible because of advances in how reinforcement learning works.

Finally, planning is not simply a matter of smart algorithms, because when it comes to execution, things aren't likely to go as planned. Think about this issue from a human perspective. When you're blindfolded, even if you want to go straight in front of you, you won't unless you have a constant source of corrections. The result is that you start going in loops. Your legs, which are the actuators, don't always perfectly execute instructions. Robots face the same problem. In addition, robots face issues such as delays in the system (technically called *latency*) or they don't execute instructions exactly on time, thus messing things up. However, most often the issue is a problem with the robot's environment, in one of the following ways:

>> **Uncertainty:** The robot isn't sure where it is, or it can partially observe the situation but can't figure it out exactly. Because of uncertainty, developers say that the robot operates in a *stochastic environment*.

>> **Adversarial situations:** People or moving objects are in the way. In some situations, these objects even become hostile (see an earlier article from Business Insider at `https://tinyurl.com/r3mkw23y`). This is the *multiagent problem*. An ongoing study in this area is described in the article in iScience at `https://tinyurl.com/f8zsdwm4`.

REMEMBER

Robots have to operate in environments that are partially unknown, changeable, mostly unpredictable, and in a constant flow, meaning that all actions are chained, and the robot has to continuously manage the flow of information and actions in real time. Being able to adjust to this kind of environment can't be fully predicted or programmed, and such an adjustment requires learning capabilities, which AI algorithms provide more and more to robots.

Chapter **13**

Flying with Drones

D rones are mobile robots that move in the environment by flying around. Initially connected to warfare, drones have become a powerful innovation for leisure, exploration, commercial delivery, and much more. However, military development still lurks behind developments and causes concern from many AI experts and public figures who foresee them as possibly unstoppable killing machines.

Flying is something that people have done since the Wright brothers first flew on December 17, 1903 (see https://tinyurl.com/3pnfzkv9). However, humans have always wanted to fly, and as far back as ancient times, legendary thinkers such as Leonardo da Vinci, a Renaissance genius, put their minds to the task (see this article from the Smithsonian Museum: https://tinyurl.com/45kktr55.) Nowadays, flying technology is advanced, so drones are more mature than other mobile robots because the key technology to make them work is well understood. The drones' frontier is to incorporate AI. Moving by flying poses some important limits on what drones can achieve, such as the weight they can carry or the actions they can take when arriving at a destination.

This chapter discusses the present state of drones: consumer, commercial, and military. It also explores the roles drones might play in the future. These roles for drones depend partly on integration with AI solutions, which will give them more autonomy and extended capabilities in moving and operating.

Acknowledging the State of the Art

Drones are mobile robots that fly. This type of robot has existed for a long time, especially for military uses (where the technology originated). The official military name for such flying machines is Unmanned Aircraft System (UAS), which includes the Unmanned Aerial Vehicle (UAV) and the associated support systems. More commonly, the public knows such mobile robots as "drones" because their sound resembles the male bee, but you won't find the term in many official papers because officials prefer names like UAS; or Unmanned Aerial Combat Vehicles (UACV); or Unmanned Aerial Vehicles (UAV); or even RPA (Remotely Piloted Aircraft).

TIP

There is a lot in a name. This article from *ABC News* can help you understand common acronyms and official names reserved for drones: https://tinyurl.com/mvv3f9yf.

Flying unmanned to missions

Resembling a standard airplane (but generally in smaller form), military drones are flying wings; that is, they have wings and one or more propellers (or jet engines) and to some extent aren't very different from airplanes that civilians use for travel. The military versions of drones are now in their sixth generation, as described at https://tinyurl.com/5ay5auaj. Military drones are unmanned and remotely controlled using satellite communications, even from the other side of the earth. Military drone operators acquire telemetry information and vision as transmitted from the drone they control, and the operators can use that information to operate the machine by issuing specific commands. Some military drones perform surveillance and recognizance tasks, and thus they simply carry cameras and other devices to acquire information. Others are armed with weapons and can carry out deadly attacks on objectives. Some of the deadliest of these aircraft match the capabilities of manned aircraft (see https://tinyurl.com/sbahk6ps) and can travel anywhere on earth — even to places where a pilot can't easily go (https://tinyurl.com/2m2exx47).

Military drones have a long history. Just when they began is a topic for much debate, but the Royal Navy began using drone-like planes for target practice in the 1930s (see https://tinyurl.com/564749wp for details). The US used actual drones regularly as early as 1945 for targets (see https://tinyurl.com/5y2xwnkj for details). Starting in 1971, researchers began to apply hobbyist drones to military purposes. John Stuart Foster, Jr., a nuclear physicist who worked for the U.S. government, had a passion for model airplanes and envisioned the idea of adding weapons to them. That led to the development of two prototypes by the U.S. Defense Advanced Research Projects Agency (DARPA) in 1973, but the use of similar drones in the past decade by Israel in Middle Eastern conflicts was what spurred interest in and further development of military drones. Interestingly enough, 1973 is the year that the military first shot a drone down, using a laser, of all things (see the Popular Science article at `https://tinyurl.com/3x82766u` and a Popular Mechanics article at `https://tinyurl.com/ymjxfna5` for details). The first drone killing occurred in 2001 in Afghanistan (see `https://tinyurl.com/3363ftdy`). Of course, a human operator was at the other end of the trigger then.

Recent efforts by the militaries of the world lean toward supplying drones with AI capabilities and more sensors. (A wide spectrum of sensors is being tested, including optical, thermal, and electromagnetic.) The challenge is twofold. First, scientists are working to increase the autonomy of unmanned devices sent to the battlefield, because the enemy could disturb or jam communications. Military experts are also working on how to increase the trust of operators and commanders that will send the AI to fight. (Trust is essential to empower the drone with the appropriate role in the fighting.)

An example of such efforts is DARPA's Gremlin project, which consists of a range of unmanned reusable drones (see `https://tinyurl.com/p7smus7w` for more details). These new drones feature the capabilities for

>> Multiple deployments

>> Use as a swarm asset

>> Use for surveillance, reconnaissance, and intelligence

>> Autonomous attack after target recognition

>> The ability to continue fighting when communications with headquarters are cut off

REMEMBER

The key reason for employing unmanned drones in the battlefield in the future is their capability to operate in swarms. Swarms require smaller (and thus harder to detect and hit) drones. Will Roper, the 13th assistant secretary of the Air Force for acquisition, explains the technology and logistics in this interview: `https://tinyurl.com/7bez5rnn`.

People debate whether to give military drones AI capabilities. Some feel that doing so would mean that drones could bring destruction and kill people through their own decision-making process. However, AI capabilities could also enable drones to more easily evade destruction or perform other nondestructive tasks, just as AI helps guide cars today. It could even steady a pilot's movements in harsh weather, similar to how the da Vinci system works for surgeons (see the "Assisting a surgeon" section of Chapter 7 for details). Presently, military drones with killing capabilities are also controversial because the AI would tend to make the act of war abstract and further dehumanizing, reducing it to images transmitted by drones to their operators and to commands issued remotely. Yes, the operator would still make the decision to kill by unleashing the drone, but the drone would perform the actual act, distancing the operator from responsibility for the act even more than when a pilot drops bombs from a plane.

TIP

Discussions about military drones are essential in this chapter because they interconnect with the development of civilian drones and influence much of the present discussion on this technology through public opinion. Also, giving military drones full autonomy inspires stories about an AI apocalypse that have arisen outside the sci-fi field and become a concern for the public. For a more detailed technical overview of models and capabilities, see this article by Deutsche Welle: https://tinyurl.com/ntwvae68.

Meeting the quadcopter

Many people first heard about consumer and hobbyist quadcopter drones, and then about commercial quadcopter drones (such as the one employed by Amazon that is discussed at https://tinyurl.com/chwnsfn3) through the mobile phone revolution. Most military drones aren't of the copter variety today, but you can find some, such as the Duke University TIKAD drone described at https://tinyurl.com/yu9sdms2 and demonstrated at https://tinyurl.com/v3432za. The military copter drones actually started as hobbyist prototypes (see https://tinyurl.com/vknd9v7u for details).

However, mobile phones were integral to making all this work. As mobile phones got smaller, their batteries also became smaller and lighter. Mobile phones also carry miniaturized cameras and wireless connectivity — all features that are needed in a contemporary drone. A few decades ago, small drones had a host of limitations:

>> They were radio controlled using large command sets.

>> They needed a line of sight (or you would have flown blind).

>> They were fixed-wing small airplanes (with no hovering capability).

>> They ran on noisy diesel or oil engines, limiting their range and user-friendliness.

Recently, lightweight lithium–polymer batteries have allowed drones to

>> Run on smaller, quieter, and reliable electric motors

>> Be controlled by wireless remote controls

» Rely on video feedback signals from the drones (no more line-of-sight requirement)

Drones also possess GPS, accelerometers, and gyroscopes now — all of which appear as part of consumer mobile phones. These features help control position, level, and orientation, something that's useful for phone applications but also quite essential for flying drones.

Thanks to all these improvements, drones changed from being fixed-wing, airplane-like models to something similar to helicopters, but which use multiple rotors to lift themselves in the air and take a direction. Using multiple rotors creates an advantage. Contrary to helicopters, drones don't need variable-pitch rotors for orientation. Variable-pitch rotors are more costly and difficult to control. Drones instead use simple, fixed-pitch propellers, which can emulate, as an ensemble, the same functions of variable-pitch rotors. Consequently, you now see multirotor drones: tricopter, quadcopter, hexacopter, and octocopter, respectively having 3, 4, 6, or 8 rotors to use. Among the different possible configurations, the quadcopter gained the upper hand and became the most popular drone configuration for commercial and civilian use. Because the quadcopter is based on four rotors (of small size), with each one oriented to a direction, an operator can easily turn and move the drone around by applying a different spin and speed to each rotor, as shown in Figure 13-1.

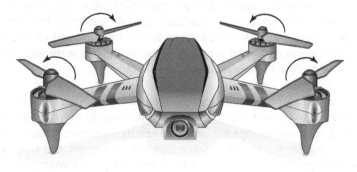

FIGURE 13-1: A quadcopter flies by opportunely spinning its rotors in the right directions.

Defining Uses for Drones

Each kind of drone type has current and futuristic applications, and consequently different opportunities to employ AI. The large and small military drones already have their parallel development in terms of technology, and those drones will likely see more use for surveillance, monitoring, and military action in the field. Experts forecast that military uses will likely extend to personal and commercial drones, which generally use different technology from the military ones. (Some overlap exists, such as Duke University's TIKAD, which actually started life in the hobbyist world.)

Apart from rogue uses of small but cheap and easily customizable drones by insurgents and terrorists groups (for an example, see https://tinyurl.com/44wubsh8), governments are increasingly interested in smaller drones for urban and indoor combat. Indoor places, like corridors or rooms, are where intervention capabilities of aircraft-size Predator and Reaper military drones are limited (unless you need to take down the entire building). The same goes for scout drones, such as Ravens and Pumas, because these drones are made for the operations on the open battlefield, not for indoor warfare. (You can read about the possible military evolution of otherwise harmless consumer drones in this article: https://tinyurl.com/6nbp5hpj that also details some of the disadvantages of doing so.) The article at https://tinyurl.com/3mn7dc3x details some of the history behind the use of drones by Violent Non-State Actors (VNSAs). It has become possible for anyone with a grudge or different point of view to use drones to engage in terrorism even without the assets that a state has for doing so.

Commercial drones are far from being immediately employed from shop shelves onto the battlefield, although they offer the right platform for the military to develop various technologies using them. An important reason for the military to use commercial drones is that off-the-shelf products are mostly inexpensive compared to standard weaponry, making them both easily disposable and employable in swarms comprising large numbers of them. Easy to hack and modify, they require more protection than their already hardened military counterparts do (their communications and controls could be jammed electronically), and they need the integration of some key software and hardware parts before being effectively deployed in any mission.

Navigating in a closed space requires enhanced abilities to avoid collisions, to get directions without needing a GPS (whose signals aren't easily caught while in a building), and to engage a potential enemy. Moreover, drones would need targeting abilities for reconnaissance (spotting ambushes and threats) and for taking out targets by themselves. Such advanced characteristics aren't found in present commercial technology, and they would require an AI solution developed specifically for the purpose. Military researchers are actively developing the required additions to gain military advantage. Recent developments in nimble deep learning networks installed on a standard mobile phone, such as YOLO (https://tinyurl.com/u7hwu88u) or Google's MobileNets (https://tinyurl.com/3rszbzsw and https://tinyurl.com/snf9va56), point out how fitting advanced AI into a small drone is achievable given the present technology advances.

Seeing drones in nonmilitary roles

Currently, commercial drones don't have a lot to offer in the way of advanced functionality found in military models. A commercial drone designed for the consumer market could possibly take a snapshot of you and your surroundings from an aerial perspective, with some benefit such as an image stabilizer and a *follow me feature* (which enables the drone to follow you without your issuing any other specific command). However, commercial drones intended for specific usage in industry and service are also becoming more sophisticated. Being equipped with more sensors, AI, and sometimes even robotic arms, commercial drones are finding their way into many applications in advanced economies, where efficiency in productivity and automation are becoming paramount.

With such enhanced commercial drones, a few innovative uses will become quite common in the near future:

» Delivering goods in a timely fashion, no matter the traffic (being developed by Google X, Amazon, and many startups)

» Performing monitoring for maintenance and project management

» Assessing various kinds of damage for insurance

» Creating field maps and counting herds for farmers

» Assisting search-and-rescue operations

» Providing Internet access in remote, unconnected areas (an idea being developed by Facebook)

» Generating electricity from high-altitude winds

» Carrying people around from one place to another

Having goods delivered by a drone is something that grabbed the public's attention early, thanks to promotion by large companies. One of the earliest and most recognized innovators is Amazon (which promises that a service, Amazon Prime Air, will become operative soon. Google promises a similar service with its Project Wing (https://tinyurl.com/3r6bfsyp). However, we may still be years away from having a feasible and scalable air delivery system based on drones. Even so, if you live in certain areas, like Virginia, you could get your Girl Scout cookies delivered by drone (https://tinyurl.com/dt3h4uma).

REMEMBER

Even though the idea would be to cut intermediaries in the logistic chain in a profitable way, many technical problems and regulatory ambiguities remain to be solved. Behind the media hype showing drones successfully delivering small parcels and other items, such as pizza or burritos, at target locations in an experimental manner (https://tinyurl.com/f2kbfw4t), the truth is that drones can't fly far or carry much weight. The biggest problem is one of regulating the flights of swarms of drones, all of which need to get an item from one point to another. There are obvious issues, such as avoiding obstacles like power lines, buildings, and other drones; facing bad weather; and finding a suitable spot to land near you. The drones would also need to avoid sensitive air space and meet all required regulatory requirements that aircraft meet. AI will be the key to solving many of these problems, but not all. For the time being, delivery drones seem to work fine on a small scale for more critical deliveries than having freshly made burritos at your home: https://tinyurl.com/kar9v9me and https://tinyurl.com/y4vn6nxx.

Drones can become your eyes, providing vision in situations that are too costly, dangerous, or difficult to see by yourself. Remotely controlled or semiautonomous (using AI solutions for image detection or processing sensor data), drones can monitor, maintain, surveil, or search and rescue because they can view any infrastructure from above and accompany and support on-demand human operators in their activities. For instance, drones have successfully inspected power lines, pipelines (https://tinyurl.com/42vxvdm5), and railway infrastructures (https://tinyurl.com/4833yxbv), allowing more frequent and less costly monitoring of vital, but not easily accessible, infrastructures. Even insurance companies find them useful for damage assessments and other purposes, such as inspecting the roof of your home before insuring it (https://tinyurl.com/2xr752ed).

Chasing crooks

Police forces and first-responders around the world have found drones useful for a variety of activities, from search-and-rescue operations to forest fire detection and localization, and from border patrol missions to crowd monitoring. Drones are already widespread in law enforcement and police are always finding newer ways to usefully employ them (https://tinyurl.com/phbr7xc), including finding traffic violators (see the article at https://tinyurl.com/4rrdy7x3).

Drones used by police are fitted with optical, zoom, and often also thermal cameras; therefore, they excel at surveillance and search from distance. This kind of aerial surveillance has proven to be the key to successfully solving a range of problems that law enforcers may encounter during their service, even though they're extremely invasive.

Not only do drones keep an eye in the sky on highly frequented locations, as well as enforce surveillance in otherwise critical areas because of crowd and car traffic, but they are also becoming indispensable for apprehending suspected criminals. When chasing suspects, a drone can report their whereabouts and whether they're carrying weapons while going unnoticed because of their low profile and low-noise engines. For instance, in this YouTube video, you can see how Daytona Beach police use a drone fitted with thermal camera to locate and seize a suspect after a burglary: https://tinyurl.com/44ynjpk3.

Finally, drones see use in many rescue situations, in which a bird's-eye view can help locate people in distress better than a squad on the ground. UAV Coach, a drone community website, reports quite a few interesting stories of people saved by drones (see https://tinyurl.com/uf238b7f). Police are also increasingly using drones for assessments that could otherwise take time and require more personnel onsite. Such tasks range from mapping areas of interest, to document-ing car accident and crime scenes, to mapping damages after a disaster.

Growing better crops

Agriculture is another important area in which drones are revolutionizing work. Not only can they monitor crops, report progress, and spot problems, but they apply pesticides or fertilizer only where and when needed, as described by MIT Technology Review (https://tinyurl.com/t5x6hsz2). Drones offer images that are more detailed and less costly to obtain than those acquired from an orbital satellite, and they can be employed to:

>> Analyze soil and map the result using image analysis and 3-D laser scanners to make seeding and planting more effective

>> Control planting by controlling tractor movements

>> Monitor real-time crop growth

>> Spray chemicals when and where needed

>> Irrigate when and where needed

>> Assess crop health using infrared vision, something a farmer can't do

Precision agriculture uses AI capabilities for movement, localization, vision, and detection. Precision agriculture could increase agriculture productivity (healthier crops and more food for everyone) while diminishing costs for intervention (no need to spray pesticides everywhere).

Organizing warehouses

Other areas where drones also shine are in logistics and manufacturing opera-tions. Drones operating in enclosed spaces can't rely on GPS geolocation to deter-mine where they are and where they're going. Recent advances in visually-based navigation and other sensors have improved the ability of drones to navigate indoors, rendering them suitable to operate in the larger warehouse spaces neces-sary for global manufacturing operations and the trading of export goods.

In warehouses, drones seem particularly apt at checking inventories. Checking inventories and counting available parts and goods is a menial activity that usually requires a large amount of time and effort from warehouse workers. It can sometimes turn dangerous when it involves climbing to reach higher shelves. Drones can handle the task perfectly by using barcodes, QR codes, or radio-frequency identification (RFID) technology. In addition, drones can engage in intralogistics, which involves moving goods among different parts of the warehouse (though a drone is limited by how much weight it can carry).

Manufacturing is undergoing a technological transformation by using AI solutions in production and organization, resulting in smart factories. In general, the possible use cases for drones increases because of the large number of potential activities they enable:

>> Replacing workers in risky operations or in less attractive activities

>> Increasing workers' productivity by supporting and speeding up their operations

>> Saving costs by replacing more costly technology or methods

>> Providing entry to inaccessible or difficult-to-reach places in the factory

Because of these reasons, market research companies like Gartner and Statista estimate that the number of drones sold for commercial purposes will increase every year and generate more revenue than consumer drones. Commercial drones are better equipped than consumer drones, and thus expensive. (You can read a comprehensive report at https://tinyurl.com/4x78rc9b.)

Drones can perform amazing feats in industries that you may never have thought about, ranging from communication to energy. The communications industry intends to move existing infrastructure to the sky using drones. Transportation plans to use drones to transport people, replacing common means of transportation, such as the car (https://tinyurl.com/uvnujv7k and https://tinyurl.com/45p7meex). Another possibility in the energy sector is to produce electricity up high where winds are stronger and no one will protest the rotor noise (https://tinyurl.com/34fhbvar).

TIP

For an updated and exhaustive list of actual uses of drones in various industries, you can skim through a complete list of 128 possible activities in 22 different areas compiled by dronegenuity, a company providing drone services: https://tinyurl.com/z72puwm5.

Powering up drones using AI

With respect to all drone applications, whether consumer, business, or military related, AI is both a game enabler and a game changer. AI allows many applications to become feasible or better executed because of enhanced autonomy and coordination capabilities. Raffaello D'Andrea, a Canadian/Italian/Swiss engineer, professor of dynamic systems and control at ETH Zurich, and drone inventor, demonstrates drone advances in this video: https://tinyurl.com/2utct3ff. The video shows how drones can become more autonomous by using AI algorithms. *Autonomy* affects how a drone flies, reducing the role of humans issuing drone commands by automatically handling obstacle detection and allowing safe navigation in complicated areas. *Coordination* implies the ability of drones to work together without a central unit to report to and get instructions from, making drones able to exchange information and collaborate in real time to complete any task.

Taken to its extreme, autonomy may even exclude any human guiding the drone so that the flying machine can determine the route to take and execute specific tasks by itself. (Humans issue only high-level orders.) When not driven by a pilot, drones rely on GPS to establish an optimal destination path, but that's possible only outdoors, and it's not always precise. Indoor usage increases the need for precision in flight, which requires increased use of other sensor inputs that help the drone understand *proximity surrounds* (the elements of a building, such as a wall protrusion, that could cause it to crash). The cheapest and lightest of these sensors is the camera that most commercial drones have installed as a default device. But having a camera doesn't suffice because it requires proficiency in processing images using computer vision and deep learning techniques (discussed in this book, for instance, in Chapter 11 when discussing convolutional networks).

Companies expect autonomous execution of tasks for commercial drones, for instance, making them able to deliver a parcel from the warehouse to the customer and handling any trouble along the way. (As with robots, something always goes wrong that the device must solve using AI on the spot.) Researchers at NASA's Jet Propulsion Laboratory in Pasadena, California, have recently tested automated drone flight against a high-skilled professional drone pilot (see https://tinyurl.com/panpurf9 for details). Interestingly, the human pilot had the upper hand in this test until he became fatigued, at which point the slower, steadier, and less error-prone drones caught up with him. In the future, you can expect the same as what happened with chess and Go games: Automated drones will outrun humans as drone pilots in terms of both flying skills and endurance.

We could take coordination to extremes as well, permitting hundreds, if not thousands, of drones to fly together. Such capability could make sense for commercial and consumer drones when drones crowd the skies. Using coordination would be beneficial in terms of collision avoidance, information sharing on obstacles, and traffic analysis in a manner similar to that used by partially or fully automated interconnected cars (Chapter 14 discusses AI-driven cars).

Rethinking existing drone algorithms is already going on, and some solutions for coordinating drone activities already exist. For instance, MIT developed a decentralized coordination algorithm for drones in 2016 (see https://tinyurl.com/cs5d4urk). Most research is, however, proceeding unnoticed because a possible use for drone coordination is military in nature. Drone swarms may be more effective in penetrating enemy defenses unnoticed and carrying out strike actions that are difficult to fend off. The enemy will no longer have a single large drone to aim at, but rather hundreds of small ones flying around. Fortunately, there are solutions for taking down drone swarms (see https://tinyurl.com/9app5ntc). A test on a swarm of 100 drones (model Perdix, a custom-made model for the United States Department of Defense) released from three F/A-18 Super Hornets and executing recognizance and intercept missions was made public (https://tinyurl.com/247xsepk), but other countries are also involved in this new arms race.

When entrepreneur Elon Musk, Apple cofounder Steve Wozniak, physicist Stephen Hawking, and many other notable public figures and AI researchers raised alarms on recent AI weaponry developments, they didn't think of robots as shown in films like *Terminator* or *I, Robot,* but rather of armed flying drones and other automated weapons. Autonomous weapons could start an arms race and forever change the face of warfare. You can discover more about this topic at https://tinyurl.com/a8ckvrm8.

Understanding regulatory issues

Drones are not the first and only things to fly over clouds, obviously. Decades of commercial and military fights have crowded the skies, requiring both strict regulation and human monitoring control to guarantee safety. In the United States, the Federal Aviation Administration (FAA) is the organization with the authority to regulate all civil aviation, making decisions about airports and air traffic management. The FAA has issued a series of rules for the UAS (drones), and you can read those regulations at https://tinyurl.com/c355drrw.

The FAA issued a set of rules known as *Part 107* in August 2016. These rules outline the use of commercial of drones during daylight hours. The rules come down to these five straightforward rules:

>> Fly below 400 feet (120 meters) altitude.

>> Fly at speeds less than 100 mph.

>> Keep unmanned aircraft in sight all times.

>> The operator must have an appropriate license.

>> Never fly near manned aircraft, especially near airports.

UNDERSTANDING TEACHING ORIENTATION

Much of this book is about creating an environment and providing data so that an AI can learn. In addition, you spend a great deal of time considering what is and isn't possible using an AI from a purely teaching perspective. Some parts of the book even consider morality and ethics as they apply to AI and its human users. However, the orientation of the teaching provided to an AI is also important.

In the movie *WarGames* (https://tinyurl.com/w6sf3edm), the War Operation Plan Response (WOPR) computer contains a strong AI capable of determining the best course of action in responding to a threat. During the initial part of the movie, WOPR goes from being merely an advisor to the executor of policy. Then along comes a hacker who wants to play a game: thermonuclear war. Unfortunately, WOPR assumes that all games are real and actually starts to create a plan to engage in thermonuclear war with the Soviet Union. The movie seems to be on the verge of confirming every worst fear that could ever exist regarding AI and war.

Here's the odd part of this movie. The hacker, who is now found out and working for the good guys, devises a method to teach the AI futility. That is, the AI enters an environment in which it learns that winning some games — tic-tac-toe, in this case — isn't possible. No matter how well one plays, in the end, the game ends in stalemate after stalemate. The AI then goes to test this new learning on thermonuclear war. In the end, the AI concludes that the only winning move is not to play at all.

Most of the media stories you hear, the sci-fi you read, and the movies you watch never consider the learning environment. Yet, the learning environment is an essential part of the equation, because how you configure the environment determines what the AI will learn. When dealing with military equipment, it's probably a good idea to teach the AI to win, but also to show it that some scenarios simply aren't winnable, so the best move is not to play at all.

>> Never fly over groups of people, stadiums, or sporting events.

>> Never fly near emergency response efforts.

The FAA will soon issue additional rules for drone flight at night that pertain to when it can be out of the line of sight and in urban settings, even though it's currently possible to obtain special waivers from the FAA. The Operations Over People rule (https://tinyurl.com/4h88ea2j) became effective in April 2021 and it allows pilots that meet certain standards to fly at night over people and moving vehicles without waiver as long as they meet certain requirements. The purpose of such regulatory systems is to protect the public safety, given that the impact of drones on our lives still isn't clear. These rules also allow innovation and economic growth to be derived from such a technology.

Presently, the lack of AI means that drones may easily lose their connection and behave erratically, sometimes causing damage. Consequently, you see articles like this one: `https://tinyurl.com/bhh635xn` that discuss what to do when your drone loses a connection. Even though most drones now have safety measures in case of a lost connection with the controller, such as having them automatically return to the exact point at which they took off, the FAA restricts their usage to staying within the line of sight of their controller unless the pilot meets certain criteria.

Another important safety measure is one called *geo-fencing.* Drones using GPS service for localization have software that limits their access to predetermined perimeters described by GPS coordinates, such as airports, military zones, and other areas of national interest. You can get the list of parameters at `https://tinyurl.com/ar9yeazw` or read more about this topic at `https://tinyurl.com/ynw4f3cx`.

Algorithms and AI are coming to the rescue by preparing a suitable technological setting for the safe usage of a host of drones that deliver goods in cities. NASA's Ames Research Center is working on a system called Unmanned Aerial Systems Traffic Management (UTM) that is playing the same air-traffic-control tower role for drones as we use for manned airplanes (see `https://tinyurl.com/5595ndfw`). However, this system is completely automated; it counts on the drones' capabilities to communicate with each other. UTM will help identify drones in the sky (each one will have an identifier code, just like car license plates) and will set a route and a cruise altitude for each drone, thus avoiding possible collisions, misbehavior, or potential damage for citizens. You can read about the four levels of testing and the current progress of this initiative at `https://www.nasa.gov/ames/utm`.

REMEMBER

When restrictions are not enough and rogue drones represent a menace, police and military forces have found a few effective countermeasures: taking the drone down by a shotgun; catching it by throwing a net; jamming its controls; taking it down using laser or microwaves; and even firing guided missiles at it.

Chapter **14**

Utilizing the AI-Driven Car

A self-driving car (SD car) is an *autonomous vehicle*, which is a vehicle that can drive by itself from a starting point to a destination without human intervention. Autonomy implies not simply having some tasks automated (such as Automated Parking Assist, demonstrated in the video "Automatic Parking Assist | GM Fleet" at YouTube.com), but also being able to perform the right steps to achieve objectives independently. An SD car performs all required tasks on its own, with a human potentially there to observe (and do nothing else unless something completely unexpected happens). Because SD cars have been part of history for more than 100 years (yes, incredible as that might seem), this chapter begins with a short history of SD cars.

REMEMBER

For a technology to succeed, it must provide a benefit that people see as necessary and not as easily obtained using other methods. That's why SD cars are so exciting. They offer many things of value, other than just driving. The next section of the chapter tells you how SD cars will change mobility in significant ways and helps you understand why this is such a compelling technology.

When SD cars become a bit more common and the world comes to accept them as just a part of everyday life, they will continue to affect society. The next part of the chapter helps you understand issues surrounding acceptance and the common use of SD cars, and considers why these issues are important. It answers the question of what it will be like to get into an SD car and assume that the car will get you from one place to another without problems.

Finally, SD cars require many sensor types to perform their task. Yes, in some respects you could group these sensors into those that see, hear, and touch, but that would be an oversimplification. The final section of the chapter helps you understand how the various SD car sensors function and what they contribute to the SD car as a whole.

Getting a Short History

Developing cars that can drive by themselves has long been part of the futuristic vision provided by sci-fi narrative and film since early experiments in the 1920s with radio-operated cars. You can read more about the long, fascinating history of autonomous cars in "We've had driverless cars for almost a hundred years" at qz.com. The problem with these early vehicles is that they weren't practical; someone had to follow behind them to guide them using a radio controller. Consequently, even though the dream of SD cars has been cultivated for so long, the present projects have little to share with the past other than the vision of autonomy.

The modern SD cars are deeply entrenched in projects that started in the 1980s (see "In the 1980s, the Self-Driving Van Was Born" at MIT Technology Review. com — which may require a subscription). These newer efforts leverage AI to remove the need for radio control found in earlier projects. Many universities and the military (especially the U.S. Army) fund these efforts. At one time, the goal was to win at the DARPA Grand Challenge, which ended in 2007. However, now the military and commercial concerns provide plenty of incentive for engineers and developers to continue moving forward.

The turning point in the challenge was the creation of the autonomous car called Stanley, designed by scientist and entrepreneur Sebastian Thrun and his team. They won the 2005 DARPA Grand Challenge (see the video "DARPA Grand Challenge - Stanley Wins" at YouTube.com). After the victory, Thrun started the development of SD cars at Google. Today you can see the Stanley on exhibit in the Smithsonian Institution's National Museum of American History.

REMEMBER

The military isn't the only one pushing for autonomous vehicles. For a long time, the automotive industry suffered from overproduction because it could produce more cars than required by market demand (though the realities of Covid-19 intervened). Market demand can go down or up as a result of all sorts of pressures, such as car longevity. In the 1930s, car longevity averaged 6.75 years, but cars today average 10.8 or more years and allow drivers to drive 250,000 or more miles. Although circumstances changed at least temporarily during the coronavirus pandemic, the decrease in sales led some makers to exit the industry or fuse together and form larger companies. SD cars are the silver bullet for the industry, offering a way to favorably reshape market demand and convince consumers to upgrade. This necessary technology will result in an increase in the production of a large number of new vehicles.

Understanding the Future of Mobility

SD cars aren't a disruptive invention simply because they'll radically change how people perceive cars, but also because their introduction will have a significant impact on society, economics, and urbanization. At present, no SD cars are on the road yet — only prototypes. (You may think that SD cars are already a commercial reality, but the truth is that they're all prototypes. Look, for example, at "Uber May Be Aflame, but Its Self-Driving Cars Are Getting Good" at Wired.com and you see phrases such as *pilot projects* used, which you should translate to mean prototypes that aren't ready for prime time.) Many people believe that SD car introduction will require at least another decade, and replacing all the existing car stock with SD cars will take significantly longer. The many articles on driverless cars at The Conversation.com will help you track SD car progress (or regression in some cases). However, even if SD cars are still in the future, you can clearly expect great things from them, as described in the following sections.

Climbing the six levels of autonomy

Foretelling the shape of things to come isn't possible, but many people have at least speculated on the characteristics of SD cars. For clarity, Society of Automotive Engineers (SAE) International (http://www.sae.org/), an automotive standardization body, published a classification standard for autonomous cars (see the J3016 standard at https://tinyurl.com/2vpnxctt). Having a standard creates car automation milestones. Here are the five levels of autonomy specified by the SAE standard:

>> **Level 1 – driver assistance:** Control is still in the hands of the driver, yet the car can perform simple support activities such as controlling the speed.

This level of automation includes cruise control, when you set your car to go a certain speed, the stability control, and precharged brakes.

>> **Level 2 – partial automation:** The car can act more often in lieu of the driver, dealing with acceleration, breaking, and steering if required. The driver's responsibility is to remain alert and maintain control of the car. A partial automation example is the automatic braking that certain car models execute if they spot a possible collision ahead (a pedestrian crossing the road or another car suddenly stopping). Other examples are adaptive cruise control (which doesn't just control car speed, but also adapts speed to situations such when a car is in front of you), and lane centering. This level has been available on commercial cars since 2013.

>> **Level 3 – conditional automation:** Most automakers are working on this level as of the writing of this book. *Conditional automation* means that a car can drive by itself in certain contexts (for instance, only on highways or on unidirectional roads), under speed limits, and under vigilant human control. The automation could prompt the human to resume driving control. One example of this level of automation is recent car models that drive themselves when on a highway and automatically brake when traffic slows because of jams (or gridlock).

>> **Level 4 – high automation:** The car performs all the driving tasks (steering, throttle, and brake) and monitors any changes in road conditions from departure to destination. This level of automation doesn't require human intervention to operate, but it's accessible only in certain locations and situations, so the driver must be available to take over as required. Vendors had originally expected to introduce this level of automation around 2020, but a quick read only will tell you that they're still a long way to seeing this level as a reality.

>> **Level 5 – full automation:** The car can drive from departure to destination with no human intervention, with a level of ability comparable or superior to a human driver. Level-5 automated cars won't have a steering wheel. This level of automation is expected five or more years after Level 4 cars become a reality. You can read about what's taking a while in "What's Holding Back Fully Autonomous Driving?" at Thomasnet.com.

Even when SD cars achieve level-5 autonomy, you won't see them roaming every road. Such cars are still far in the future, and there could be difficulties ahead. The "Overcoming Uncertainty of Perceptions" section, later in this chapter, discusses some of the obstacles that an AI will encounter when driving a car. The SD car won't happen overnight; it'll probably come about through a progressive mutation, starting with the gradual introduction of more and more automatic car models. Humans will keep holding the wheel for a long time. What you can expect to see is an AI that assists in both ordinary driving and dangerous conditions to make the driving experience safer. Even when vendors commercialize SD cars, replacing actual stock may take years. The process of revolutionizing road use in urban settings with SD cars may take 30 years.

WARNING

This section contains a lot of dates, and some people are prone to thinking that any date appearing in a book must be precise. All sorts of things could happen to speed or retard adoption of SD cars. For example, the insurance industry is currently suspicious of SD cars because it is afraid that its motor insurance products will be dismissed in the future as the risk of having a car accident becomes rarer. (The McKinsey consulting firm predicts that SD cars will reduce accidents by 90 percent; see "Ten ways autonomous driving could redefine the automotive world" at McKinesey.com). Lobbying by the insurance industry could retard acceptance of SD cars. Also, consumers might put up some resistance because of lack of openness to the new technology (some consumers look for gradual product improvements, not for radical changes, as described in "Consumers Don't Really Want Self-Driving Cars, MIT Study Finds" at wbur.org). On the other hand, people who have suffered the loss of a loved one to an accident are likely to support anything that will reduce traffic accidents. They might be equally successful in speeding acceptance of SD cars. Consequently, given the vast number of ways in which social pressures change history, predicting a precise date for acceptance of SD cars isn't possible.

Rethinking the role of cars in our lives

Mobility is inextricably tied to civilization. It's not just the transportation of people and goods, but also ideas flowing around to and from distant places. When cars first hit the roads, few believed that they would soon replace horses and carriages. Yet, cars have many advantages over horses: They're more practical to keep, offer faster speeds, and run longer distances. Cars also require more control and attention by humans, because horses are aware of the road and react when obstacles or possible collisions arise, but humans accept this requirement for obtaining greater mobility.

Today, car use molds both the urban fabric and economic life. Cars allow people to commute long distances from home to work each day (making suburban real estate development possible). Businesses easily send goods farther distances; cars create new businesses and jobs; and factory workers in the car industry have long since become the main actors in a new redistribution of riches. The car is the first real mass-market product, made by workers for other workers. When the car business flourishes, so do the communities that support it; when it perishes, catastrophe can ensue. Trains and airplanes are bound to predetermined journeys, whereas cars are not. Cars have opened and freed mobility on a large scale, revolutionizing, more than other long-range means of transportation, the daily life of people. As Henry Ford, the founder of the Ford Motor Company, stated, "cars freed common people from the limitations of their geography."

As when cars first appeared, civilization is on the brink of a new revolution brought about by SD cars. When vendors introduce autonomous driving-level 5 and SD cars become mainstream, you can expect significant new emphasis on how humans design cities and suburbs, on economics, and on everyone's lifestyle. There are obvious and less obvious ways that SD cars will change life. The most obvious and often noted ways are the following:

>> **Fewer accidents:** Fewer accidents will occur because AI will respect road rules and conditions; it's a smarter driver than humans are. Accident reduction will deeply affect the way vendors build cars, which are now more secure than in the past because of structural passive protections. In the future, given their absolute safety, SD cars could be lighter because of fewer protections than now. They may even be made of plastic. As a result, cars will consume fewer resources than today. In addition, the lowered accident rate will mean reduced insurance costs, creating a major impact on the insurance industry, which deals with the economics of accidents.

>> **Fewer jobs involving driving:** Many driving jobs will disappear or require fewer workers. That will bring about cheaper transportation labor costs, thus making the transportation of goods and people even more accessible than now. It will also raise problems for finding new jobs for people. (In the United States alone, 3 million people are estimated to work in transportation.)

>> **More time:** SD cars will help humans obtain more of the most precious things in life, such as time. SD cars won't help people to go farther, but it will help them put the time they would have spent driving to use in other ways (because the AI will be driving). Moreover, even if traffic increases (because of smaller transportation costs and other factors), traffic will become smoother, with little or no traffic congestion. In addition, the transportation capacity of existing roads will increase. It may sound like a paradox, but this is the power of an AI when humans remain out of the picture, as illustrated by this video "The Simple Solution to Traffic" at YouTube.com.

TIP

>> There are always opposing points of view when it comes to technology, and it's important to maintain an open mind when hearing them. For example, instead of reducing traffic congestion, some people say that SD cars will actually increase traffic congestion because more people will opt to drive, rather than carpool, take a train, or rely on a bus. In addition, given the nature of people, you might see weird behavior like having a car continue driving in circles around a block while the owner eats at a restaurant when parking spaces are limited.

Apart from these immediate effects are the subtle implications that no one can determine immediately, but which can appear evident after reflection. Benedict Evans points outs a few of them in his blog post "Cars and second order consequences" at ben-evans.com). This insightful article looks deeper into consequences of the introduction of both electric cars and level-5 autonomy for SD cars on the market. As one example, SD cars could make the dystopian Panopticon a reality (see "What does the panopticon mean in the age of digital surveillance?" at The Guardian.com. The Panopticon is the institutional building theorized by the English philosopher Jeremy Bentham at the end of the eighteenth century, where everyone is under surveillance without being aware of it. When SD cars roam the streets in large number, car cameras will appear everywhere, watching and possibly reporting everything they happen to witness. Your car may spy on you and others when you least expect it.

Thinking of the future isn't an easy exercise because it's not simply a matter of cause and effect. Even looking into more remote orders of effects could prove ineffective when the context changes from the expected. For instance, a future Panopticon may never happen because the legal system could force SD cars not to communicate the images they capture. For this reason, prognosticators rely on scenarios that are approximate descriptions of a possible future; these scenarios may or may not be capable of happening, depending on different circumstances. Experts speculate that a car enabled with autonomous driving capabilities could engage in four different scenarios, each one redefining how humans use or even own a car:

>> **Autonomous driving on long journeys on highways:** When drivers can voluntarily allow the AI to do the driving and take them to their destination, the driver can devote attention to other activities. Many consider this first scenario as a possible introductory scenario for autonomous cars. However, given the high speeds on highways, giving up control to an AI isn't completely risk-free because other cars, guided by humans, could cause a crash. People have to consider consequences such as the current inattentive driving laws found in most locations. The question is one of whether the legal system would see a driver using an AI as inattentive. This is clearly a level-3 autonomy scenario. Fatalities occur (see "2 Killed in Driverless Tesla Car Crash, Officials Say" at the nytimes.com).

>> **Acting as a chauffeur for parking:** In this scenario, the AI intervenes when the passengers have left the car, saving them the hassle of finding parking. The SD car offers a time-saving service to its occupants as it opens the possibility of both parking-lot optimization (the SD car will know where best to park) and car sharing. (After you leave the car, someone else can use it; later, you hail another car left nearby in the parking lot.) Given the limitations of autonomous driving used only for car fetching, this scenario involves a transition from level-3 to level-4 autonomy.

>> **Acting as a chauffeur for any journey, except those locations where SD cars remain illegal:** This advanced scenario allows the AI to drive in any areas but ones that aren't permitted for safety reasons (such as new road infrastructures that aren't mapped by the mapping system used by the car). This scenario takes SD cars to near maturity (autonomy level 4).

>> **Playing on-demand taxi driver:** This is an extension of scenario 2, when the SD cars are mature enough to drive by themselves all the time (level-5 autonomy), with or without passengers, providing a transportation service to anyone requiring it. Such a scenario will fully utilize cars (in this era, cars are parked 95 percent of the time; see "Today's Cars Are Parked 95% of the Time" at Fortune.com) and revolutionize the idea of owning a car because you won't need one of your own.

Taking a step back from unmet expectations

At this point, you may expect to ride an SD car soon because it can clearly bring safety and many advantages. At least, you may expect more automation in existing cars. Vendors have, in fact, made quite a few announcements in past years that raised expectations and made many hope for the introduction of autonomous vehicles on the road:

>> In 2016, Elon Musk, Tesla's CEO, announced that "by the end of 2017, one of Tesla's cars will be able to drive from New York to Los Angeles without the driver having to do anything" (which you can read about at https://tinyurl.com/2368ccj4).

>> Apart from Tesla, a lot of automakers, such as General Motors, have made bold statements (https://tinyurl.com/yf74m3h3). Audi (https://tinyurl.com/netjs52d) and Nissan (https://tinyurl.com/3uvz2xbc) have also made announcements.

>> In 2016, Business Insider Intelligence forecast 10 million autonomous vehicles on roads by 2020, and it wasn't the only business intelligence service to forward such ambitious targets (see https://tinyurl.com/k8jn9xsk).

Yet, in spite of such intense hype about SD cars between 2016 and 2017, current cars haven't changed all that much. At this point, you may even wonder whether the technology will be commercialized anytime soon, with new car models or aftermarket kits capable of transforming your old car into a self-driving one.

Actually, the technology behind SD cars did improve in the recent years, and security issues didn't limit such development all that much. Yet, everyone working on the technology will now tell you that things appear much more tricky and difficult than they looked back in those 2016–2017 years, and they postpone the introduction of SD cars to the end of the 2020 decade (or possibly beyond).

SD cars are being introduced today in limited parts of the United States. These vehicles have limited scope, such as the cars from Waymo. Waymo is an Alphabet company, heir of the Google Self-Driving Car Project, previously led by Sebastian Thrun, and it has opened its fully driverless service to residents in the metropolitan area of Phoenix, Arizona (see "Waymo is opening its fully driverless service to the general public in Phoenix" at blog.waymo.com). Access to this technology by the general public seems delayed, and it will probably first occur in particular areas and sectors, involving large fleets of cars such as taxis, shuttles, and truck transportation. The problems with SD cars reside in two areas:

>> **Perception** is necessary for the car to determine where it is, and it relies on various technologies discussed by the end of the chapter. The problem with these technologies is that the more reliable they are, the more expensive, and the more maintenance and care they require.

>> **Prediction** helps to elaborate on the perceptions and to provide the car with an idea of what will happen, which is the key to making good decisions on the road and avoiding collisions and other accidents. For instance, such skill is learned when the SD car is engaged in traffic and has to navigate across lanes of oncoming traffic or when, at a crossing, it must perform an unprotected left turn. Determining the behavior of other cars is critical. Unfortunately, what is natural for a human car driver, relying on experience and social cues between drivers, doesn't seem to come easily for a SD car.

Believed to be the most challenging prediction task, predictions involving other cars are solved at present by forcing an overly cautious behavior on SD cars. Scientists are currently working on reinforcement learning solutions and imitation learning to solve these issues.

REMEMBER

Imitation learning techniques try to mimic human behavior in a specific task. This is done in a similar way to reinforcement learning (which consists of an environment and a set of rewards for correct behavior in the environment). The imitation learning approach instead resembles machine learning because it's supervised and based on data. Usually, experts curate the data for imitation learning manually, and it resembles laboratory data more than real-world data.

SD CARS AND THE TROLLEY PROBLEM

Some say that insurance liability and the trolley problem will seriously hinder SD car use. The insurance problem involves the question of who takes the blame when something goes wrong. Accidents happen now, and SD cars should cause fewer accidents than humans do, so the problem seems easily solved by automakers if the insurance industry won't insure SD cars. (The insurance industry is wary of SD cars because SD car use could reshape its core business.) SD car automakers such as Audi, Volvo, Google, and Mercedes-Benz have already pledged to accept liability if their vehicles cause an accident (see "Potential liability ramifications of self-driving cars" at cohen-lawyers.com and "The Laws and Liabilities of Autonomous Vehicles" at Cornell Policy Review.com). This means that automakers will become insurers for the greater good of introducing SD cars to the market.

The *trolley problem* is a moral challenge introduced by the British philosopher Philippa Foot in 1967 (but it is an ancient dilemma). In this problem, a runaway trolley is about to kill a number of people that are on the track, but you can save them by diverting the trolley to another track, where unfortunately another person will be killed in their place. Of course, you need to choose which track to use, knowing that someone is going to die. Quite a few variants of the trolley problem exist, and there is even a Massachusetts Institute of Technology (MIT) website https://www.moralmachine.net/ that proposes alternative situations more suited to those that an SD car may experience.

The point is that situations arise in which someone will die, no matter how skilled the AI is that's driving the car. In some cases, the choice isn't between two unknown people, but between the driver and someone on the road. Such situations do happen even now, and humans resolve them by leaving the moral choice to the human at the steering wheel. Some people will save themselves, some will sacrifice for others, and some will choose what they see as the lesser evil or the greater good. Most of the time, it's a matter of an instinctive reaction made under life-threatening pressure and fear, although the culture you are from plays an important role (as this MIT study points out: https://tinyurl.com/tmu4thty). Mercedes-Benz, the world's oldest car maker, has stated that it will give priority to passengers' lives (see https://tinyurl.com/kfybmkes). Car makers might consider that a trolley-problem type of catastrophic situation is already so rare — and SD cars will make it even rarer — and that self-protection is something so innate in us that most SD car buyers will agree upon this choice.

Getting into a Self-Driving Car

Creating an SD car, contrary to what people imagine, doesn't consist of putting a robot into the front seat and letting it drive the car. Humans perform myriad tasks to drive a car that a robot wouldn't know how to perform. To create a human-like intelligence requires many systems connecting to each other and working harmoniously together to define a proper and safe driving environment. Some efforts are under way to obtain an end-to-end solution, rather than rely on separate AI solutions for each need. The problem of developing an SD car requires solving many single problems and having the individual solutions work effectively together. For example, recognizing traffic signs and changing lanes require separate systems.

REMEMBER

End-to-end solution is something you often hear when discussing deep learning's role in AI. This means that a single solution will provide an answer to an entire problem, rather than some aspect of a problem. Given the power of learning from examples, many problems don't require separate solutions, which are essentially a combination of many minor problems, with each one solved by a different AI solution. Deep learning can solve the problem as a whole by solving examples and providing a unique solution that encompasses all the problems that required separate AI solutions in the past.

NVIDIA, the deep learning GPU producer, is working on end-to-end solutions. Check out the video at https://tinyurl.com/5a3zu5vd, which shows the effectiveness of the solution as an example. Yet, as is true for any deep learning application, the goodness of the solution depends heavily on the exhaustiveness and number of examples used. To have an SD car function as an end-to-end deep learning solution requires a dataset that teaches the car to drive in an enormous number of contexts and situations, which aren't available yet but could be in the future.

TECHNICAL STUFF

Nevertheless, hope exists that end-to-end solutions will simplify the structure of SD cars. The article at https://tinyurl.com/kuar48td explains how the deep learning process works. You may also want to read the original NVIDIA paper on how end-to-end learning helps steer a car at https://tinyurl.com/3enk2f82.

Putting all the tech together

Under the hood of an SD car are systems working together according to the robotic paradigm of sensing, planning, and acting. Everything starts at the sensing level, with many different sensors telling the car different pieces of information:

>> The GPS tells where the car is in the world (with the help of a map system), which translates into latitude, longitude, and altitude coordinates.

>> The radar, ultrasound, and lidar devices spot objects and provide data about their location and movements in terms of changing coordinates in space.

» The cameras inform the car about its surroundings by providing image snapshots in digital format.

TIP

Many specialized sensors appear in an SD car. The "Overcoming Uncertainty of Perceptions" section, later in this chapter, describes them at length and discloses how the system combines their output. The system must combine and process the sensor data before the perceptions necessary for a car to operate become useful. Combining sensor data therefore defines different perspectives of the world around the car.

Localization is knowing where the car is in the world, a task mainly done by processing the data from the GPS device. GPS is a space-based satellite navigation system originally created for military purposes. When used for civilian purposes, it has some inaccuracy embedded (so that only authorized personal can use it to its full precision). The same inaccuracies also appear in other systems, such as GLONASS (the Russian navigation system), GALILEO (or GNSS, the European system), or the BeiDou (or BDS, the Chinese system). Consequently, no matter what satellite constellation you use, the car can tell that it's on a certain road, but it can miss the lane it's using (or even end up running on a parallel road). In addition to the rough location provided by GPS, the system processes the GPS data with lidar sensor data to determine the exact position based on the details of the surroundings.

The *detection system* determines what is around the car. This system requires many subsystems, with each one carrying out a specific purpose by using a unique mix of sensor data and processing analysis:

» Lane detection is achieved by processing camera images using image data analysis or deep learning specialized networks for *image segmentation,* in which an image is partitioned into separated areas labeled by type (that is, road, cars, and pedestrians).

» Traffic signs and traffic lights detection and classification are achieved by processing images from cameras using deep learning networks that first spot the image area containing the sign or light and then labeling them with the right type (the type of sign or the color of lights). This NVIDIA article helps you understand how an SD car sees: https://tinyurl.com/ph5kdm.

» Combined data from radar, lidar, ultrasound, and cameras help locate external objects and track their movements in terms of direction, speed, and acceleration.

» Lidar data is mainly used for detecting free space on the road (an unobstructed lane or parking space).

Letting AI into the scene

After the sensing phase, which involves helping the SD car determine where it is and what's going on around it, the planning phase begins. AI fully enters the scene at this point. Planning for an SD car boils down to solving these specific planning tasks:

>> **Route:** Determines the path that the car should take. Because you're in the car to go somewhere specific (well, that's not always true, but it's an assumption that holds true most of the time), you want to reach your destination in the fastest and safest way. In some cases, you also must consider cost. Routing algorithms, which are classic algorithms, are there to help.

>> **Environment prediction:** Helps the car to project itself into the future because it takes time to perceive a situation, decide on a maneuver, and complete it. During the time necessary for the maneuver to take place, other cars could decide to change their position or initiate their own maneuvers, too. When driving, you also try to determine what other drivers intend to do to avoid possible collisions. An SD car does the same thing using machine learning prediction to estimate what will happen next and take the future into account.

>> **Behavior planning:** Provides the car's core intelligence. It incorporates the practices necessary to stay on the road successfully: lane keeping; lane changing; merging or entering into a road; keeping distance; handling traffic lights, stop signs and yield signs; avoiding obstacles; and much more. All these tasks are performed using AI, such as an expert system that incorporates many drivers' expertise, or a probabilistic model, such as a Bayesian network, or even a simpler machine learning model.

>> **Trajectory planning:** Determines how the car will actually carry out the required tasks, given that usually more than one way exists to achieve a goal. For example, when the car decides to change lanes, you'll want it to do so without harsh acceleration or by getting too near other cars, and instead to move in an acceptable, safe, and pleasant way.

Understanding that it's not just AI

After sensing and planning, it's time for the SD car to act. Sensing, planning, and acting are all part of a cycle that repeats until the car reaches its destination and stops after parking. Acting involves the core actions of acceleration, braking, and steering. The instructions are decided during the planning phase, and the car simply executes the actions with controller system aid, such as the Proportional-Integral-Derivative (PID) controller or Model Predictive Control (MPC), which are algorithms that check whether prescribed actions execute correctly and, if not, immediately prescribe suitable countermeasures.

It may sound a bit complicated, but it's just three systems acting, one after the other, from start to end at destination. Each system contains subsystems that solve a single driving problem, as depicted in Figure 14-1, using the fastest and most reliable algorithms.

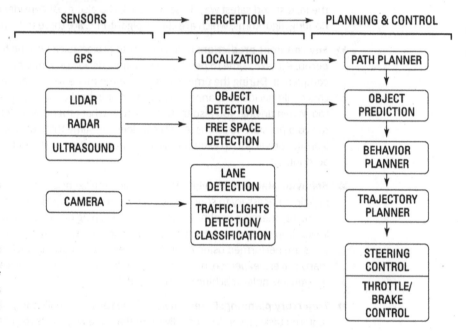

FIGURE 14-1:
An overall, schematic view of the systems working in an SD car.

At the time of writing, this framework is the state of the art. SD cars will likely continue as a bundle of software and hardware systems housing different functions and operations. In some cases, the systems will provide redundant functionality, such as using multiple sensors to track the same external object, or relying on multiple perception processing systems to ensure that you're in the right lane. Redundancy helps to ensure zero errors and therefore reduce fatalities. For instance, even when a system like a deep learning traffic-sign detector fails or is tricked (see https://tinyurl.com/ufn9ephc), other systems can back it up and minimize or nullify the consequences for the car.

Overcoming Uncertainty of Perceptions

Steven Pinker, professor in the Department of Psychology at Harvard University, says in his book *The Language Instinct: How the Mind Creates Language* that "in robotics, the easy problems are hard and the hard problems are easy." In fact, an AI playing chess against a master of the game is incredibly successful; however, more mundane activities, such as picking up an object from the table, avoiding a collision with a pedestrian, recognizing a face, or properly answering a question over the phone, can prove quite hard for an AI.

REMEMBER

The *Moravec paradox* says that what is easy for humans is hard for AI (and vice versa), as explained in the 1980s by robotics and cognitive scientists Hans Moravec, Rodney Brooks, and Marvin Minsky. Humans have had a long time to develop skills such as walking, running, picking up an object, talking, and seeing; these skills developed through evolution and natural selection over millions of years. To survive in this world, humans do what all living beings have done since life has existed on earth — they develop skills that enhance their ability to interact with the world as a whole based on species goals. Conversely, high abstraction and mathematics are relatively new discoveries for humans when you consider the first humans appeared on earth around 315,000 years ago and most experts agree that mathematics only appears 2,500 years go. We aren't naturally adapted for either mathematics or abstractions; it's something that an AI can often perform better than we can.

Cars have some advantages over robots, which have to make their way in buildings and on outside terrain. Cars operate on roads specifically created for them, usually well-mapped ones, and cars already have working mechanical solutions for moving on road surfaces.

Actuators aren't the greatest problem for SD cars. Planning and sensing are what pose serious hurdles. Planning is at a higher level (what AI generally excels in). When it comes to general planning, SD cars can already rely on GPS navigators, a type of AI specialized in providing directions. Sensing is the real bottleneck for SD cars because without it, no planning and actuation are possible. Drivers sense the road all the time to keep the car in its lane, to watch out for obstacles, and to respect the required rules.

REMEMBER

Sensing hardware is updated continuously at this stage of the evolution of SD cars to find more reliable, accurate, and less costly solutions. On the other hand, both processing sensor data and using it effectively rely on robust algorithms, such as the *Kalman filter* (see `https://tinyurl.com/2ken4zjx`), which have already been around a few decades.

Introducing the car's senses

Sensors are the key components for perceiving the environment, and an SD car can sense in two directions, internal and external:

>> **Proprioceptive sensors:** Responsible for sensing vehicle state, such as systems status (engine, transmission, braking, and steering) and the vehicle's position in the world by using GPS localization, rotation of the wheels, the speed of the vehicle, and its acceleration

>> **Exteroceptive sensors:** Responsible for sensing the surrounding environment by using sensors such as camera, lidar, radar, and ultrasonic sensors

Both proprioceptive and exteroceptive sensors contribute to SD car autonomy. GPS localization, in particular, provides a guess (possibly viewed as a rough estimate) as to the SD car's location, which is useful at a high level for planning directions and actions aimed at getting the SD car to its destination successfully. The GPS helps an SD car in the way it helps any human driver: by providing the right directions.

The exteroceptive sensors (shown in Figure 14-2) help the car specifically in driving. They replace or enhance human senses in a given situation. Each of them offers a different perspective of the environment; each suffers specific limitations; and each excels at different capabilities.

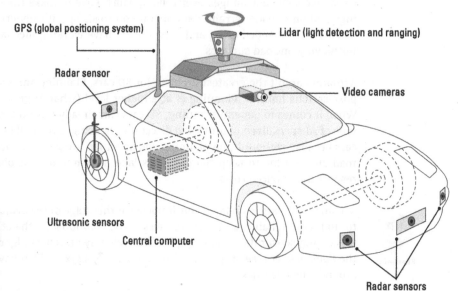

FIGURE 14-2: A schematic representation of exteroceptive sensors in an SD car.

GPS (global positioning system)

Lidar (light detection and ranging)

Radar sensor

Video cameras

Ultrasonic sensors

Central computer

Radar sensors

Limitations come in a number of forms. As you explore what sensors do for an SD car, you must consider cost, sensitivity to light, sensitivity to weather, noisy recording (which means that sensitivity of the sensor changes, affecting accuracy), range, and resolution. On the other hand, capabilities involve the capability to track the velocity, position, height, and distance of objects accurately, as well as the skill to detect what those objects are and how to classify them.

Camera

Cameras are passive, vision-based sensors. They can provide mono or stereo vision. Given their low cost, you can place plenty of them on the front windshield, as well as on front grilles, side mirrors, the rear door, and the rear windshield. Commonly, stereo vision cameras mimic human perception and retrieve information on the road and from nearby vehicles, whereas mono vision cameras are usually specialized in detecting traffic signs and traffic lights. The data they capture is processed by algorithms for image processing or by deep learning neural networks to provide detection and classification information (for instance, spotting a red light or a speed-limit traffic signal). Cameras can have high resolution (they can spot small details) but are sensitive to light and weather conditions (night, fog, or snow).

Lidar (LIght Detection And Ranging)

Lidar uses infrared beams (about 900 nanometer wavelength, invisible to human eyes) that can estimate the distance between the sensor and the hit object. They use a rotating swivel to project the beam around and then return estimations in the form of a cloud of collision points, which helps estimate shapes and distances. Depending on price (with higher generally meaning better), lidar can have higher resolution than radar. However, lidar is frailer and easier to get dirty than radar because it's exposed outside the car. (Lidar is the rotating device you see on top of the Google car in this CBS report: https://tinyurl.com/42rmwvrj.)

Radar (RAdio Detection And Ranging)

Based on radio waves that hit a target and bounce back, and whose time of flight defines distance and speed, radar can be located in the front and rear bumper, as well as on the sides of the car. Vendors have used it for years in cars to provide adaptive cruise control, blind-spot warning, collision warning, and avoidance. In contrast to other sensors that need multiple successive measurements, radar can detect an object's speed after a single ping because of the Doppler effect (see https://tinyurl.com/4a567s23). Radar comes in short-range and long-range versions, and can both create a blueprint of surroundings and be used for localization purposes. Radar is least affected by weather conditions when compared to other types of detection, especially rain or fog, and has 150 degrees of sight and

30–200 meters of range. Its main weakness is the lack of resolution (radar doesn't provide much detail) and inability to detect static objects properly.

Ultrasonic sensors

Ultrasonic sensors are similar to radar but use high-frequency sounds (ultra-sounds, inaudible by humans, but audible by certain animals) instead of microwaves. The main weakness of ultrasonic sensors (used by manufacturers instead of the frailer and more costly lidars) is their short range.

Putting together what you perceive

When it comes to sensing what is around an SD car, you can rely on a host of different measurements, depending on the sensors installed on the car. Yet, each sensor has different resolution, range, and noise sensitivity, resulting in different measures for the same situation. In other words, none of them is perfect, and their sensory weaknesses sometimes hinder proper detection. Sonar and radar signals might be absorbed; lidar's rays might pass through transparent solids. In addition, it's possible to fool cameras with reflections or bad light, as described by this article at MIT Technology Review.com at https://tinyurl.com/yfudnv9c.

SD cars are here to improve our mobility, which means preserving our lives and those of others. An SD car can't be permitted to fail to detect a pedestrian who suddenly appears in front of it. For safety reasons, vendors focus much effort on sensor fusion, which combines data from different sensors to obtain a unified measurement that's better than any single measurement. Sensor fusion is most commonly the result of using Kalman filter variants (such as the Extended Kalman Filter or the even more complex Unscented Kalman Filter). Rudolf E. Kálmán was a Hungarian electrical engineer and an inventor who immigrated to the United States during World War II. Because of his invention, which found so many applications in guidance, navigation, and vehicle control, from cars to aircraft to spacecraft, Kálmán received the National Medal of Science in 2009 from U.S. President Barack Obama.

A Kalman filter algorithm works by filtering multiple and different measurements taken over time into a single sequence of measurements that provide a real estimate (the previous measurements were inexact manifestations). It operates by first taking all the measurements of a detected object and processing them (the state prediction phase) to estimate the current object position. Then, as new measurements flow in, it uses the new results it obtains and updates the previous ones to obtain a more reliable estimate of the position and velocity of the object (the measurement update phase), as shown in Figure 14-3.

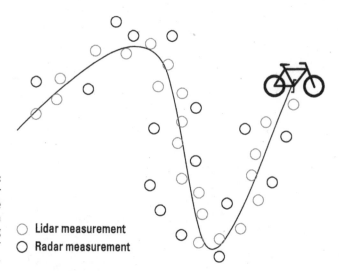

FIGURE 14-3:
A Kalman filter
estimates the
trajectory of a
bike by fusing
radar and lidar
data.

○ Lidar measurement
○ Radar measurement

In this way, an SD car can feed the algorithm the sensor measurements and use them to obtain a resulting estimate of the surrounding objects. The estimate combines all the strengths of each sensor and avoids their weaknesses. This is possible because the filter works using a more sophisticated version of probabilities and Bayes' theorem, which are described in Chapter 10.

5

Considering the Future of AI

Chapter **15**

Understanding the Nonstarter Application

P revious chapters in this book explore what AI is and what it isn't, along with which problems it can solve well and which problems are seemingly out of range. Even with all this information, you can easily recognize a potential application that won't ever see the light of day because AI simply can't address that particular need. This chapter explores the nonstarter application. Perhaps the chapter should be retitled as "Why We Still Need Humans," but the current title is clearer.

As part of this chapter, you discover the effects of attempting to create nonstarter applications. The most worrisome of those effects is the AI winter. An *AI winter* occurs whenever the promises of AI proponents exceed their capability to deliver, resulting in a loss of funding from entrepreneurs.

AI can also fall into the trap of developing solutions to problems that don't really exist. Yes, the wonders of the solution really do look quite fancy, but unless the solution addresses a real need, no one will buy it. Technologies thrive only when they address needs that users are willing to spend money to obtain. This chapter finishes with a look at solutions to problems that don't exist.

Using AI Where It Won't Work

Table 1-1 in Chapter 1 lists the seven kinds of intelligence. A fully functional society embraces all seven kinds of intelligence, and different people excel in different kinds of intelligence. When you combine the efforts of all the people, you can address all seven kinds of intelligence in a manner that satisfies society's needs.

REMEMBER

You'll quickly note from Table 1-1 that AI doesn't address two kinds of intelligence at all, and provides only modest capability with three more. AI excels when it comes to math, logic, and kinesthetic intelligence, limiting its ability to solve many kinds of problems that a fully functional society needs to address. The following sections describe situations in which AI simply can't work because it's a technology — not a person.

Defining the limits of AI

When talking to Alexa, you might forget that you're talking with a machine. The machine has no idea of what you're saying, doesn't understand you as a person, and has no real desire to interact with you; it only acts as defined by the algorithms created for it and the data you provide. Even so, the results are amazing. It's easy to anthropomorphize the AI without realizing it and see it as an extension of a human-like entity. However, an AI lacks the essentials described in the following sections.

Creativity

You can find an endless variety of articles, sites, music, art, writings, and all sorts of supposedly creative output from an AI. The problem with AI is that it can't create anything. When you think about creativity, think about patterns of thought. For example, Beethoven had a distinct way of thinking about music. You can recognize a classic Beethoven piece even if you aren't familiar with all his works because the music has a specific pattern to it, formed by the manner in which Beethoven thought.

An AI can create a new Beethoven piece by viewing his thought process mathematically, which the AI does by learning from Beethoven music examples. The resulting basis for creating a new Beethoven piece is mathematical in nature. In fact, because of the mathematics of patterns, in "Hear AI play Beethoven like The Beatles," at TechCrunch.com, you can hear an AI play Beethoven from the perspective of the Beatles, as well as other music genres.

The problem of equating creativity to math is that math isn't creative. To be creative means to develop a new pattern of thought — something that no one has seen before (see "What is creativity?" at CSUN.edu for more details). Creativity isn't just the act of thinking outside the box; it's the act of defining a new box.

Creativity also implies developing a different perspective, which is essentially defining a different sort of dataset (if you insist on the mathematical point of view). An AI is limited to the data you provide. It can't create its own data; it can only create variations of existing data — the data from which it learned. The "Understanding teaching orientation" sidebar in Chapter 13 expounds on this idea of perspective. To teach an AI something new, something different, something amazing, a human must decide to provide the appropriate data orientation.

Imagination

To create is to define something real, whether it's music, art, writing, or any other activity that results in something that others can see, hear, touch, or interact with in other ways. Imagination is the abstraction of creation, and is therefore even further outside the range of AI capability than creativity. Someone can imagine things that aren't real and can never be real. Imagination is the mind wandering across fields of endeavor, playing with what might be if the rules didn't get in the way. True creativity is often the result of a successful imagination.

From a purely human perspective, everyone can imagine something. Imagination sets us apart from everything else and often places us in situations that aren't real at all. The *Huffington Post* article "5 Reasons Imagination Is More Important Than Reality" provides five reasons that imagination is critical in overcoming the limits of reality.

Just as an AI can't create new patterns of thought or develop new data without using existing sources, it must also exist within the confines of reality. Consequently, it's unlikely that anyone will ever develop an AI with imagination. Not only does imagination require creative intelligence, it also requires intrapersonal intelligence, and an AI possesses neither form of intelligence.

Imagination, like many human traits, is emotional. AI lacks emotion. In fact, when viewing what an AI can do, versus what a human can do, it often pays to ask the simple question of whether the task requires emotion.

Original ideas

To imagine something, create something real from what was imagined, and then to use that real-world example of something that never existed in the past is to develop an idea. To successfully create an idea, a human needs good creative, intrapersonal, and interpersonal intelligence. Creating something new is great if you want to define one-off versions of something or to entertain yourself. However, to make it into an idea, you must share it with others in a manner that allows them to see it as well.

Data deficiencies

The "Considering the Five Mistruths in Data" section of Chapter 2 tells you about data issues that an AI must overcome to perform the tasks that it's designed to do. The only problem is that an AI typically can't recognize mistruths in data with any ease unless there is an accompanying wealth of example data that lacks these mistruths, which might be harder to come by than you think. Humans, on the other hand, can often spot the mistruths with relative ease. Having seen more examples than any AI will ever see, a human can spot the mistruths through both imagination and creativity. A human can picture the mistruth in a manner that the AI can't because the AI is stuck in reality.

REMEMBER

Mistruths are added into data in so many ways that listing them all is not even possible. Humans often add these mistruths without thinking about it. In fact, avoiding mistruths can be impossible, caused as they are by perspective, bias, and frame-of-reference at times. Because an AI can't identify all the mistruths, the data used to make decisions will always have some level of deficiency. Whether that deficiency affects the AI's capability to produce useful output depends on the kind and level of deficiency, along with the capabilities of the algorithms.

The oddest sort of data deficiency to consider, however, is when a human actually wants a mistruth as output. This situation occurs more often that most people think, and the only way to overcome this particular human issue is through the subtle communication provided by interpersonal intelligence that an AI lacks. For example, someone buys a new set of clothes. They look hideous — to you, at least, (and clothes can be amazingly subjective). However, if you're smart, you'll say that the clothes look amazing. The person isn't looking for your unbiased opinion — the person is looking for your support and approval. The question then becomes not one of "How do these clothes look?" — which is what the AI would hear — but one of "Do you approve of me?" or "Will you support my decision to buy these clothes?" You can partially overcome the problem by suggesting accessories that complement the clothes or by using other means, such as subtly getting the person to see that they might not even wear the clothes publicly.

There is also the issue of speaking a hurtful truth that an AI will never be able to handle because an AI lacks emotion. A *hurtful truth* is one in which the recipient gains nothing useful, but instead receives information that causes harm — whether emotional, physical, or intellectual. For example, a child may not know that one parent was unfaithful to another. Because both parents have passed on, the information isn't pertinent any longer, and it would be best to allow the child to remain in a state of bliss. However, someone comes along and ensures that the child's memories are damaged by discussing the unfaithfulness in detail. The child doesn't gain anything, but is most definitely hurt. An AI could cause the same sort of hurt by reviewing family information in ways that the child would never consider. Upon discovering the unfaithfulness through a combination of police reports, hotel records, store receipts, and other sources, the AI tells the child about the unfaithfulness, again causing hurt by using the truth. However, in the case of the AI, the truth is presented because of a lack of emotional intelligence (empathy); the AI is unable to understand the child's need to remain in a blissful state about the parent's fidelity. Unfortunately, even when a dataset contains enough correct and truthful information for an AI to produce a usable result, the result can prove more hurtful than helpful.

Applying AI incorrectly

The limits of AI define the realm of possibility for applying AI correctly. However, even within this realm, you can obtain an unexpected or unhelpful output. For example, you could provide an AI with various inputs and then ask for a probability of certain events occurring based on those inputs. When sufficient data is available, the AI can produce a result that matches the mathematical basis of the input data. However, the AI can't produce new data, create solutions based on that data, imagine new ways of working with that data, or provide ideas for implementing a solution. All these activities reside within the human realm. All you should expect is a probability prediction.

REMEMBER

Many of the results of AI are based on probability or statistics. Unfortunately, neither of these mathematical methods applies to individuals; these methods work only with groups. In fact, using statistics creates myriad problems for just about any purpose other than concrete output, such as driving a car. The article "The Problems with Statistics" at public.wsu.edu discusses the problems with using statistics. When your AI application affects individuals, you must be prepared for the unexpected, including complete failure to achieve any of the goals that you had set out to achieve.

Another issue is whether the dataset contains any sort of opinion, which is far more prevalent than you might think. An opinion differs from a fact in that the fact is completely provable and everyone agrees that a fact is truthful (at least, everyone with an open mind). Opinions occur when you don't have enough scientific fact to back up the data. In addition, opinions occur when emotion is involved. Even when faced with conclusive proof to the contrary, some humans would rather rely on opinion than fact. The opinion makes us feel comfortable; the fact doesn't. AI will nearly always fail when opinion is involved. Even with the best algorithm available, someone will be dissatisfied with the output.

Entering a world of unrealistic expectations

The previous sections of the chapter discuss how expecting an AI to perform certain tasks or applying it in less than concrete situations will cause problems. Unfortunately, humans don't seem to get the idea that the sort of tasks that many of us think an AI can perform will never come about. These unrealistic expectations have many sources, including

>> **Media:** Books, movies, and other forms of media all seek to obtain an emotional response from us. However, that emotional response is the very source of unrealistic expectations. We imagine that an AI can do something, but it truly can't do those things in the real world.

>> **Anthropomorphization:** Along with the emotions that media generates, humans also tend to form attachments to everything. People often name their cars, talk to them, and wonder if they're feeling bad when they break down. An AI can't feel, can't understand, can't communicate (really), can't do anything other than crunch numbers — lots and lots of numbers. When the expectation is that the AI will suddenly develop feelings and act human, the result is doomed to failure.

>> **Undefined problem:** An AI can solve a defined problem, but not an undefined one. You can present a human with a set of potential inputs and expect a human to create a matching question based on extrapolation. Say that a series of tests keeps failing for the most part, but some test subjects do achieve the desired goal. An AI might try to improve test results through interpolation by locating new test subjects with characteristics that match those who survived. However, a human might improve the test results through extrapolation by questioning why some test subjects succeeded and finding the cause, whether the cause is based on test subject characteristics or not (perhaps environmental conditions have changed or the test subject simply has a different attitude). For an AI to solve any problem, however, a human must be able to express that problem in a manner that the AI understands. Undefined problems, those that represent something outside human experience, simply aren't solvable using an AI.

>> **Deficient technology:** In many places in this book, you find that a problem wasn't solvable at a certain time because of a lack of technology. It isn't realistic to ask an AI to solve a problem when the technology is insufficient. For example, the lack of sensors and processing power would have made creating a self-driving car in the 1960s impossible, yet advances in technology have made such an endeavor possible today.

Considering the Effects of AI Winters

AI winters occur when scientists and others make promises about the benefits of AI that don't come to fruition within an expected time frame, causing funding for AI to dry up and research to continue at only a glacial pace. (Scare tactics employed by those who have no idea of how AI works have likely had an effect on AI winters as well.) Since 1956, the world has seen two AI winters. (Right now, the world is in its third AI summer.) The following sections discuss the causes, effects, and results of AI winter in more detail.

Understanding the AI winter

It's hard to say precisely when AI began. After all, even the ancient Greeks dreamed of creating mechanical men, such as those presented in the Greek myths about Hephaestus and Pygmalion's Galatea, and we can assume that these mechanical men would have some sort of intelligence. Consequently, one could argue that the first AI winter actually occurred sometime between the fall of the Roman empire and the time in the middle ages when people dreamed of an alchemical way of placing the mind into matter, such as Jābir ibn Hayyān's Takwin, Paracelsus' homunculus (see ancient-origins.net), and Rabbi Judah Loew's Golem (see "Golem: A myth of perfection in an imperfect world" at blogs.timesofisrael.com. However, these efforts are unfounded stories and not of the scientific sort that would appear later in 1956 with the founding of government-funded artificial intelligence research at Dartmouth College.

REMEMBER

An AI winter occurs when funding for AI dwindles. The use of the word *winter* is appropriate because, like a tree in winter, AI didn't stop growing altogether. When you view the rings of a tree, you see that the tree does continue to grow in winter — just not very fast. Likewise, during the AI winters from 1974 to 1980 and again from 1987 to 1993, AI did continue to grow, but at a glacial pace.

Defining the causes of the AI winter

The cause of an AI winter could easily be summarized as resulting from outlandish promises that are impossible to keep. At the outset of the efforts at Dartmouth College in 1956, the soon-to-be leaders of AI research predicted that a computer as intelligent as a human would take no more than a generation. Sixty-plus years later, computers still aren't nearly as smart as humans. In fact, if you've read previous chapters, you know that computers are unlikely to ever be as smart as humans, at least not in every kind of intelligence (and by now have exceeded human capability only in a very few kinds and only in limited situations).

REMEMBER

Part of the problem with overpromising capabilities is that early proponents of AI believed that all human thought could be formalized as algorithms. In fact, this idea goes back to the Chinese, Indian, and Greek philosophers. However, as shown in Table 1-1 of Chapter 1, only some components of human intelligence are formalized. In fact, the best possible outcome is that human mathematical and logical reasoning could be mechanized. Even so, in the 1920s and 1930s, David Hilbert challenged mathematicians to prove that all mathematical reasoning can be formalized. The answer to this challenge came from Gödel's incompleteness proof, Turing's machine, and Church's Lambda calculus. Two outcomes emerged: Formalizing *all* mathematical reasoning isn't possible; and in the areas in which formalization is possible, you can also mechanize the reasoning, which is the basis of AI.

Another part of the problem with overpromising is excessive optimism. During the early years of AI, computers solved algebra word problems, proved theorems in geometry, and learned to speak English. The first two outputs are reasonable when you consider that the computer is simply parsing input and putting it into a form that the computer can manipulate. The problem is with the third of these outputs. The computer wasn't truly speaking English; instead, it was converting textual data into digital patterns that were in turn converted to analog and output as something that seemed like speech, but wasn't. The computer didn't understand anything about English, or any other language for that matter. Yes, the scientists did indeed hear English, but the computer simply saw 0s and 1s in a specific pattern that the computer didn't see as language at all.

WARNING

Even the researchers were often fooled into thinking that the computer was doing more than it really was. For example, Joseph Weizenbaum's ELIZA at psych.fullerton.edu appeared to hear input and then respond in an intelligent manner. Unfortunately, the responses were canned and the application wasn't hearing, understanding, or saying anything. Yet, ELIZA was the first chatterbot and did represent a step forward, albeit an incredibly small one. The hype was simply significantly greater than the actual technology — a problem that AI faces today. People feel disappointed when they see that the hype isn't real, so scientists and promoters continue to set themselves up for failure by displaying glitz rather than real technology. The first AI winter was brought on by predictions such as these:

>> **H.A. Simon:** "Within ten years, a digital computer will be the world's chess champion" (1958) and "machines will be capable, within twenty years, of doing any work a man can do." (1965)

>> **Allen Newell:** "Within ten years, a digital computer will discover and prove an important new mathematical theorem." (1958)

>> **Marvin Minsky:** "Within a generation . . . the problem of creating 'artificial intelligence' will substantially be solved" (1967) and "In from three to eight years, we will have a machine with the general intelligence of an average human being." (1970)

Oddly enough, a computer did become chess champion in 1997, though not within ten years (see "How 22 Years of AI Superiority Changed Chess" at Towards Data Science.com), but the other predictions still aren't true. In viewing these outlandish claims today, it's easy to see why governments withdrew funding. The "Considering the Chinese Room argument" section of Chapter 5 outlines just one of many counterarguments that even people within the AI community made against these predictions.

The second AI winter came as a result of the same issues that created the first AI winter — overpromising, overexcitement, and excessive optimism. In this case, the boom started with the expert system (see "Leveraging expert systems" in Chapter 3 for more details on expert systems), a kind of AI program that solves problems using logical rules. In addition, the Japanese entered the fray with their Fifth Generation Computer project, a computer system that offered massively parallel processing. The idea was to create a computer that could perform a lot of tasks in parallel, similar to the human brain. Finally, John Hopfield and David Rumelhart resurrected connectionism, a strategy that models mental processes as interconnected networks of simple units.

The end came as sort of an economic bubble. The expert systems proved brittle, even when run on specialized computer systems. The specialized computer systems ended up as economic sinkholes that newer, common computer systems could easily replace at a significantly reduced cost. In fact, the Japanese Fifth Generation Computer project was also a fatality of this economic bubble. It proved extremely expensive to build and maintain.

Rebuilding expectations with new goals

An AI winter does not necessarily prove devastating. Quite the contrary: Such times can be viewed as an opportunity to stand back and think about the various issues that came up during the rush to develop something amazing. Two major areas of thought benefitted during the first AI winter (along with minor benefits to other areas of thought):

>> **Logical programming:** This area of thought involves presenting a set of sentences in logical form (executed as an application) that expresses facts and rules about a particular problem domain. Examples of programming

languages that use this particular paradigm are Prolog, Answer Set Programming (ASP), and Datalog. This is a form of rule-based programming, which is the underlying technology used for expert systems.

>> **Common-sense reasoning:** This area of thought uses a method of simulating the human ability to predict the outcome of an event sequence based on the properties, purpose, intentions, and behavior of a particular object. Common-sense reasoning is an essential component in AI because it affects a wide variety of disciplines, including computer vision, robotic manipulation, taxonomic reasoning, action and change, temporal reasoning, and qualitative reasoning.

The second AI winter brought additional changes that have served to bring AI into the focus that it has today. These changes included:

>> **Using common hardware:** At one point, expert systems and other uses of AI relied on specialized hardware. The reason is that common hardware didn't provide the necessary computing power or memory. However, these custom systems proved expensive to maintain, hard to program, and extremely brittle when faced with unusual situations. Common hardware is general purpose in nature and is less prone to issues of having a solution that's attempting to find a problem (see the upcoming "Creating Solutions in Search of a Problem" section of the chapter for details).

TECHNICAL STUFF

It's important to realize that common hardware indicates hardware that you can buy anywhere and that other groups use. For example, machine learning benefits greatly from the inclusion of a Graphics Processing Unit (GPU) in the host system (see "What is a GPU and do you need one in Deep Learning?" at Towards Data Science.com for details). However, gaming and other graphics-intensive tasks also rely on these devices (find out more at https://www.hp.com/us-en/shop/tech-takes/gpu-vs-cpu-for-pc-gaming), so the hardware is theoretically common, but not every system has one.

>> **Seeing a need to learn:** Expert systems and other early forms of AI required special programming to meet each need, thereby making them extremely inflexible. It became evident that computers would need to be able to learn from the environment, sensors, and data provided.

>> **Creating a flexible environment:** The systems that did perform useful work between the first and second AI winters did so in a rigid manner. When the inputs didn't quite match expectations, these systems were apt to produce grotesque errors in the output. It became obvious that any new systems would need to know how to react to real-world data, which is full of errors, incomplete, and often formatted incorrectly.

>> **Relying on new strategies:** Imagine that you work for the government and have promised all sorts of amazing things based on AI, except that none of them seemed to materialize. That's the problem with the second AI winter: Some governments had tried various ways of making the promises of AI a reality. When the current strategies obviously weren't working, these same governments started looking for other ways to advance computing, some of which have produced interesting results, such as advances in robotics.

The point is that AI winters aren't necessarily bad for AI. In fact, these occasions to step back and view the progress (or lack thereof) of current strategies are important. Taking these thoughtful moments is hard when one is rushing head-long into the next hopeful achievement.

REMEMBER

When considering AI winters and the resulting renewal of AI with updated ideas and objectives, an adage known as Amara's law, coined by American scientist and futurist Roy Charles Amara, is worth remembering: "We tend to overestimate the effect of a technology in the short run and underestimate the effect in the long run." After all the hype and disillusionment, there is always a time when people can't perceive the long-term impact of a new technology clearly and understand the revolutions it brings about with it. As a technology, AI is here to stay and will change our world for better and worse, no matter how many winters it still has to face.

Creating Solutions in Search of a Problem

Two people are looking at a mass of wires, wheels, bits of metal, and odd, assorted items that appear to be junk. The first person asks the second, "What does it do?" The second answers, "What doesn't it do?" Yet, the invention that apparently does everything ends up doing nothing at all. The media is rife with examples of the solution looking for a problem. We laugh because everyone has encountered the solution that's in search of a problem before. These solutions end up as so much junk, even when they do work, because they fail to answer a pressing need. The following sections discuss the AI solution in search of a problem in more detail.

Defining a gizmo

When it comes to AI, the world is full of gizmos. Some of those gizmos really are useful, but many aren't, and a few fall between these two extremes. For example, Alexa comes with many useful features, but it also comes with a hoard of gizmos that will leave you scratching your head when you try to use them. The article at https://www.digitaltrends.com/home/what-is-amazons-alexa-and-what-can-it-do/ provides you with a balanced view of what Alexa is and how it can be helpful in a gizmo sort of a way. The review at https://www.prologic-technologies.com/blog/pros-cons-of-amazon-alexa/ points out some interesting aspects of using Alexa that you might not consider at first. However, what you might find even more interesting is actual user reviews of Alexa (off Amazon), which you can find at https://www.trustradius.com/products/alexa/reviews?qs=pros-and-cons.

An *AI gizmo* is any application that seems on first glance to do something interesting, but ultimately proves unable to perform truly useful tasks. Here are some of the common aspects to look for when determining whether something is a gizmo. (The first letter of the each bullet in the list spells the acronym CREEP, meaning, don't create a creepy AI application):

>> **Cost effective:** Before anyone decides to buy into an AI application, it must prove to cost the same or less than existing solutions. Everyone is looking for a deal. Paying more for a similar benefit will simply not attract attention.

>> **Reproducible:** The results of an AI application must be reproducible, even when the circumstances of performing the task change. In contrast to procedural solutions to a problem, people expect an AI to adapt — to learn from doing, which means that the bar is set higher on providing reproducible results.

>> **Efficient:** When an AI solution suddenly consumes huge amounts of resources of any sort, users look elsewhere. Businesses, especially, have become extremely focused on performing tasks with the fewest possible resources.

>> **Effective:** Simply providing a practical benefit that's cost effective and efficient isn't enough; an AI must also provide a solution that fully addresses a need. Effective solutions enable someone to allow the automation to perform the task without having to constantly recheck the results or prop the automation up.

>> **Practical:** A useful application must provide a practical benefit. The benefit must be something that the end user requires, such as access to a road map or reminders to take medication.

Avoiding the infomercial

Bedazzling potential users of your AI application is a sure sign that the application will fail. Oddly enough, the applications that succeed with the greatest ease are those whose purpose and intent are obvious from the outset. A voice recognition application is obvious: You talk, and the computer does something useful in exchange. You don't need to sell anyone on the idea that voice recognition software is useful. This book is filled with a number of these truly useful applications, none of which requires the infomercial approach of the hard sell. If people start asking what something does, it's time to rethink the project.

Understanding when humans do it better

This chapter is all about keeping humans in the loop while making use of AI. You've seen sections about things we do better than AI, when an AI can master them at all. Anything that requires imagination, creativity, the discernment of truth, the handling of opinion, or the creation of an idea is best left to humans. Oddly enough, the limits of AI leave a lot of places for humans to go, many of which aren't even possible today because humans are overly engaged in repetitive, boring tasks that an AI could easily do.

Look for a future in which AI acts as an assistant to humans. In fact, you'll see this use of AI more and more as time goes on. The best AI applications will be those that look to assist, rather than replace, humans. Yes, it's true that robots will replace humans in hazardous conditions, but humans will need to make decisions as to how to avoid making those situations worse, which means having a human at a safe location to direct the robot. It's a hand-in-hand collaboration between technology and humans.

CONSIDERING THE INDUSTRIAL REVOLUTION

The human/AI collaboration won't happen all at one time. In addition, the new kinds of work that humans will be able to perform won't appear on the scene immediately. However, the vision of humans just sitting around waiting to be serviced by a machine is farfetched and obviously not tenable. Humans will continue to perform various tasks. Of course, the same claims of machines taking over were made during all major human upheavals in the past, with the industrial revolution being the more recent and more violent of those upheavals (see "The Industrial Revolution" at History Doctor.net). Humans will always do certain things better than an AI, and you can be certain that we'll continue to make a place for ourselves in society. We just need to hope that this upheaval is less violent than the industrial revolution was.

Looking for the simple solution

The Keep It Simple, Stupid (KISS) principle is the best idea to keep in mind when it comes to developing AI applications. You can read more about KISS at Techopedia.com, but the basic idea is to ensure that any solution is the simplest you can make it. All sorts of precedents exist for the use of simple solutions. However, of these, Occam's Razor is probably the most famous (https://science.howstuffworks.com/innovation/scientific-experiments/occams-razor.htm).

Of course, the question arises as to why KISS is so important. The easiest answer is that complexity leads to failure: The more parts something has, the more likely it is to fail. This principle has its roots in mathematics and is easy to prove.

REMEMBER

When it comes to applications, however, other principles come into play. For most people, an application is a means to an end. People are interested in the end and don't really care about the application. If the application were to disappear from view, the user would be quite happy because then just the end result is in view. Simple applications are easy to use, tend to disappear from view, and don't require any complex instructions. In fact, the best applications are obvious. When your AI solution has to rely on all sorts of complex interactions to use, you need to consider whether it's time to go back to the drawing board and come up with something better.

Chapter **16**

Seeing AI in Space

Peope have been observing the heavens since time immemorial. Many of the names of constellations and stars come from the Greeks or other ancients (depending on where you live). The Big Dipper alone has many different names and may be seen as a bear when grouped with other stars (see `https://tinyurl.com/ymumd3xb` for details). People love gazing at the stars and thinking about them, which is why many cultures have thought about actually seeing what the stars look like. As people have become capable of space travel, the universe, as a whole, has taken on new meaning, as described in this chapter. AI enables people to see the universe more clearly and view it in new ways.

Over the years, humans have begun living in space (such as at the International Space Station: `https://tinyurl.com/2r2hrbjm`) as well as visiting other places, such as the moon and possibly beyond (see `https://tinyurl.com/cr92patb` and `https://tinyurl.com/aftwt6xh`). Humans have also begun working in space. Of course, various experiments have produced materials that people can produce only in space. A company, Made In Space (`https://madeinspace.us/`) actually specializes in this activity. Outside these activities, the use of robots and specialized AI enables the mining of all sorts of materials in space. In fact, the U.S. Congress passed legislation in 2015 making such activity financially feasible by giving companies rights to sell what they mine (`https://tinyurl.com/7ajr5v56`). This space-mining trend is continuing, but not without some hiccups (see `https://tinyurl.com/2jsrud8c` and `https://tinyurl.com/9zbjss6w`). In addition to all of these considerations, this chapter also looks at the role of AI in making space mining work.

The universe holds nearly infinite secrets. One recently discovered secret is the existence of exoplanets, those that exist outside our solar system (see https://tinyurl.com/j69hyp8e for details). Quite a few of them are habitable from our perspective (https://tinyurl.com/z5nrazrf), although scientists think that even uninhabitable for us might still support life for others. The existence of exoplanets means that humans might eventually find life on other planets, but even finding the exoplanets requires AI. The ways in which AI will make all these possibilities visible is truly amazing.

Living and working in space is one thing, but vacationing in space is quite another. As early as 2011, people began talking about the possibility of creating a hotel in near-Earth orbit (https://tinyurl.com/v5eysc7k) or the moon, but the date of the first opening has moved a bit since early hype (https://tinyurl.com/j286e9pz). Some people can take a trip to space now, albeit for just a few minutes, courtesy of Blue Origin's New Shepard rocket (https://tinyurl.com/d8z4hu8). The point is, AI will enable people to live, work, and even vacation in space using specialized structures, as described in this chapter.

Observing the Universe

A Dutch eyeglass maker named Hans Lippershey is credited with inventing a telescope (which at that time, in about 1600, was called *Dutch perspective glasses*). (Actually, just who invented the telescope is a subject for significant debate; see https://tinyurl.com/762wc3h3.) Scientists such as the Italian astronomer Galileo Galilei immediately began to scan the skies with something more than their eyes. Thus, telescopes have been around for a long time and have become larger, more complex, and even space based over the years.

REMEMBER

The reason for sticking telescopes in space is that the earth's atmosphere makes it impossible to obtain clear images of anything too far away. The Hubble telescope is one of the first and most famous of the space-based telescopes (see https://tinyurl.com/3pcdhrdv), but many others have followed and more are planned (https://tinyurl.com/2u4yest4 and https://tinyurl.com/x587knmv). As described in the following sections, using modern telescopes requires AI in a number of ways, such as scheduling time to use the Hubble (see https://www.stsci.edu/hst).

Seeing clearly for the first time

One way to avoid earth's atmosphere is to put your telescope in space. However, this approach is a little on the expensive side, and maintenance can become a nightmare. Most people observing the heavens need another alternative, such as a telescope that can adjust for the blurring action of the earth's atmosphere by warping the telescope's mirror (see https://tinyurl.com/46zrn98r).

TECHNICAL STUFF

Imagine having to calculate the blurring effect of the earth's atmosphere based on the light from something like a laser thousands of times a second. The only way to make such a huge number of calculations and then move the mirror's actuators in just the right way is to use AI, something that is quite adept at performing the sort of math required to make adaptive optics possible. The article at https://tinyurl.com/r2a7bwsb provides just one example of the use of AI in adaptive optics. The sites at https://tinyurl.com/3bchhr2a and https://tinyurl.com/5hwhj53b provide additional resources for discovering how neural networks are used in adaptive optic systems.

To provide even better optics, future telescopes will feature 3-D correction of blurring effects using Multiconjugate Adaptive Optics (MCAO) (https://tinyurl.com/k96suruf and https://tinyurl.com/bwmfh6bn). This new technology will correct the narrow field of view suffered by current telescopes, but will require even greater (and more precise) control of multiple actuator levels through multiple mirrors. Telescopes such as the Giant Magellan Telescope, the Thirty-Meter Telescope, and the European Extremely Large Telescope (see https://tinyurl.com/yjfrzx59) will rely on this technology to make their $1 billion-plus investment price worth the effort. (Efforts are ongoing with MAVIS, the MCAO-Assisted Visible Imager and Spectrograph, described at https://tinyurl.com/245ap3nr.)

Finding new places to go

Before the eighteenth century, people were tied to the surface of the earth, but they still gazed at the heavens and dreamed. Humans tried all sorts of odd experiments to leave earth, such as tower jumping (see https://tinyurl.com/5e4sywva), but before hot air balloons, any sort of true flight seemed out of reach. We still explored, though, and humans continue to explore today, looking for new places to go.

REMEMBER

The idea of having places to visit really didn't become much of a reality before the first moon landing on July 20, 1969 (see https://tinyurl.com/m8unzp9s). Yes, we could look, but we couldn't touch. Even so, since that time people have looked at all sorts of places to go and have, through robots, reached a few of them, such as Mars (https://tinyurl.com/382b95d4 and https://tinyurl.com/3nb345wd) and the Rosetta comet (see https://tinyurl.com/5px86sr5). Each of these explorations serves to stimulate the human desire to go to still other new places. More important, none of them would have happened without the complex math that AI can perform.

Finding things in space used to rely on telescopes. However, NASA and other organizations increasingly rely on other approaches, such as using AI, as described at https://tinyurl.com/u44vey2p. In this case, machine learning made it possible to locate an eighth planet around Kepler 90. Of course, the problem with finding so many places to go is determining whether we can actually reach some of the more exotic places. Voyager 1, the probe farthest from Earth, has recently picked up a new signal (https://tinyurl.com/4nmcunwu) created by plasma waves from other worlds. Yet, it's only 14 billion miles away (0.0024 light years), just a walk in the galactic park, and Kepler 90 is 2,545 light years away, so any interstellar travel will take a long time and require the use of AI.

Fortunately, our own solar system contains all kinds of places that might be reachable. For example, the *Encyclopaedia Britannica* recommends visiting places like the Caloris Basin on Mercury (see https://tinyurl.com/5dzfft8f). You might also want to check out the *MIT Technology Review* (https://tinyurl.com/rmp6th7s) for the top-five locations today (the list changes a bit all the time as we learn more).

Considering the evolution of the universe

Humans have stared at the universe for a long time and still have no real idea of precisely what the universe is, except to know that we live in it. Of course, the observations continue, but the essence of the universe is still a huge unknown. Scientists use AI to carefully plot the motions of various parts of the universe to try to discover just how the universe works (see https://tinyurl.com/bfknhdc).

Creating new scientific principles

Ultimately, the research that humans perform in learning more about space, the local solar system, the galaxy, and the universe must pay some dividend. Otherwise, no one will want to continue funding it. The AI winters discussed in Chapter 15 are an example of what happens to a technology, no matter how promising, when it fails to deliver on expectations. Consequently, given the long history of space exploration, people must be deriving some benefit. In most cases, these benefits are in the form of new scientific principles — an increase in the understanding of how things work. By applying the lessons learned from space exploration and travel, people can make life here on earth better. In addition, space-based technologies often find their way into products that people use daily.

Consider just one exploration: the Apollo 11 moon landing. People still feel the effects of the technology explosion that occurred during the workup for that mission. For example, the need to conserve space prompted the government to spend lots of money on technologies such as integrated circuits (ICs) that we take for granted today (see https://tinyurl.com/myebdcnr). Depending on what source you read, every dollar invested in research by the government in NASA nets Americans $7 to $8 in goods and services today.

However, the space race generated new technology beyond the creation of actual capsules and their associated components. For example, the movie *Hidden Figures* (https://tinyurl.com/4bjerd5n) presents a view of NASA that most people don't think about: All that math requires a lot of computing power. In the movie, you see the evolution of NASA math from human computers to electronic computers. However, if you watch the movie carefully, you see that the computer ends up working alongside the human, much as AI will work alongside humans as our knowledge of the universe increases.

REMEMBER

Today we have data about space coming from everywhere. This data is helping us create new scientific principles about things we can't even see, such as *dark matter* (an area of space with mass but no visible presence) and *dark energy* (an unknown and unidentified form of energy that counteracts the effects of gravitation between bodies in space). By understanding these invisible entities using technologies like the dark emulator (https://tinyurl.com/pvf7pyy7), we build new knowledge about how forces work on our own planet. Researchers are so buried in data, however, that they must use AI just to make sense of a small part of it (see https://tinyurl.com/yvuxk8fu). The point is that the future of space and our use of technologies created for space depend on making use of all that data we're collecting, which requires AI at this point.

Performing Space Mining

Space mining has received more than a little attention in the media and the scientific community as well. Movies such as *Alien* (https://tinyurl.com/acdyp4ya) provide a glimpse as to what a future mining ship might look like. (With luck, space mining won't involve hostile aliens.) People and organizations have a number of reasons to want to exploit space mining, such as to save planet Earth from further ecological damage (https://tinyurl.com/kcj4tzrt). Of course, there is the money aspect as well (https://tinyurl.com/244w6s7d). Countries of all sizes are getting involved in space mining (see https://tinyurl.com/88dsakfb and https://tinyurl.com/r3hty7yw for details). There are also detractors who think the idea will never take solid form (https://tinyurl.com/2df2krsk). With all this in mind, the following sections take a deeper look at space mining.

Harvesting water

Water covers about 71 percent of the earth. In fact, the earth has so much water that we often find it difficult to keep it out of places where we don't want it. However, earth is an exception to the rule. Space doesn't have an overabundance of water. Of course, you might wonder why you'd even need water in space, other than of the sort needed to keep astronauts hydrated and potentially to keep plants irrigated. The fact is that water makes great rocket fuel. Separating H_2O into its constituent components produces hydrogen and oxygen, which are both components of rocket fuel today (see `https://tinyurl.com/23jpp9b5` for details). Consequently, that big, dirty ice ball in the sky could end up being a refueling station at some point.

Obtaining rare earths and other metals

Mining has always been dirty, but some mining is much dirtier than other mining, and rare earths fall into that category. Rare-earth mining is so dirty (see `https://tinyurl.com/mnbh7ayy` and `https://tinyurl.com/zue7deyk`) that all the rare-earth mines in the U.S. were closed until the U.S. government saw a need to reopen the Mountain Pass rare-earth mine as a strategic reserve for the military because of a Chinese chokehold on rare earths (`https://tinyurl.com/4asedrzj`). One of the worst parts of rare-earth mining is that it irradiates the surrounding areas with thorium radiation.

USING DRONES AND ROBOTS FOR MINING

You can't determine what an asteroid contains until you get really close to it. In addition, the number of asteroids that require exploration before finding anything worthwhile is significant — far more than human pilots could ever explore. Also, getting close to any object that might be rotating in an odd way and have strange characteristics involves dangers. For all these reasons, most asteroid exploration for mining purposes will occur by using autonomous drones of various sorts. These drones will go from asteroid to asteroid, looking for needed materials. When a drone finds a needed material, it will alert a centralized station with precise location information and other asteroid characteristics.

As this point, a robot will be dispatched to do something with the asteroid. Most people feel that mining will occur in place, but actually, mining in place would prove both dangerous and costly. Another idea is to move the asteroid to a safer location, such as in orbit around the moon, to perform the required mining. The point is that robots would do the moving, and possibly other robots would perform the mining. Humans might be involved in robot repair and likely involved in monitoring both drone and robot activities. Think about it as safer, less polluting, and more interesting mining than could happen here on earth.

One of the more interesting developments is that a company in China recently sent a space-mining robot into near-Earth orbit to clean up the mess there (`https://tinyurl.com/3r8u3hpv`). This might seem like an unimportant step, but it's a step nonetheless, and scientists will gain essential information from this step into a much larger world of mining.

The cellphone you carry, the tablet you use, the car you drive, the television you watch, and the solar panel and windmill that provide electricity to your house all rely on extremely hazardous materials in the form of rare earths (see https://tinyurl.com/yt6hak4s for just a few examples of usage). Most people aren't even aware that these materials aren't sustainable because of the way we currently use them (https://tinyurl.com/9df6xu25). Given the track record of these minerals, they represent the best reason to mine minerals off planet, where the toxins won't affect us any longer. In fact, mining should be only the first step; all manufacturing should move off planet as well (yes, the potential for pollution is that great).

REMEMBER

AI is essential to efforts to find better sources of rare earths that won't pollute our planet into oblivion. One of the interesting oddities of rare earths is that the moon has a significant supply of them (see https://tinyurl.com/c67pkc68) and mining could start there as early as 2025. In fact, many politicians now see mining the moon for rare earths as a strategic need (see https://tinyurl.com/7j9hxczz). The problem is that efforts to discover precisely what the moon is made of haven't been altogether successful so far, and it's important to know what to expect. The Moon Minerology Mapper (https://tinyurl.com/yw8ns87p) is just one of many efforts to discover the composition of the moon. (An upcoming project, Trailblazer (https://tinyurl.com/2xsr55jf), will look for water.) The probes, robots, data analysis, and all the required planning will require use of AI because the issues are a lot more complicated than you might think.

Finding new elements

The periodic table that contains a list of all available elements has received a number of updates over the years. In fact, four new elements appeared in the table in 2016 (see https://tinyurl.com/2ab23chb). However, finding those four new elements required the work of a minimum of a hundred scientists using advanced AI (see https://tinyurl.com/337etd7z) because they typically last a fraction of a second in a lab environment. Interestingly enough, space could provide an environment in which these new elements exist naturally, rather than a fraction of a second, as they do on earth, because the protons in the nucleus repel each other.

REMEMBER

As this story shows, we're still finding new elements to add to the periodic table, and space will almost certainly provide even more. Supernovas and other space phenomena can help replicate elements that scientists create by using particle accelerators or reactors. In fact, particle physicists have used AI in their work since the 1980s (see https://tinyurl.com/26phwpku).

Combining the elements provides new materials. AI is also directly responsible for helping chemists find new ways to combine elements into interesting new crystals (see https://tinyurl.com/z6jutf9s). In one case, scientists discovered

2 million new kinds of crystals using just four elements, but those discoveries relied on the use of AI. Just imagine what will happen in the future as scientists start opening the door to AI and deep learning (which will be able to determine whether the resulting crystals are actually useful).

Enhancing communication

Any undertaking in space that is as complex as mining requires the use of advanced communications. Even if the probes and robots used for mining include deep learning capability to handle most of the minor and some of the major incidents that will occur during the mining process, humans will still need to solve problems that the AI can't. Waiting for hours only to discover that a problem exists, and then spending yet more hours trying to determine the source of the problem, will spell disaster for space-based mining. Current manual communication techniques require an upgrade that, odd as it might seem, also includes AI (see https://tinyurl.com/rp7anumz).

REMEMBER

Cognitive radio relies on AI to make decisions automatically about the need to improve radio efficiency in various ways (see https://tinyurl.com/3xcffd3p). The human operator need not worry about precisely how the signal gets from one place to another; it simply does so in the most efficient manner possible. In many cases, cognitive radio relies on unused or underused spectrum to achieve its goal, but it can rely on other methods as well. In other words, the current methods to control probes such as those listed at https://tinyurl.com/5dmvkewz just won't work in the future when it's necessary to do more, in less time, with less spectrum (because of the increased communication load).

Exploring New Places

Space is vast. Humans are unlikely to ever explore it all. Anyone who tells you that all the frontiers are gone has obviously not looked up at the sky. Even the sci-fi authors seem to think that the universe will continue to hold places to explore for humans. Of course, if multiverse theory is true (https://tinyurl.com/4thxmsyf), the number of places to explore may be infinite. The problem isn't even one of finding somewhere to go; rather, it's one of figuring out which place to go first. The following sections help you understand the role of AI in moving people from planet earth, to other planets, and then to the stars.

Starting with the probe

Humans have already starting putting probes out everywhere to explore everything. In fact, using probes is older than many people think. As early as 1916, Dr. Robert H. Goddard, an American rocket pioneer, calculated that a rocket could be sent to the moon with an explosive payload that could be seen from earth. However, it was E. Burgess and C. A. Cross who gave the world the term *probe* as part of a paper they wrote entitled *The Martian Probe* in 1952. Most people consider a space probe to be a vehicle designed to escape earth and explore some other location. The first probe to make a soft landing on the moon was Luna 9 in 1966.

Probes today aren't just trying to reach some location. When they arrive at the location, they perform complex tasks and then radio the results of those tasks back to scientists on earth. For example, NASA designed the Mars Curiosity probe to determine whether Mars ever hosted microbial life. (The search for life continues with the Perseverance rover: https://tinyurl.com/3j6kuv85). To perform this task, both rovers have complex computer systems that can perform many tasks on their own and Perseverance has a complex set of goals to achieve (https://mars.nasa.gov/mars2020/mission/science/goals/). Of course, the highlight of current Mars visitors is Ingenuity, which is the first helicopter on the planet (https://mars.nasa.gov/technology/helicopter/). In all three cases, waiting for humans simply isn't an option in many cases; some issues require immediate resolution.

It doesn't take much to imagine the vast amount of information that individual probes, such as Curiosity, generate. Just analyzing the Curiosity data requires the same big data analytics used by organizations such as Netflix and Goldman Sachs (see https://tinyurl.com/7bb2xc5x). The difference is that the data stream comes from Mars, not from local users, so any data analysis must consider the time required to actually obtain the information. In fact, the time delay between Earth and Mars is as much as 24 minutes (and when the two planets are in conjunction for a couple of weeks every few years, no communication is possible). With this in mind, Curiosity and other probes must think for themselves (https://tinyurl.com/rffj8j29) even when it comes to performing certain kinds of analysis.

After data arrives back on Earth, scientists store and then analyze it. The process, even with the help of AI, will take years. Obviously, reaching the stars will take patience and even more computing power than humans currently possess. With the universe being such a messy place, the use of probes is essential, but the probes may need more autonomy just to find the right places to search.

CONSIDERING EXISTING COLONIZATION TARGETS

Depending on which article you read, scientists are already considering likely places for humans to colonize sometime in the future. Colonization will become essential for numerous reasons, but the burgeoning population of planet earth figures highly in the math. Of course, the potential factories and mining operations on other planets are also part of the consideration. Plus, having another place to live does improve our chances should another killer asteroid strike earth. With these thoughts in mind, here is a list of the commonly considered colonization targets (your list may differ):

- Moon
- Mars
- Europa
- Enceladus
- Ceres
- Titan

All these potential candidates come with special requirements that AI can help solve. For example, colonizing the moon requires the use of domes. In addition, colonists must have a source of water — enough water to split into oxygen for breathing and hydrogen to use as a heat source and fuel. So, probes will provide some information, but modeling the colonization environment will require time and a great deal of processing power here on earth before humans can move to some other location.

Relying on robotic missions

Humans aren't likely to ever actually visit a planet directly as a means of learning more about it, sci-fi books and movies notwithstanding. It makes more sense to send robots to planets to discover whether sending humans there is even worth the time, because robots are less expensive and easier to deploy. Humans have actually sent robots to a number of planets and moons in the solar system already, but Mars seems to be a favorite target for a number of reasons:

>> A robotic mission can leave for Mars every 26 months.

>> Mars is in the solar system's habitable zone, so it makes a likely target for colonization.

>> Many scientists believe that life once existed on Mars.

The human love affair with Mars started in October 1960 when the Soviet Union launched Marsnik 1 and Marsnik 2. Unfortunately, neither probe even made it into Earth's orbit, much less to Mars. The U.S. tried next, with the Mariner 3 spacecraft in 1964 and the Mariner 4 spacecraft in 1965. The Mariner 4 fly-by succeeded by sending 12 photos of the red planet back to Earth. Since that time, humans have sent myriad probes to Mars and a host of robots as well, and the robots are starting to reveal the secrets of Mars. (The success rate for trips to Mars, however, is less than 50 percent, according to https://tinyurl.com/2djdb6um.) Besides probes designed to perform fly-bys and observe Mars from space, robots land on Mars in three forms:

» **Lander:** A robotic device designed to sit in one place and perform relatively complex tasks.

» **Rover:** A robotic device that moves from one location to another — increasing the amount of ground covered.

» **Flyer:** A robotic device that is able to fly from one location to another—covering large amounts of ground relatively fast and from an aerial vantage point.

You can find a list of the landers and rovers sent to Mars since 1971 at https://tinyurl.com/5h9y7jzs and https://tinyurl.com/423ataen. Even though most landers and rovers come from the United States, China, or the former Soviet Union (which actually wasn't successful), at least one rover is from England (Japan has one planned for the near future). As the techniques required for a successful landing become better known, you can expect to see other countries participate in the race to Mars (even if only by remote control).

REMEMBER

As landers and rovers become more capable, the need for AI increases. For example, Perseverance has a relatively complex AI that helps it choose new targets for exploration autonomously, as described at https://tinyurl.com/3yyzyjdx. Don't get the idea, though, that this AI is replacing the scientists on Earth. The scientists still determine the properties of the rocks that the AI will search for when used. In addition, a scientist can override the AI and choose a different target. The AI is there to assist, not replace, the scientist and provides an example of how people and AI will work together in the future.

Adding the human element

Humans want to visit places beyond Earth. Of course, the only place that we've actually visited is the moon. The first such visit occurred on July 20, 1969, with the Apollo 11 mission. Since then, people have landed on the moon six times, ending with the Apollo 17 flight on December 7, 1972. China, India, and Russia all have future plans for moon landings. The Russian-manned flight is scheduled to occur around 2030. NASA plans to land on the moon in the future, but has no reliable schedule for this event yet (there are rumors of sometime in 2024).

NASA does have plans for Mars. An actual human visit to Mars will likely have to wait until the 2030s (https://www.nasa.gov/topics/moon-to-mars/overview). As you might imagine, data science, AI, machine learning, and deep learning will figure prominently in any effort to reach Mars. Because of the distance and environment, people will require a lot of support to make a Mars landing feasible. In addition, getting back from Mars will be considerably harder than getting back from the moon. Even the lift-off will be harder because of the presence of some atmosphere and greater gravity on Mars.

WARNING

In 1968, Arthur C. Clarke released the book *2001: A Space Odyssey*. The book must have struck a chord, because it spawned a movie and a television series, not to mention three additional books. In *2001: A Space Odyssey*, you find the Heuristically programmed ALgorithmic (HAL) 9000 computer that ends up running amok because of a conflict in its mission parameters. The main purpose of the computer was to help the space travelers complete their mission, but the implied purpose was to also keep the space travelers from going nuts from loneliness. Whatever hopes you have of seeing a HAL-like computer on any space flights are likely doomed to failure. For one thing, any AI programmed for space isn't likely to purposely keep the crew in the dark about the mission parameters. Space flights will use an AI, no doubt about it, but it will be of a more practical and mundane construction than the HAL 9000.

Building Structures in Space

Just visiting space won't be enough at some point. The reality of space travel is that everything is located so far from everything else that we need waypoints between destinations. Even with waypoints, space travel will require serious effort. However, the waypoints are important even today. Imagine that people actually do start mining the moon. Having a warehouse in near-Earth orbit will be a requirement because of the immense cost of getting mining equipment and other resources moved from the earth's surface. Of course, the reverse trip also has to happen to get the mined resources and finished products from space to earth. People also want to take vacations in space, and scientists already rely on various structures to continue their investigations. The following sections discuss the use of various structures in different ways to help humanity move from planet Earth to the stars.

Taking your first space vacation

Companies have promised space vacations for some time now. Orbital Technologies made one of the first of these promises in 2011, which had an original expected date of 2016 (see https://tinyurl.com/rhxujxpc for details). The date has slipped a little to 2027 (https://tinyurl.com/ysvjmxdb). Even though you can't take a space vacation yet, the video at https://tinyurl.com/5c6eaa73 tells you about the technology required to make such a vacation possible. Most of the concepts found in these sites are feasible, at least to some extent, but aren't really around today. What you're seeing is *vaporware* (a promised product that doesn't actually exist yet but is probable enough to attract attention), but it's interesting, anyway.

TIP

Blue Origin, the company founded by Jeff Bezos, actually does have a functional rocket and quarters (https://tinyurl.com/7ry9fej6). The rocket has made a number of trips to date without any passengers and at least one with Jeff Bezos aboard (https://tinyurl.com/jh5pphu4). This trip didn't actually take people to space but rather into a near-Earth orbit of 100 kilometers. Companies such as Blue Origin (https://www.blueorigin.com/)and SpaceX (www.spacex.com) have the best chance right now of making a space vacation a reality. In fact, SpaceX is actually discussing plans for a vacation to Mars (http://www.spacex.com/mars).

Whatever the future holds, people will eventually end up in space for various reasons, including vacations. You should count on a cost as astronomical as your distance from earth. Space travel won't be cheap for the foreseeable future. In any case, companies are working on space vacations now, but you can't take one yet.

Performing scientific investigation

A lot of scientific investigation already occurs in space, all of which is currently aided by AI in some way. Everything from the International Space Station to the Hubbard Telescope depends heavily on AI (https://tinyurl.com/rvbe7hrt). Regarding the future, you can envision entire labs in space, or short-term hops into space to conduct experiments. Zero Gravity currently offers what it terms a *parabolic vomit comet flight* to perform near weightless experiments (https://www.gozerog.com/). The flight actually occurs in a plane that goes into a dive from high altitude. This trend is likely to continue, and at higher altitudes.

Industrializing space

Making space travel pay comes in several forms. Humans already enjoy considerable benefits from technologies developed for space flight and adopted for civilian use here on Earth. (Just one of many articles emphasizing the importance of space to life here on Earth is at https://tinyurl.com/zr2nmapn.) However, even with the technology transfers, space is still very expensive, and a better payback could occur by adapting what we know in other ways, such as by creating space factories (https://tinyurl.com/bexux4kr).

In fact, we may find that space factories provide the only way to produce certain materials and products (see https://tinyurl.com/87d2pt5t as an example). Having a zero-gravity environment affects how materials react and combine, which means that some of what's impossible here on earth suddenly becomes quite possible in space. In addition, some processes are easily performed only in space, such as making a completely round ball bearing (https://tinyurl.com/bhapjsb).

Using space for storage

People will eventually store some items in space, and that makes sense. As space travel becomes more prevalent and humans begin industrializing space; the need to store items such as fuel and mined materials will increase. Because people won't know where mined materials will see use (space factories will require materials, too), keeping the materials in space until a need for them occurs on Earth will actually be less expensive than storing them on Earth. The Orbit Fab space gas station (https://tinyurl.com/24hcypny) has already been launched. We may need it as part of our quest to visit Mars (https://tinyurl.com/28xhuzmj and https://tinyurl.com/kvfjhks2).

Although no current plans exist for the storage of hazardous materials in space, the future could also see humans storing such waste there, where it can't pollute the planet. Of course, the question of why we'd store hazardous waste, rather than do something like incinerate it in the sun, comes to mind. For that matter, logical minds might question the need to keep producing hazardous waste at all. As long as humans exist, however, we'll continue to produce hazardous waste. Storing such waste in space would give us a chance to find some means of recycling it into something useful, while keeping it out of the way.

Chapter **17**

Engaging in Human Endeavors

When people view news about robots and other automation created by advances in technology, such as AI, they tend to see the negative more than the positive. For example, the article at https://www.theverge.com/2017/11/30/16719092/automation-robots-jobs-global-800-million-forecast states that using automation will cost between 400 million and 800 million jobs by 2030. It then goes on to tell how these jobs will disappear. A somewhat more measured article at https://mitsloan.mit.edu/ideas-made-to-matter/a-new-study-measures-actual-impact-robots-jobs-its-significant states that robots have cost us 400,000 so far, but it also states bluntly that robots are also lowering wages. The problem is that most of these articles are quite definite when it comes to job losses, but nebulous, at best, when speaking of job creation. The overall goal of this chapter is to clear away the hype, disinformation, and outright fear mongering with some better news.

This chapter looks at interesting new human occupations. But first, don't assume that your job is on the line. (See Chapter 18 for just a few examples of AI-safe occupations.) Unless you're involved in something mind-numbingly simple and extremely repetitive, an AI isn't likely to replace you. Quite the contrary, you may find that an AI augments you, enabling you to derive more enjoyment from your occupation. Even so, after reading this chapter, you may just decide to get a little more education and some job training in some truly new and amazing occupation.

REMEMBER

Some of the jobs noted in this chapter are a bit on the dangerous side, too. AI will also add a host of mundane applications to the list that you'll perform in an office or perhaps even your home. These are the more interesting entries on the list, and you shouldn't stop looking for that new job if an AI does manage to grab yours. The point is that humans have been in this place multiple times in our history — the most disruptive of which was the industrial revolution — and we've managed to continue to find things to do. If you get nothing else from this chapter, be aware that all the fear mongering in the world is just that: someone trying to make you afraid so that you'll believe something that isn't true.

Keeping Human Beings Popular

The headline for an online advertisement in the future reads, "Get the New and Improved Human for Your Business!" It's one of those advertising gimmicks that many people find annoying. For one thing, something is either new or it's improved, but it isn't both. For another, aren't humans simply humans? However, the headline does have merit. Humans are constantly evolving, constantly adapting to change. We're the most amazing of species because we're always doing the unexpected in order to survive. Part of the reason for this chapter is to ensure that people think about the future — that is, where we're headed as a species, because we're certainly going to evolve as AI generally invades every aspect of our lives.

Children (and many adults) love video games! For many people, video games are only so much wasted time, yet they have a profound effect on children (or anyone else playing them), as described at `https://www.raisesmartkid.com/3-to-6-years-old/4-articles/34-the-good-and-bad-effects-of-video-games`. In fact, playing games permanently changes the brain, as described at `https://interestingengineering.com/playing-video-games-can-actually-change-the-brain`. Video games are just one of many aspects of life that AI changes, and these changes aren't generally appearing in new software, so the human of tomorrow is very unlikely to be mentally the same as the human of today. This likelihood leads to the idea that humans will remain popular and that AI won't take over the world.

When you extend the effects of brain changes due to game playing, it's not too difficult to assume that brain changes also occur for other uses of technology, especially technology that creates a Brain-Computer Interface (BCI), as described at `https://hbr.org/2020/09/are-you-ready-for-tech-that-connects-to-your-brain`. Currently, BCI enables people to do things like move limbs or overcome spinal cord injuries, but there is nothing preventing a BCI from letting humans interact directly with an AI in ways that we can't even imagine yet. Far from being replaced by AI, humans are evolving to work with AI to perform amazing things that were never possible in the past.

Living and Working in Space

The media has filled people's heads with this idea that we'll somehow do things like explore the universe or fight major battles in space with aliens who have come to take over the planet. The problem is that most people wouldn't know how to do either of those things. Yet, you can get a job with SpaceX today that involves some sort of space-oriented task (see https://www.spacex.com/careers/index.html). The list of potential job opportunities is huge (https://www.spacex.com/careers/index.html?department=), and many of them are internships so that you can get your feet wet before diving deeply into a career. Of course, you might expect them to be quite technical, but look down the list and you see a bit of everything — including a barista, at the time of this writing. The fact is that space-based careers will include everything that other careers include; you just have the opportunity to eventually work your way up into something more interesting.

TIP

Companies like SpaceX are also involved in providing their own educational opportunities and interacting with universities on the outside (https://www.spacex.com/internships/). Space represents a relatively new venture for humans, so everyone is starting at about the same level, in that everyone is learning something new. One of the most thrilling parts of entering a new area of human endeavor is that we haven't done the things that we're doing now, so there is a learning curve. You could find yourself in a position to make a really big contribution to the human race, but only if you're willing to take on the challenge of discovering and taking the risks associated with doing something different.

Today, the opportunities to actually live and work in space are limited, but the opportunities will improve over time. Chapter 16 discusses all sorts of things that humans will do in space eventually, such as mining or performing research. Yes, we'll eventually found cities in space after visiting other planets. Mars could become the next Earth. Many people have described Mars as potentially habitable (see https://www.planetary.org/articles/can-we-make-mars-earth-like-through-terraforming as an example) with the caveat that we'll have to re-create the Mars magnetosphere (https://phys.org/news/2017-03-nasa-magnetic-shield-mars-atmosphere.html).

Some of the ideas that people are discussing about life in space today don't seem feasible, but they're quite serious about those ideas and, theoretically, they're possible. For example, after the Mars magnetosphere is restored, it should be possible to terraform the planet to make it quite habitable. (Many articles exist on this topic; the one at https://futurism.com/nasa-were-going-to-try-and-make-oxygen-from-the-atmosphere-on-mars/ discusses how we could possibly provide an oxygen environment.) Some of these changes would happen automatically; others would require intervention from us. Imagine what being part of a terraforming team might be like. To make endeavors like this work, though, humans will rely heavily on AIs, which can actually see things that humans can't and react in ways that humans can't even imagine today. Humans and AIs will work together to reshape places like Mars to meet human needs. More important, these efforts will require huge numbers of people here on Earth, on the moon, in space, and on Mars. Coordination will be essential.

Creating Cities in Hostile Environments

As of this writing, Earth is currently host to 7.8 billion people (https://www.worldometers.info/world-population/), and that number will increase. Today the Earth will add about 156,000 people. In 2030, when NASA plans to attempt the first trip to Mars, the Earth will have about 8.5 billion people. In short, a lot of people inhabit Earth today, and there will be more of us tomorrow. Eventually, we'll need to find other places to live. If nothing else, we'll need more places to grow food. However, people also want to maintain some of the world's wild places and set aside land for other purposes, too. Fortunately, AI can help us locate suitable places to build, discover ways to make the building process work, and maintain a suitable environment after a new place is available for use.

As AI and humans become more capable, some of the more hostile places to build become more accessible. Theoretically, we might eventually build habitats in a volcano, but there are certainly a few locations more ideal than that to build before then. The following sections look at just a few of the more interesting places that humans might eventually use as locations for cities. These new locations all provide advantages that humans have never had before — opportunities for us to expand our knowledge and ability to live in even more hostile places in the future.

Building cities in the ocean

There are multiple ways to build cities in the ocean. However, the two most popular ideas are building floating cities and building cities that sit on the ocean floor. In fact, a floating city is in the planning stages right now off the coast of Tahiti (https://www.dailymail.co.uk/sciencetech/article-4127954/Plans-world-s-floating-city-unveiled.html and https://www.greenprophet.com/2020/12/seasteading-floating-cities/ for an update). The goals for floating cities are many, but here are the more attainable:

>> Protection from rising sea levels

>> Opportunities to try new agricultural methods

>> Growth of new fish-management techniques

>> Creation of new kinds of government

People who live on the oceans in floating cities are *seasteading* (sort of like home-steading, except on the ocean). The initial cities will exist in relatively protected areas. Building on the open ocean is definitely feasible (oil platforms already rely on various kinds of AI to keep them stable and perform other tasks; see `https://emerj.com/ai-sector-overviews/artificial-intelligence-in-oil-and-gas/` for details) but expensive.

Underwater cities are also quite feasible, and a number of underwater research labs currently exist (`https://interestingengineering.com/7-things-you-should-know-about-the-future-of-underwater-cities`). None of these research labs is in truly deep water, but even at 60 feet deep, they're pretty far down. According to a number of sources, the technology exists to build larger cities, further down, but they'd require better monitoring. That's where AI will likely come into play. The AI could monitor the underwater city from the surface and provide the safety features that such a city would require.

REMEMBER

It's important to consider that cities in the ocean might not look anything like cities on land. For example, some architects want to build an underwater city near Tokyo that will look like a giant spiral (`https://constructionglobal.com/construction-projects/underwater-construction-concept-could-harness-seabed-energy-resources`). This spiral could house up to 5,000 people. This particular city would sit at 16,400 feet below the ocean and rely on advanced technologies to provide things like power. It would be a full-fledged city, with labs, restaurants, and schools, for example.

No matter how people eventually move to the ocean, the move will require extensive use of AI. Some of this AI is already in the development stage (`https://www.5gtechnologyworld.com/unlocking-the-mysteries-of-the-deep-sea-with-ai-enhanced-underwater-vehicles/`) as companies develop underwater autonomous vehicles. As you can imagine, robots like these will be part of any underwater city development because they will perform various kinds of maintenance that would be outright impossible for humans to perform.

Creating space-based habitats

A *space habitat* differs from other forms of space station in that a space habitat is a permanent settlement. The reason to build a space habitat is to provide long-term accommodations for humans. The assumption is that a space habitat will provide a *closed-loop* environment, one in which people can exist without resupply indefinitely (or nearly so). Consequently, a space habitat would need air and water recycling, a method of growing food, and the means to perform other tasks that short-term space stations don't provide. Although all space stations require an AI to monitor and tune conditions, the AI for a space habitat would be an order of magnitude (or greater) more complex.

Chapter 16 offers some discussion of space-based habitats in the "Taking your first space vacation" section of the chapter. Of course, short visits will be the first way in which people interact with space. A space vacation would certainly be interesting! However, a near-Earth vacation is different from a long-term habitat in deep space, which NASA will need if it actually succeeds in making a trip to Mars a reality. NASA has already commissioned six companies to start looking into the requirements for creating habitats in deep space (https://www.nasa.gov/press-release/nasa-selects-six-companies-to-develop-prototypes-concepts-for-deep-space-habitats and https://www.nasa.gov/feature/nasa-begins-testing-habitation-prototypes).

For some organizations, space-based habitats aren't so much a means for enhancing exploration but rather for protecting civilization. At this moment, if a giant asteroid impacts Earth, most of humanity will perish. People on the International Space Station (ISS) might survive, however — at least, if the asteroid didn't hit it as well. However, the ISS isn't a long-term survival strategy for humans, and the number of people on the ISS at any given time is limited. So, people like the Lifeboat Foundation (https://lifeboat.com/ex/spacehabitats) are looking into space habitats as a means for ensuring humanity's survival. Their first attempt at a space habitat is Ark I (https://lifeboat.com/ex/arki), which is designed for 1,000 permanent residents and up to 500 guests. Theoretically, the technology can work, but it will require a great deal of planning.

Another use for space habitats is as a *generational ship,* a kind of vessel to explore interstellar space using technologies we have available today (https://scienceline.org/2021/02/novel-science-talkin-bout-my-generation-ship/). People would live on this ship as it traveled to the stars. They'd have children in space in order to make long voyages feasible. The idea of generational ships isn't new. They have appeared in both movies and books for years. The problem with a generational ship is that the ship would require a consistent number of people who are willing to work in each of the various trades needed to keep the ship moving. Even so, growing up knowing that you have an essential job waiting for you would be an interesting change from what humans have to deal with today.

TECHNICAL STUFF

Rather than build space habitat components on Earth and then move them into space, the current strategy is to mine the materials needed from asteroids and use space factories to produce the space habitats. The solar system's main asteroid belt is currently estimated to contain enough material to build habitats containing the same area as 3,000 Earths. That's a lot of human beings in space.

HABITATS VERSUS TERRAFORMING

Significant use of AI will occur no matter how we decide to live and work in space. The way we create the AI will differ depending on where we go and when. People currently have the idea that we could be living on Mars in a relatively short period. However, when reviewing sites such as https://phys.org/news/2017-03-future-space-colonization-terraforming-habitats.html, it becomes obvious that terraforming Mars will take a very long time indeed. Just to warm the planet (after we build the technology required to re-create the Mars magnetosphere) will take about a hundred years. Consequently, we don't really have a choice between habitats and terraforming; habitats will come first, and we'll likely use them extensively to make any plans we have for Mars work. Even so, the AI for both projects will be different, and seeing the sorts of problems that the AI will help address should be interesting.

Constructing moon-based resources

It's not a matter of *if* we go back to the moon and build bases there; it's *when*. Many of the current strategies for colonizing space depend on moon-based resources of various sorts, including the NASA effort to eventually send people to Mars. We don't suffer from any lack of moon base designs, either. You can see a few of these designs at https://interestingengineering.com/8-interesting-moon-base-proposals-every-space-enthusiast-should-see.

REMEMBER

At times, people have talked of military bases on the moon (http://www.todayifoundout.com/index.php/2017/01/project-horizon/), but the Outer Space Treaty, signed by 60 nations as a way to keep politics out of space (https://www.cfr.org/report/outer-space-treaty), has largely put an end to that idea. Moon-based structures and the services they provide will more likely answer exploration, mining, and factory needs at first, followed by complete cities. Even though these projects will likely rely on robots, they will still require humans to perform a wide range of tasks, including robot repair and robot management. Building bases on the moon will also require a host of new occupations that you won't likely see as part of habitats or in scenarios that deal exclusively with working in space. For example, someone will have to deal with the aftermath of moonquakes (see https://www.nasa.gov/press-release/goddard/2019/moonquakes for details).

Using existing moon features to build housing is also a possibility. The recent discovery of moon structures suitable to colonization uses would make building bases on the moon easier. For example, you can read about a huge cave that's suitable for colonization at http://time.com/4990676/moon-cave-base-lunar-colony-exploration/. In this case, Japan discovered what appears to be a lava tube that would protect colonists from a variety of environmental threats.

Making Humans More Efficient

An AI can make a human more efficient in lots of different ways. Most of the chapters in this book have some sort of example of a human relying on an AI to do things more efficiently. One of the more interesting chapters, though, is Chapter 7, which points out how an AI will help with medical needs in various ways. All these uses of an AI assume that a human remains in charge but uses the AI to become better at performing a task. For example, the da Vinci Surgical System doesn't replace the surgeon; it simply makes the surgeon able to perform the task with greater ease and less potential for errors. A new occupation that goes along with this effort is a trainer who shows professionals how to use new tools that include an AI.

REMEMBER

In the future, you should plan to see consultants whose only job is to find new ways to incorporate AIs into business processes to help people become more efficient. To some extent, this profession already exists, but the need will increase at some point when generic, configurable AIs become common. For many businesses, the key to profitability will hinge on finding the right AI to augment human workers so that workers can complete tasks without error and as quickly as possible. Think about these people as part script programmer/application packager, part salesperson, and part trainer all wrapped into one. You can see an example of this kind of thinking in the article at http://www.information-age.com/harness-ai-improve-workplace-efficiency-123469118/.

When dealing with human efficiency, you should think about areas in which an AI can excel. For example, an AI wouldn't work well in a creative task, so you leave the creativity to a human. However, an AI does perform searches exceptionally well, so you might train a human to rely on an AI to perform search-related tasks while the human does something creative. Here are some ways in which you may see humans using an AI to become more efficient in the future:

>> **Hiring:** Currently, a person hiring people for an organization may not know all the candidate's real credentials and history. An AI could research candidates before an interview so that the hiring person has more information to use during the interview. In addition, because the AI would use the same search methodology for every candidate, the organization can ensure that each candidate is treated both fairly and equally.

>> **Scheduling:** Today, a business is constantly at risk because someone didn't think about the need to schedule a task. In fact, people might not have had time to even think about the need for the task in the first place. Secretaries and assistants used to manage schedules, but in the new, flattened hierarchies, these assistants have all but disappeared, and individual employees perform their own scheduling tasks. Thus, overworked employees often miss

opportunities to help a business excel because they're too busy managing a schedule. Coupling an AI with a human frees the human from actually performing the scheduling. Instead, the human can look ahead and see what will need to be scheduled. It's a matter of focus: By focusing the human where the human can excel, the business gets more out of the human. The AI makes this focus on human excellence possible.

>> **Locating hidden information:** More than ever today, businesses get blindsided by the competition because of hidden information. Information overload and ever growing science, technology, business, and societal complexity are at the root of the problem. Perhaps a new way to package goods exists that reduces costs significantly, or the structure of a business changes as a result of internal politics. Knowing what is available and what's going on at all times is the only way that businesses can truly succeed, but the job is simply not feasible. If a human were to take the time required to become all-knowing about everything that a particular job requires, no time would be left to actually do the job.

Als, however, are exceptional at finding things. By incorporating machine learning into the mix, a human could train an AI to look for precisely the right issues and requirements to keep a business afloat without wasting quite so much time in manual searches.

>> **Adaptive help:** Anyone using products today will have to admit that having to remember how to perform a certain task is incredibly frustrating at times, especially when rediscovering how to perform the task requires using application help. You can already see how an AI becomes an adaptive aid when it comes to typing certain kinds of information into forms. However, an AI could go much further. By using machine learning techniques to discover patterns of use, an AI could eventually provide adaptive help that would help users get past hard-to-remember parts of an application. Because every user is different, an application that is hardwired to provide adaptive help would never work. Using machine learning enables people to customize the help system to fit each individual user.

>> **Adaptive learning:** Today you can take an adaptive exam that tailors itself to ask questions about perceived weak areas in your knowledge. The adaptive exam either discovers that you really do know enough or asks enough questions to verify that you need more training. Eventually, applications will be able to sense how you use them and then provide automated training to make you better. For example, the application may discover that you could perform a task using five fewer clicks, so it could show you how to perform the task using this approach. By constantly training people to use the most efficient approach when interacting with computers or performing other tasks, the person becomes more efficient but the need for the human in that particular role remains.

Fixing Problems on a Planetary Scale

Regardless of whether you believe in global warming, think that pollution is a problem, or are concerned about overpopulation, the fact is that we have only one planet Earth, and it has problems. The weather is most definitely getting stranger; large areas are no longer useful because of pollution; and some areas of the world have, frankly, too many people. An out-of-control storm or forest fire doesn't care what you think; the result is always the same: destruction of areas where humans live. The act of trying to cram too many people into too little space usually results in disease, crime, and other problems. The issues aren't political or defined by personal beliefs. The issues are real, and AI can help solve them by helping knowledgeable people look for the right patterns. The following sections discuss planetary problems from the perspective of using an AI to see, understand, and potentially fix them. We're not stating or implying any political or other kind of message.

Contemplating how the world works

Sensors monitor every aspect of the planet today. In fact, so much information exists that it's amazing that anyone can collect all of it in one place, much less do anything with it. In addition, because of the interactions among various Earth environments, you can't really know which facts have a causal effect on some other part of the environment. For example, it's hard to know precisely how much wind patterns affect sea warming, which in turn affects currents that potentially produce storms. If humans actually understood all these various interactions, the weather report would be more accurate. Unfortunately, the weather report is usually sort of right — if you squint just right and hold your mouth a certain way. The fact that we accept this level of performance from the people who predict the weather testifies to our awareness of the difficulty of the task.

Over the years, weather prediction has become a lot more reliable. Part of the reason for this increase in reliability is all those sensors out there. The weather service has also created better weather models and amassed a much larger store of data to use for predictions. However, the overriding reason that the weather report is more accurate is the use of AI to handle the number crunching and look for identifiable patterns in the resulting data (see https://emerj.com/ai-sector-overviews/ai-for-weather-forecasting/ for details).

The weather is actually one of the better understood Earth processes. Consider the difficulty in forecasting earthquakes. The use of machine learning has made it more likely that scientists will know when an earthquake will happen (https://www.wired.co.uk/article/ai-predicting-earthquakes), but only time will tell whether the new information is actually useful. At one time, people thought that the weather could affect earthquakes, but this isn't the case. On the other hand, earthquakes can affect the weather by changing the environmental conditions. Also, earthquakes and weather can combine to make a situation even worse (https://www.usatoday.com/story/news/nation/2015/05/02/kostigen-earthquake-weather/26649071/).

Even more difficult to predict are volcanic eruptions. At least NASA can now detect and obtain images of volcanic eruptions with great accuracy (https://www.livescience.com/58423-nasa-artificial-intelligence-captures-volcano-eruption.html). Volcanic eruptions often cause earthquakes, so knowing about one helps to predict the other (https://www.dw.com/en/volcanoes-and-earthquakes-the-pacific-ring-of-fire/a-36676363). Of course, volcanoes also affect the weather (https://www.sciencedaily.com/releases/2020/09/200911110809.htm).

The natural events that this section has covered so far are just the tip of the iceberg. If you're getting the idea that Earth is so complex that no one person could ever understand it, you're right. That's why we need to create and train AIs to help humans do a better job of understanding how the world works. By creating this sort of knowledge, avoiding catastrophic events in the future may be possible, along with reducing the effects of certain manmade ills.

WARNING

No matter what you've read, no way currently exists to prevent bad weather, earthquakes, or volcanoes. The best that humans can hope to achieve today is to predict these events and then act to reduce their impact. However, even the ability to reduce the impact of natural events is a major step forward. Before AI, humans were at the mercy of whatever event occurred because prediction was impossible before it was too late to truly act in a proactive manner to reduce the effects of the natural disaster.

Likewise, even though preventing all manmade disasters might seem possible, it often isn't. No amount of planning will keep accidents from happening. This said, most human-made events are controllable and potentially preventable with the correct insights, which can be provided through the pattern matching that an AI can provide.

Locating potential sources of problems

With all the eyes in the sky today, you'd think that satellite data could provide an absolute source of data for predicting problems on earth. However, this viewpoint has a number of problems:

» The Earth is huge, so detecting a particular event means scouring millions of pictures every second of every day.

>> The pictures must appear at the correct resolution to actually find an event.

>> Using the right light filter is essential because some events become visible only in the right light.

>> Weather can prevent the acquisition of certain types of images.

Even with all these problems, scientists and others use AI to scan through the pictures taken each day, looking for potential problems (https://www.cnet.com/news/descartes-labs-satellite-imagery-artificial-intelligence-geovisual-search/). However, the AI can show possible problem areas and perform analysis only when the images appear in the correct form. A human still has to determine whether the problem is real and needs to be addressed. For example, a major storm in the middle of the Pacific Ocean away from the transportation routes or any landmass probably won't be considered a high-priority problem. The same storm over the top of a landmass is a cause for concern. Of course, when it comes to storms, detecting the storm before it becomes an issue is always better than trying to do something about it later.

TIP

Besides scanning images for potential problems, AI can also enhance images. The article at https://www.jdsupra.com/legalnews/artificial-intelligence-and-satellite-72364/ talks about how AI can increase the resolution and usability of images taken from space. By enhancing the images, the AI can make better determinations of specific kinds of events based on the event pattern (such as carbon tracking). Of course, if the AI hasn't seen a particular pattern before, it still can't make any sort of prediction. Humans will always need to check the AI and ensure that an event really is what the AI purports it to be.

Defining potential solutions

The solution to planetary problems depends on the problem. For example, with a storm, earthquake, or volcanic eruption, preventing the event isn't even a consideration. The best that humans can hope to achieve today is to get the area of the event evacuated and provide people with another place to go. However, by knowing as much about the event as possible as far in advance as possible, people can act proactively rather than react to the event after total chaos breaks out.

Other events don't necessarily require an evacuation. For example, with current technology and a bit of luck, people can reduce the effects of something like a forest fire. In fact, some fire professionals are now using AI to actually predict forest fires before they occur (https://www.ctvnews.ca/sci-tech/artificial-intelligence-can-better-predict-forest-fires-says-alberta-researcher-1.3542249). Using AI to enable people to see the problem and then create a solution for it based on historical data is feasible because humans have recorded so much information about these events in the past.

Using historical data to work through planetary problems is essential. Having just one potential solution is usually a bad idea. The best plans for solving a problem include several solutions, and an AI can help rank the potential solutions based on historical results. Of course, here again, a human may see something in the solutions that makes one option preferable to another. For example, a particular solution may not work because the resources aren't available or the people involved don't have the right training.

Seeing the effects of the solutions

Tracking the results of a particular solution means recording data in real time, analyzing it as quickly as possible, and then displaying the effects in a way that humans understand. An AI can gather data, analyze it, and provide several presentations of that data far faster than any human can do it. Humans are still setting the criteria for performing all these tasks and making the final decisions; the AI simply acts as a tool to enable the human to act in a reasonable amount of time.

TIP

In the future, some people might specialize in interacting with AIs to make them work with data better. Getting the right results often means knowing what question to ask and how to ask it. People today often get poor results from an AI because they aren't familiar enough with how the AI works to ask reasonable questions of it.

Humans who assume that AIs think in a human-like manner are doomed to fail at getting good results from the AI. Unfortunately, that's what our society promotes today. The Siri and Alexa commercials make the AI appear to be human, but it isn't, of course. In an emergency, even with an AI accessible to the humans who are dealing with the event, the humans must know how to ask appropriate questions and in what way to ask them to get the required results. You can't see the effect of a solution if you don't know what to expect from the AI.

Trying again

The Earth is a complicated place. Various factors interact with other factors in ways that no one can anticipate. Consequently, the solution you created may not actually solve a problem. In fact, if you read the news very often, you find that many solutions don't solve anything at all. Failure is the hallmark of many geniuses in the world, even technical writers, as described at http://blog.johnmuellerbooks.com/2013/04/26/defining-the-benefits-of-failure/. Trial and error help people understand what does and doesn't work. However, by using an AI to recognize patterns of failure — those solutions that didn't work, and why — you can reduce the number of solutions that you need to try to find one that works. In addition, an AI can look for similar scenarios for solutions that have worked in the past, sometimes saving time and effort in trying to find new solutions to try. AI isn't a magic wand that you can wave to create a solution that works the first time you try it. The reason that humans will always remain in the picture is that only humans can see the results for what they are.

REMEMBER

An AI is always programmed to win today. The "Understanding teaching orientation" sidebar in Chapter 13 discusses the potential for creating an AI that understands futility — that is, the no-win scenario. However, such an AI doesn't currently and may never exist. Humans, however, do understand the no-win scenario and can therefore often create a less-than-optimal solution that works well enough. In assessing why a solution doesn't work, considering the no-win scenario is essential because the AI will never present it to you.

The AIs you use in creating solutions will eventually run out of ideas, at which point the AI becomes basically useless. That's because an AI isn't creative. The patterns that an AI works with already exist. However, those patterns may not address a current need (one that you can see today, but haven't creatively thought out), which means that you need new patterns. Humans are adept at creating new patterns to apply to problems. Consequently, trying again becomes essential as a means to create new patterns that an AI can then access and use to help a human remember something that worked in the past. In short, humans are an essential part of the problem-solving loop.

6 The Part of Tens

IN THIS PART . . .

Find an occupation that AI can't perform.

Discover how AI mostly helps society.

Understand why AI must fail in some situations.

Chapter **18**

Ten Occupational Categories that AI Can't Replace

This book has spent a lot of time telling you about how AI and humans differ and demonstrating that humans have absolutely nothing to worry about. Yes, some jobs will go away, but as described in Chapter 17, the use of AI will actually create a wealth of new jobs — most of them a lot more interesting than working on an assembly line. The new jobs that humans will have rely on the areas of intelligence (as described in Chapter 1) that an AI simply can't master. In fact, the inability of AI to master so many areas of human thought will keep many people in their current occupations, which is the point of this chapter.

REMEMBER

You may find that your current occupation is safe from AI replacement when it falls into specific categories, with human interaction, creativity, and using intuition being the most prevalent. However, this chapter touches on only the tip of the iceberg. Fear mongering by certain individuals (see "Humans wouldn't be able to control a superintelligent AI" at Business Insider.com for details) has people worried that their job will go away tomorrow. Fear mongering will also keep people from using the full potential of AI to make their lives easier (see "Head of A.I. at Google slams the kind of 'A.I. apocalypse' fear-mongering Elon Musk has been doing" at CNBC.com). The overall message of this chapter is this: Don't be afraid. AI is a tool that, like any other tool, is designed to make your life easier and better.

Performing Human Interaction

Robots already perform a small amount of human interaction and will likely perform more human interaction tasks in the future. However, if you take a good look at the applications that robots are used in, they're essentially doing things that are ridiculously boring: performing like a kiosk in directing people where to go; serving as an alarm clock to ensure that the elderly take their medications; and so on. Most human interaction isn't this simple. The following sections look at some of the more interactive and demanding forms of human interaction — activities that an AI has no possibility whatsoever of mastering.

Teaching children

Spend some time at a grade school and watch the teachers herd the children. You'll be amazed. Somehow, teachers manage to get all the kids from Point A to Point B with a minimum of fuss, apparently by sheer force of will. Even so, one child will need one level of attention while another child needs another level. When things go wrong, the teacher might end up having to deal with several problems at the same time. All these situations would overwhelm an AI today because an AI relies on cooperative human interaction. Think for a minute about the reaction that Alexa or Siri would have to a stubborn child (or try to simulate such a reaction with your own unit). It simply won't work. An AI can, however, help a teacher in these areas:

>> Grading papers

>> Using adaptive educational software

>> Improving courses based on student patterns

>> Providing students with tutors

>> Showing students how to find information

>> Creating a safe environment for trial-and-error learning

>> Helping guide students in making decisions about courses to take and after-school activities to do based on their skill set

>> Providing students with homework help

Nursing

A robot can lift a patient, saving a nurse's back. However, an AI can't make a decision about when, where, and how to lift the patient because it can't judge all the required, nonverbal patient input correctly or understand patient psychology, such as a penchant for telling mistruths (see the "Considering the Five Mistruths in Data" section of Chapter 2). An AI could ask the patient questions, but probably not in a manner best suited to elicit useful answers. A robot can clean up messes, but it's unlikely to do so in a manner that preserves patient dignity and helps the patient feel cared for. In short, a robot is a good hammer: great for performing hard, coarse tasks, but not particularly gentle or caring.

REMEMBER

The use of AIs will undoubtedly increase in the medical profession, but these uses are extremely specific and limited. Chapter 7 gives you some good ideas on where an AI can help in the medical field. Few of these activities have anything to do with human interaction. They're more along the lines of human augmentation and medical data collection.

Addressing personal needs

You may think that your AI is a perfect companion. After all, it never talks back, is always attentive, and never leaves you for someone else. You can tell it your deepest thoughts and it won't laugh. In fact, an AI such as Alexa or Siri may well make the perfect companion, as depicted in movies such as *Her* (find details of it as Amazon.com). The only problem is that an AI doesn't actually make a very good companion at all. What it really does is provide a browser application with a voice. Anthropomorphizing the AI doesn't make it real.

The problem with having an AI address personal needs is that it doesn't understand the concept of a personal need. An AI can look for a radio station, find a news article, make product purchases, record an appointment, tell you when it's time to take medication, and even turn your lights on and off. However, it can't tell you when a thought is a really bad idea and likely to cause you a great deal of woe. To obtain useful input in situations that offer no rules to follow, you need someone with real-life experience to present something approximating an answer. In other words, you need a human. That's why people like counselors, doctors, nurses, and even that lady you talk with at the coffee shop are necessary. Some of these people are paid monetarily; others just depend on you to listen when they need help in turn. Human interaction is always required when addressing personal needs that truly are personal.

Solving developmental issues

People with special needs require a human touch. Often, the need turns out to be a special gift, but only when the caregiver recognizes it as such. Someone with a special need might be fully functional in all but one way, and it takes creativity and imagination to discover the means to getting over the hurdle. Finding a way to use the special need in a world that doesn't accept special needs as normal is even harder. For example, most people wouldn't consider color blindness (which is actually color shifting) an asset when creating art. However, someone came along and turned it into an advantage (see "Dealing with Color Blindness as an Artist: Advantages You Can Have" at Colorblind Guide.com).

An AI might be able to help people with special needs in specific ways. For example, a robot can help someone perform their occupational or physical therapy to become more mobile. The absolute patience of the robot would ensure that the person would receive the same even-handed help every day. However, it would take a human to recognize when the occupational or physical therapy isn't working and requires a change.

WARNING

Helping with developmental issues is one area in which an AI, no matter how well programmed and trained, could actually prove detrimental. A human can see when someone is overdoing it, even when they appear to succeed at various tasks. A host of nonverbal messages help, but it's also a matter of experience and intuition, qualities that an AI can't provide in abundance because some situations would require the AI to *extrapolate* (extend its knowledge to an unknown situation) rather than *interpolate* (use knowledge between two well-known points) to succeed. In short, not only will humans have to monitor a person that they and the AI are helping, they'll also need to monitor the AI to ensure that it works as anticipated.

Creating New Things

As noted in Table 1-1 of Chapter 1, robots can't create. It's essential to view the act of creating as one of developing new patterns of thought. A good deep learning application can analyze existing patterns of thought, rely on an AI to turn those patterns into new versions of things that have happened before, and produce what appears to be original thought, but no creativity is involved. What you're seeing is math and logic at work analyzing what is, rather than defining what could be. With this limitation of AI in mind, the following sections describe the creation of new things — an area where humans will always excel.

Inventing

When people talk about inventors, they think about people like Thomas Edison, who held 2,332 patents worldwide (1,093 in the United States alone) for his inventions see "15 Inventions From Thomas Edison That Changed The World" at Business Insider.com). You may still use one of his inventions, the light bulb, but many of his inventions, such as the phonograph, truly changed the world. Not everyone is an Edison. Some people are like Bette Nesmith Graham (described at

Famous Women Inventors.com), who invented Whiteout (also known as Liquid Paper and by other names) in 1956. At one point, her invention appeared in every desk drawer on the planet as a means for correcting typing errors. Both of these people did something that an AI can't do: create a new thought pattern in the form of a physical entity.

Yes, each of these people drew inspiration from other sources, but the idea was truly their own. The point is that people invent things all the time. You can find millions and millions of ideas on the Internet, all created by people who simply saw something in a different way. If anything, people will become more inventive as they have time to do so. An AI can free people from the mundane so that they can do what people do best: invent still more new things.

Being artistic

Style and presentation make a Picasso (https://www.pablopicasso.org/) different from a Monet (https://www.claudemonetgallery.org/). Humans can tell the difference because we see the patterns in these artists' methods: everything from choosing a canvas, to the paint, to the style of presentation, to the topics displayed. An AI can see these differences, too. In fact, with the precise manner in which an AI can perform analysis and the greater selection of sensors at its disposal (in most cases), an AI can probably describe the patterns of artistry better than a human can, and mimic those patterns in output that the artist never provided. However, the AI advantage ends here.

An AI will stick with what it knows, but humans experiment. In fact, you can find 59 examples of human experimentation at https://tinyurl.com/ztk63cfy with just materials alone. Only a human would think to create art from chicken wire (https://tinyurl.com/rfkkp9aa) or leaves (https://tinyurl.com/36ph3xmd). If a material is available, someone has created art from it — art that an AI could never reproduce.

Imagining the unreal

Humans constantly extend the envelope of what is real by making the unreal possible. At one time, no one thought that humans would fly by coming up with heavier-than-air machines. In fact, experiments tended to support the theory that even attempting to fly was foolish. Then came the Wright brothers (http://www.history.com/topics/inventions/wright-brothers). Their flight at Kitty Hawk changed the world. However, it's important to realize that the Wright brothers merely made the unreal thoughts of many people (including themselves) real. An AI would never have an unreal output, much less turn it into reality. Only humans can do this.

Making Intuitive Decisions

Intuition is a direct perception of a truth, independent of any reasoning process. It's the truth of illogic, making it incredibly hard to analyze. Humans are adept at intuition, and the most intuitive people usually have a significant advantage over those who aren't intuitive. AI, which is based on logic and math, lacks intuition. Consequently, an AI usually has to plod through all the available logical solutions and eventually conclude that no solution to a problem exists, even when a human finds one with relative ease. Human intuition and insight often play a huge role in making some occupations work, as described in the following sections.

Investigating crime

If you watch fictional crime dramas on television, you know that the investigator often finds one little fact that opens the entire case, making it solvable. Real-world crime-solving works differently. Human detectives rely on fully quantifiable knowledge to perform their task, and sometimes the criminals make the job all too easy as well. Procedures and policies, digging into the facts, and spending hours just looking at all the evidence play important roles in solving crime. However, sometimes a human will make that illogical leap that suddenly makes all the seemingly unrelated pieces fit together.

A detective's work involves dealing with a wide range of issues. In fact, some of those issues don't even involve illegal activities. For example, a detective may simply be looking for someone who seems to be missing. Perhaps the person even has a good reason for not wanting to be found. The point is that many of these detections involve looking at the facts in ways that an AI would never think to look because it requires a leap — an extension of intelligence that doesn't exist for an AI. The phrase *thinking outside the box* comes to mind.

Monitoring situations in real time

An AI will monitor situations using previous data as a basis for future decisions. In other words, the AI uses patterns to make predictions. Most situations work fine using this pattern, which means that an AI can actually predict what will happen in a particular scenario with a high degree of accuracy. However, sometimes situations occur when the pattern doesn't fit and the data doesn't seem to support the conclusion. Perhaps the situation currently lacks supporting data — which happens all the time. In these situations, human intuition is the only fallback. In an emergency, relying only on an AI to work through a scenario is a bad idea. Although the AI does try the tested solution, a human can think outside the box and come up with the alternative idea.

Separating fact from fiction

An AI will never be intuitive. Intuition runs counter to every rule that is currently used to create an AI. Consequently, some people have decided to create Artificial Intuition (see `https://thenextweb.com/news/the-fourth-generation-of-ai-is-here-and-its-called-artificial-intuition` as an example). In reading the materials that support Artificial Intuition, it quickly becomes obvious that there is some sort of magic taking place (that is, the inventors are engaged in wishful thinking) because the theory simply doesn't match the proposed implementation.

REMEMBER

Some essential issues are involved with Artificial Intuition, the first of which is that all programs, even those that support AI, run on processors whose only capability is to perform the simplest of math and logic functions. That AI works as well as it does given the hardware currently available is nothing short of amazing.

The second issue is that AI and all computer programs essentially rely on math to perform tasks. The AI understands nothing. The "Considering the Chinese Room argument" section of Chapter 5 discusses just one of the huge problems with the whole idea of an AI's capacity for understanding. The point is that intuition is illogical, which means that humans don't even understand the basis for it. Without understanding, humans can't create a system that mimics intuition in any meaningful way.

Chapter **19**

Ten Substantial Contributions of AI to Society

This book helps you understand the history of AI, where it is today, and where it could go tomorrow. However, a technology is useful only as long as it makes some sort of substantial contribution to society. Moreover, the contribution must come with a strong financial incentive, or investors won't contribute to it. Although the government may contribute to a technology that it sees as useful for military or other purposes for a short time, long-term technological health relies on investor support. Consequently, this chapter focuses on AI components that are useful today, meaning that they're making a substantial contribution to society right now.

REMEMBER

Some people say that the overpromising of AI benefits today could cause another AI winter tomorrow (see "AI winter is coming?" at AI Futures.org). In addition, the fear mongering by certain influential people is causing people to rethink the value of AI, as discussed in "Will Artificial Intelligence Ever Live Up to Its Hype? Scientific American.com. (Fortunately, those with a better view often counter the fear mongering, such as with the view expressed in "Artificial intelligence problem isn't computers; it's humanity" at the Daily Illini.com.) Both of these issues are countered by others who feel that a balanced view of AI is ultimately desirable (see "Let's Not Regulate A.I. Out of Existence" at OneZero.com). Discussion is valuable in assessing any technology, but investors aren't interested in words; investors are interested in results. This chapter is about results that demonstrate that AI has become integrated into society in a significant enough manner to make another AI winter truly unlikely. Of course, getting rid of the hype so that people can really understand what AI can do for them would be a plus at this point.

Considering Human-Specific Interactions

People drive sales of products. In addition, people decide what to talk about most, which creates buzz, which in turn creates sales. Although you probably won't hear about the technologies discussed in the following sections on the radio, the level at which they affect people is amazing. In the first case, an active human foot, people will actually be able to walk using prosthetics with nearly the same ease as they walk with a natural foot. Even though the group needing this product is relatively small, the effects can be widely known. The second and third cases have the potential for affecting millions, perhaps billions, of people. They're mundane offerings, but often the mundane is what becomes expected, which again drives sales. In all three cases, the technologies won't work without AI, which means that stopping AI research, development, and sales is likely to be met with disdain by the people using the technologies.

Devising the active human foot

Prosthetics are big money. They cost a fortune to make and are a necessary item for anyone missing a limb. Many prosthetics rely on passive technology, which means that they provide no feedback and don't automatically adjust their functionality to accommodate personal needs. All that has changed in recent years as scientists such as Hugh Herr have created active prosthetics that can simulate the actions of real limbs and automatically adjust to the person using them (see "MIT's Hugh Herr Reveals Joys (and Challenges) of Commercializing Bionic Limbs" at Robotics Business Review.com). Even though Hugh Herr grabbed major headlines, you can find active technology in all sorts of prosthetics today, including knees, arms, and hands. (See Chapter 7 for a link to Hugh Herr's TED talk.)

REMEMBER

You may wonder about the potential value of using active over passive prosthetics. Medical suppliers are already doing the research (see some results in the report "Economic Value of Advanced Transfemoral Prosthetics" at Rand.org). It turns out that microprocessor-based prosthetics that rely on an AI to ensure that the device interacts properly with the user are a huge win. Not only do people who use active technology prosthetics live longer, but these prosthetics have also reduced direct and indirect medical costs. For example, a person using an active technology prosthetic is less likely to fall. Even though the initial cost of an active technology prosthetic is higher, the costs over time are much smaller.

Performing constant monitoring

Chapter 7 discusses a host of monitoring devices used by medicine to ensure that people get their medications at the right time and in the correct dosage. In addition, medical monitoring can help patients receive care faster after a major incident and even predict when a patient will have a major incident, such as a heart attack. Most of these devices, especially those that are predictive in nature, rely on an AI of some sort to perform the work. However, the question of whether these devices provide a financial incentive for the people creating and using them remains.

Studies are hard to come by, but the study results in "Clinical and economic impact of HeartLogic compared with standard care in heart failure patients" (found at Wiley Online Library) show that remote monitoring of heart patients saves considerable medical costs (besides helping the patient live a happier, longer life). In fact, the use of remote monitoring, even for healthy people, has a significant impact on medical costs (see "Benefits of Remote Patient Monitoring" at blog.prevounce.com). The impact of the savings is so high that remote monitoring is actually changing how medicine works.

Administering medications

Sick people who forget to take their medications cost the medical establishment huge amounts of money. According to this 2016 article, "Patients skipping meds cost $290 billion per year—can 'smart' pills help?" at CNBC.com, the cost in the United States alone at that time was $290 billion a year. (There are ongoing efforts to reduce this waste, as described in papers like "The Prevalence of Unused Medications in Homes" at NCBI.gov. By combining technologies such as Near Field Communication (NFC) (see "Smart Packaging: Looks to Move Forward" at Jones Healthcare Group.com) with apps that rely on an AI, you can track how people take their medications, and when. In addition, the AI can help people remember when to take medications, which ones to take, and how much to use. When coupled with monitoring, even people with special monitoring needs can obtain the right dose of their medications (see "AI Informed Solutions to Promote Medical Adherence" at Xyonix.com).

Developing Industrial Solutions

People drive a ton of small sales. However, when you think about an individual's spending power, it pales in comparison to what just one organization can spend. The difference is in quantity. However, investors look at both kinds of sales because both generate money — lots of it. Industrial solutions affect organizations. They tend to be expensive, yet industry uses them to increase productivity, efficiency, and most of all, income. It's all about the bottom line. The following sections discuss how AI affects the bottom line of organizations that use the supplied solutions.

Using AI with 3-D printing

3-D printing began as a toy technology that produced some interesting, but not particularly valuable, results. However, that was before NASA used 3-D printing on the International Space Station (ISS) to produce tools (see "International Space Station's 3-D Printer" at NASA.gov). Most people will think that the ISS should have taken all the tools it needs when it left Earth. Unfortunately, tools get lost or broken. In addition, the ISS simply doesn't have enough space to store absolutely every required tool. Three-dimensional printing can also create spare parts, and the ISS certainly can't carry a full complement of spare parts. Three-dimensional printers work the same in microgravity as they do on Earth (check out the Space Station Research Explorer page at NASA.gov), so 3-D printing is a technology that scientists can use in precisely the same manner in both places.

Meanwhile, industry uses 3-D printing to meet all sorts of demands. Adding an AI to the mix lets the device create an output, see what it has created, and learn from its mistakes (see "3D printers with an AI brain – ENGINEERING.com" at FR24 News.com). This means that industry will eventually be able to create robots that correct their own mistakes — at least to an extent, which will reduce mistakes and increase profits. AI also helps to reduce the risk associated with 3-D printing through products such as Business Case, explained in "The Artificial Intelligence for your 3D Printing Projects" at Sculpteo.com.

Advancing robot technologies

This book contains a wealth of information on how robots are being used, from in the home to medicine to industry. The book also talks about robots in cars, space, and under water. If you're getting the idea that robots are a significant driving force behind AI, you're right. Robots are becoming a reliable, accessible, and known technology with a visible presence and a track record of success, which is why so many organizations are investing in even more advanced robots.

Many existing traditional businesses rely on robots today, which is something many people may not know. For example, the oil industry relies heavily on robots to search for new oil sources, perform maintenance, and inspect pipes. In some cases, robots also make repairs in places that humans can't easily access; such as in pipes (see "Robotics and AI in Oil & Gas" at OGV Energy. Using AI enables engineers to reduce overall risk, which means that oil will also have a potentially smaller environmental impact because of fewer spills.

TIP

The reduced price for oil is part of what has driven the oil industry to adopt AI (see "AI in Oil and Gas Market - Growth, Trends, COVID-19 Impact, and Forecasts (2021 - 2026)" at Intrado Global News Wire.com). Because the oil industry is so risk averse, its use of AI makes a good test case for seeing how other businesses will adopt AI. By reviewing articles on the oil industry, you realize that the oil industry waited for successes in the healthcare, finance, and manufacturing industries before making investments of its own. You can expect to see an uptick in AI adoption as successes in other industries grow.

REMEMBER

This book covers all sorts of robotic solutions — some mobile, some not. Part 4 of the book covers robots in general, flying robots (which is what drones truly are when you think about it), and self-driving, or SD, cars. Generally, robots can make a profit when they perform a specific kind of task, such as sweeping your floor (the Roomba) or putting your car together. Likewise, drones are money makers now for defense contractors and will eventually become profitable for a significant number of civilian uses as well.

Creating New Technology Environments

Everyone generally looks for new things to buy, which means that businesses need to come up with new things to sell. AI helps people look for patterns in all sorts of things. Patterns often show the presence of something new, such as a new element or a new process for creating something. In the realm of product development, AI's purpose is to help discover the new product (as opposed to focusing on selling an existing product). By reducing the time required to find a new product to sell, AI helps business improve profits and reduces the cost of research associated with finding new products. The following sections discuss these issues in more detail.

Developing rare new resources

As you can see throughout the book, an AI is especially adept at seeing patterns, and patterns can indicate all sorts of things, including new mineral elements (the "Finding new elements" section of Chapter 16 talks about this aspect of AI). New elements mean new products, which translate into product sales. An organization that can come up with a new material has a significant advantage over the competition. The article "An Economic Perspective on Revolutionary US Inventions" at the blog Virulent Word of Mouse tells you about the economic impact of some of the more interesting inventions out there. Many of these inventions rely on a new process or material that AI can help find with significant ease.

Seeing what can't be seen

Human vision doesn't see the broad spectrum of light that actually exists in nature. And even with augmentation, humans struggle to think at a very small scale or a very large scale. Biases keep humans from seeing the unexpected. Sometimes a random pattern actually has structure, but humans can't see it. An AI can see what humans can't see and then act upon it. For example, when looking for stresses in metal (see "Automatic Inspection of Metallic Surface Defects Using Genetic Algorithms" at ResearchGate.net), an AI can see the potential for fatigue and act upon it. The cost savings can be monumental when dealing with precision metal surfaces, which are scanned using a waveguide sensor (explained in "Intelligent Detection of Cracks in Metallic Surfaces Using a Waveguide Sensor Loaded with Metamaterial Elements at NCBI.gov.)

Working with AI in Space

Chapter 16 takes you on a tour of what AI can potentially do in space. Even though plans for performing these tasks are on the drawing board, most of them are government sponsored, which means that they provide an opportunity that may not necessarily result in a profit. You also find some business-related research projects in Chapter 16. In this case, the business is actually looking to make a profit but may not be making one today. The following sections look at space in another way and point to what's happening today. AI is currently enabling businesses to earn money working in space, which gives businesses an incentive to keep investing in both AI and in space-related projects.

Delivering goods to space stations

Perhaps the greatest AI commercial success story in space so far is the resupply of the ISS by companies such as SpaceX and Orbital ATK (see "Commercial Resupply Services Overview" at NASA.gov).

The organizations make money with each trip, of course, but NASA benefits as well. In fact, the United States as a whole has enjoyed these benefits from the venture:

>> Reduced cost for delivering materials, instead of using vehicles from other countries to resupply the ISS

>> Increased use of U.S.-based facilities such as the Kennedy Space Center, which means that the cost of these facilities is amortized over a long time frame

>> Added launch centers for future space flights

>> More available payload capacity for satellites and other items

SpaceX and Orbital ATK interact with lots of other businesses. Consequently, even though only two companies might appear to benefit from this arrangement, many others benefit as subsidiary partners. The use of AI makes all this possible, and it's happening right this second. Companies are earning money from space today, not waiting until tomorrow, as you might think from news reports. That the earnings come from what is essentially a mundane delivery service doesn't make any difference.

REMEMBER

Space deliveries are essentially new. Many Internet-based businesses ran at a deficit for years before becoming profitable. However, SpaceX, at least, appears to be in a position to possibly earn money after some early losses (see "Revisiting SpaceX's $36-Billion Valuation After Its First Manned Mission" at Forbes.com). Space-based businesses will take time to ramp up to the same financial impact that earth-based businesses of the same sort enjoy today.

Mining extraplanetary resources

Space mining is currently undergoing the equivalent of an AI winter (see "How the asteroid-mining bubble burst" at MIT Technology Review.com — may be available only to subscribers). However, the problem that space mining is supposed to fix still remains: The Earth still has limited resources that are growing more limited by the day (see "Is space mining the eco-friendly choice?" at Astronomy.com). Consequently, people are still looking for ways to make space mining work because the potential for making a profit are so huge. One current idea is to mine the moon (see "Arcs of 'lightning' on the moon could be the future of lunar mining" at Space.com) using a number of intriguing techniques, such as ablative arc mining (explained in "Ablative Arc Mining for In-Situ Resource Utilization" at NASA.gov). The point is that AI will most definitely be part of any space-mining endeavor (see "Artificial Intelligence and Space Mining: the Gateway to Infinite Riches" at aidaily.co.uk).

Exploring other planets

It seems likely that humans will eventually explore and even colonize other planets, with Mars being the likely first candidate. Elon Musk recently made the headlines by offering to use his wealth in the colonization effort (https://www. businessinsider.com/worlds-richest-person-elon-musk-dedicate-wealth-mars-colony-2021-1). After people get to other worlds, including the moon, many people think that the only way to make money will be through the sale of intellectual property or possibly the creation of materials that only that particular world will support (see "Is There A Fortune To Be Made On Mars?" at Forbes.com).

WARNING

Unfortunately, although some people are making money on space exploration today, we likely won't see any actual profit from space exploration for a while. Still, some companies are making a profit today by providing the various tools needed to design the trip. Research does fund the economy. However, the world is also in a buyer-beware environment filled with scam artists. For example, 78,000 people signed up for a trip to Mars (see "78,000 People Apply for One-Way Trip to Mars" at Time.com), but the company eventually went bankrupt ("The company that promised a one-way ticket to Mars is bankrupt" at The Verge.com).

Chapter **20**

Ten Ways in Which AI Has Failed

ny comprehensive book on AI must consider the ways in which AI has failed to meet expectations. The book discusses this issue in part in other chapters, giving the historical view of the AI winters. However, even with those discussions, you might not grasp that AI hasn't just failed to meet expectations set by overly enthusiastic proponents; it has failed to meet specific needs and basic requirements. This chapter is about the failures that will keep AI from excelling and performing the tasks we need it to do to fully achieve the successes described in other chapters. AI is currently an evolving technology that is partially successful at best.

REMEMBER

One of the essential issues surrounding AI today is that people keep anthropomorphizing it and making it into something it isn't. An AI accepts cleaned data as input, analyzes it, finds the patterns, and provides a requested output. As described in the sections of this chapter, an AI doesn't understand anything, it can't create or discover anything new, and it has no intrapersonal knowledge, so it can't empathize with anyone about anything. The critical piece of information to take from this chapter is that an AI behaves as designed by a human programmer, and what you often take for intelligence is only a mix of clever programming and vast amounts of data analyzed in a specific manner. For another view of these and other issues, check out "Asking the Right Questions About AI" by Yonatan Zunger at Medium.com and "Asking the Right Questions: How Machine Learning Improves Your Insights" at Explorium.ai.

Even more important, however, is that people who claim that an AI will eventually take over the world fail to understand that doing so is impossible given current technology. An AI can't suddenly become self-aware, because it lacks any means of expressing the emotion required to become self-aware. As shown in Table 1-1 in Chapter 1, an AI today lacks some of the essential seven kinds of intelligence required to become self-aware. Simply possessing those levels of intelligence wouldn't be enough, either. Humans have a spark in them — something that scientists don't understand. Without understanding what that spark is, science can't re-create it as part of an AI.

Understanding

The ability to comprehend is innate to humans, but AIs completely lack it. Looking at an apple, a human responds to more than just a series of properties associated with a picture of an object. Humans understand apples through the use of senses, such as color, taste, and feel. We understand that the apple is edible and provides specific nutrients. We have feelings about apples; perhaps we like them and feel that they're the supreme fruit. It's also important to realize that we associate memories with objects, such as the delicious apple pies that Grandma used to bake. The AI sees an object that has properties associated with it — values that the AI doesn't understand, but only manipulates. The following sections describe how the failure to understand causes AI as a whole to fail to meet expectations.

JUST HOW MANY SENSES ARE THERE?

Many people have been taught in school that there are five senses, but scientists have now said that we have a minimum of nine and most agree that we have 21. These additions, such as color, are usually subsets of existing senses, such as sight. That's right, color is currently considered to be an addition to the sight sense, along with very strange sense names like proprioception, which is the ability to feel the space around us. The article "You Have a Lot More than Five Senses" at Medium.com (among many others), details just a few of these other than five senses, and you can find a more complete list in "Come to Your Senses" at Meditation 24-7.com. This extensive listing of senses has become so important because scientists are also starting to realize that it's nearly impossible to create good deep learning models or useful robots that deal with environmental issues without a good understanding of how we sense things. The five senses that we started with just aren't sufficient to describe how we do things like eat in darkened restaurants and climb stairs without looking at them.

Interpreting, not analyzing

As stated many times throughout the book, an AI uses algorithms to manipulate incoming data and produce an output. The emphasis is on performing an analysis of the data. However, a human controls the direction of that analysis and must then interpret the results. For example, an AI can perform an analysis of an x-ray showing a potential cancer tumor. The resulting output may emphasize a portion of the x-ray containing a tumor so that the doctor can see it. The doctor might not be able to see the tumor otherwise, so the AI undoubtedly provides an important service. Even so, a doctor must still review the result and determine whether the x-ray does indeed show cancer. As described in several sections of the book, especially with self-driving cars in Chapter 14, an AI is easily fooled at times when even a small artifact appears in the wrong place. Consequently, even though the AI is incredibly helpful in giving the doctor the ability to see something that isn't apparent to the human eye, the AI also isn't trustworthy enough to make any sort of an important decision.

Interpretation also implies the ability to see beyond the data. It's not the ability to create new data, but to understand that the data may indicate something other than what is apparent. For example, humans can often tell that data is fake or falsified, even though the data itself presents no evidence to indicate these problems. An AI accepts the data as both real and true, while a human knows that it's neither real nor true. Formalizing precisely how humans achieve this goal is currently impossible because humans don't actually understand it.

Going beyond pure numbers

Despite any appearance otherwise, an AI works only with numbers. An AI can't understand words, for example, which means that when you talk to it, the AI is simply performing pattern matching after converting your speech to numeric form. The substance of what you say is gone. Even if the AI were able to understand words, it couldn't do so because the words are gone after the tokenization process (see Chapter 4 for more about tokenizing). The failure of AIs to understand something as basic as words means that an AI's translation from one language to another will always lack that certain something needed to translate the feeling behind the words, as well as the words themselves. Words express feelings, and an AI can't do that. The same conversion process occurs with every sense that humans possess. A computer translates sight, sound, smell, taste, and touch into numeric representations and then performs pattern matching to create a data set that simulates the real-world experience. Further complicating matters, humans often experience things differently from each other. For example, each person experiences color uniquely (see "Why We Don't See the Same Colors" at Psychology Today.com). For an AI, every computer sees color in precisely the same way, which means that an AI can't experience colors uniquely. In addition, because of the conversion, an AI doesn't actually experience color at all.

Considering consequences

An AI can analyze data, but it can't make moral or ethical judgements. If you ask an AI to make a choice, it will always choose the option with the highest probability of success unless you provide some sort of randomizing function as well. The AI will make this choice regardless of the outcome. The "SD cars and the trolley problem" sidebar in Chapter 14 expresses this problem quite clearly. When faced with a choice between allowing either the occupants of a car or pedestrians to die when such a choice is necessary, the AI must have human instructions available to it to make the decision. The AI isn't capable of considering consequences and is therefore ineligible to be part of the decision-making process.

WARNING

In many situations, misjudging the ability of an AI to perform a task is merely inconvenient. In some cases, you may have to perform the task a second or third time manually because the AI isn't up to the task. However, when it comes to consequences, you might face legal problems in addition to the moral and ethical problems if you trust an AI to perform a task that is unsuited to it. For example, allowing a self-driving (SD) car to drive by itself in a place that doesn't provide the infrastructure required for safe SD car use is likely illegal, and you'll face legal problems in addition to damage and medical charges that the SD car can cause. In short, know what the legal requirements are before you trust an AI to do anything involving potential consequences.

Discovering

An AI can interpolate existing knowledge, but it can't extrapolate existing knowledge to create new knowledge. When an AI encounters a new situation, it usually tries to resolve it as an existing piece of knowledge, rather than accept that it's something new. In fact, an AI has no method for creating anything new, or seeing a situation as something unique. These are human expressions that help us discover new things, work with them, devise methods for interacting with them, and create new methods for using them to perform new tasks or augment existing tasks. The following sections describe how an AI's inability to make discoveries keeps it from fulfilling the expectations that humans have of it.

Devising new data from old

One of the more common tasks that people perform is *extrapolation* of data; for example, given A, what is B? Humans use existing knowledge to create new knowledge of a different sort. By knowing one piece of knowledge, a human can make a leap to a new piece of knowledge, outside the domain of the original knowledge, with a high probability of success. Humans make these leaps so often that they become second nature and intuitive in the extreme. Even children can make such predictions with a high rate of success.

REMEMBER

The best that an AI will ever do is to *interpolate* data; for example, given A and B, is C somewhere in between? The capability to successfully interpolate data means that an AI can extend a pattern, but it can't create new data. However, sometimes developers can mislead people into thinking that the data is new by using clever programming techniques. The presence of C looks new when it truly isn't. The lack of new data can produce conditions that make the AI seem to solve a problem, but it doesn't. The problem requires a new solution, not the interpolation of existing solutions.

Seeing beyond the patterns

Currently, an AI can see patterns in data when they aren't apparent to humans. The capability to see these patterns is what makes AI so valuable. Data manipulation and analysis is time consuming, complex, and repetitive, but an AI can perform the task with aplomb. However, the data patterns are simply an output and not necessarily a solution. Humans rely on five senses, empathy, creativity, and intuition to see beyond the patterns to a potential solution that resides outside what the data would lead one to believe. Chapter 18 discusses this aspect of the human condition in more detail.

TIP

A basic way to understand the human ability to see beyond patterns is to look at the sky. On a cloudy day, people can see patterns in the clouds, but an AI sees clouds and only clouds. In addition, two people may see different things in the same set of clouds. The creative view of patterns in the cloud may have one person seeing a sheep and another a fountain. The same holds true for stars and other kinds of patterns. The AI presents the pattern as output, but it doesn't understand the pattern; moreover, it lacks the creativity to do anything with the pattern, other than report that the pattern exists.

Implementing new senses

As humans have become more knowledgeable, they have also become aware of variances in human senses that don't actually translate well to an AI because replicating these senses in hardware isn't truly possible now. For example, the ability to use multiple senses to manage a single input (synesthesia; see "What Is Synesthesia? What It's Like to Hear Colors and See Sounds" at The Healthy.com for details) is beyond an AI.

Describing synesthesia effectively is well beyond most humans. Before they can create an AI that can mimic some of the truly amazing effects of synesthesia, humans must first fully describe it and then create sensors that will convert the experience into numbers that an AI can analyze. However, even then, the AI will see only the effects of the synesthesia, not the emotional impact. Consequently, an AI will never fully experience or understand synesthesia. (The "Shifting data spectrum" section of Chapter 8 discusses how an AI could augment human perception with a synesthetic-like experience.) Oddly enough, some studies show that adults can be trained to have synesthetic experiences, making the need for an AI uncertain (discussed in "Study: Synesthesia Can Be Learned" at Art of Memory.com).

TECHNICAL STUFF

Although most people know that humans have five senses, as noted in the sidebar "Just how many senses are there?" earlier in this chapter, many sources now contend that humans actually have far more than the standard five senses (see "Humans have a lot more than five senses — here are 18" at Considerable.com). Some of these additional senses aren't at all well understood and are just barely provable, such as *magnetoception* (the ability to detect magnetic fields, such as earth's magnetic field). This sense gives people the ability to tell direction, similar to the same sense in birds, but to a lesser degree. Because we have no method of even quantifying this sense, replicating it as part of an AI is impossible.

Empathizing

Computers don't feel anything. That's not necessarily a negative, but this chapter views it as a negative. Without the ability to feel, a computer can't see things from the perspective of a human. It doesn't understand being happy or sad, so it can't react to these emotions unless a program creates a method for it to analyze facial expressions and other indicators, and then act appropriately. Even so, such a reaction is a canned response and prone to error. Think about how many decisions you make based on emotional need rather than outright fact. The following sections discuss how the lack of empathy on the part of an AI keeps it from interacting with humans appropriately in many cases.

Walking in someone's shoes

The idea of *walking in some else's shoes* means to view things from another person's perspective and feel similar to how the other person feels. No one truly feels precisely the same as someone else, but through empathy, people can get close. This form of empathy requires strong intrapersonal intelligence as a starting point, which an AI will never have unless it develops a sense of self (the *singularity*, as described in "Why the singularity will happen – but not by 2045" at Lars Holdgaard.com). In addition, the AI would need to be able to feel, something that is currently not possible, and the AI would need to be open to sharing feelings with some other entity (generally a human, today), which is also impossible. The current state of AI technology prohibits an AI from feeling or understanding any sort of emotion, which makes empathy impossible.

REMEMBER

Of course, the question is why empathy is so important. Without the ability to feel the same as someone else, an AI can't develop the motivation to perform certain tasks. You could order the AI to perform the task, but there the AI would have no motivation on its own. Consequently, the AI would never perform certain tasks, even though the performance of such tasks is a requirement to build skills and knowledge required to achieve human-like intelligence.

Developing true relationships

An AI builds a picture of you through the data it collects. It then creates patterns from this data and, using specific algorithms, develops output that makes it seem to know you — at least as an acquaintance. However, because the AI doesn't feel, it can't appreciate you as a person. It can serve you, should you order it to do so and assuming that the task is within its list of functions, but it can't have any feeling for you.

When dealing with a relationship, people have to consider both intellectual attachment and feelings. The intellectual attachment often comes from a shared benefit between two entities. Unfortunately, no shared benefit exists between an AI and a human (or an AI and any other entity, for that matter). The AI simply processes data using a particular algorithm. Something can't claim to love something else if an order forces it to make the proclamation. Emotional attachment must carry with it the risk of rejection, which implies self-awareness.

Changing perspective

Humans can sometimes change an opinion based on something other than the facts. Even though the odds would say that a particular course of action is prudent, an emotional need makes another course of action preferable. An AI has no preferences. It therefore can't choose another course of action for any reason other than a change in the probabilities, a *constraint* (a rule forcing it to make the change), or a requirement to provide random output.

Making leaps of faith

Faith is the belief in something as being true without having proven fact to back up such belief. In many cases, faith takes the form of *trust*, which is the belief in the sincerity of another person without any proof that the other person is trustworthy. An AI can't exhibit either faith or trust, which is part of the reason that it can't extrapolate knowledge. The act of extrapolation often relies on a hunch, based on faith, that something is true, despite a lack of any sort of data to support the hunch. Because an AI lacks this ability, it can't exhibit insight — a necessary requirement for human-like thought patterns.

TIP

Examples abound of inventors who made leaps of faith to create something new. However, one of the most prominent was Edison. For example, he made 1,000 (and possibly more) attempts to create the light bulb. An AI would have given up after a certain number of tries, likely due to a constraint. You can see a list of people who made leaps of faith to perform amazing acts in "But They Did Not Give Up" at uky.edu. Each of these acts is an example of something that an AI can't do because it lacks the ability to think past the specific data you provide as input.

Index

Brain-Computer Interface (BCI), 288
branch node, 53
breadth-first search (BFS), 52, 55. *See also* state-space
search
Brockman, Greg, 201
Brooks, Rodney, 251
Bukimi no Tani Genshō, 214–217
Burgess, E., 281
bus system, 68–70, 73–74
Butterfly Network, 124

C

Čapek, Karel, 210–211
CAPTCHA (Completely Automatic Public Turing Test
to Tell Computers and Humans Apart), 14
CAT (computerized axial tomography), 15
Catanzaro, Bryan, 76
central processing unit (CPU)
  ASIC versus, 78–79
  GPU versus, 74–76
  new computational techniques and, 71
  TPU versus, 78
CGI (Computer-Generated Imagery) technology, 216
chatbots
  Mitsuku, 14, 95–96
  ML and, 152
  NLP model and, 195
  RNNs and, 194–196
  Turing Test and, 194–196
cheat sheet, 4
Chen, Tianshi, 77
chess, 65
Chinese Room argument, 88–89
chi-square tests, 143
cities, 290–293
Clarke, Arthur C., 284
classification problems, 153
classification trees, 159
climate, 296–300
CNNs. *See* Convolutional Neural Networks
cognition, 88
cognitive radio, 280
color-translation software, 115–116

commercial drones, 228–229
common-sense reasoning, 268
communication
  body language, 128, 131–132
  discussion, 127–128, 280
  emojis, 129–130
  idea exchange, 127, 133–135
  language translation, 130–131
  new alphabets, 129
Completely Automatic Public Turing Test to Tell
Computers and Humans Apart (CAPTCHA), 14
complex analysis, 20
complex system monitoring, 170
Compute Unified Device Architecture (CUDA) Core, 75
computer applications
  AI-based errors, 86, 95–96
  common, 86–89
  corrections, 91–93
  discussion, 85–86
  friendliness, 89–91
  suggestions, 85–86, 93–95
computer vision, 71, 87
Computer-Generated Imagery (CGI) technology, 216
computerized axial tomography (CAT), 15
computers
  AI and, 23–24
  architecture of, 68–70
  data and, 27
  history of, 17
  intelligence and, 10–11
"Computing Machinery and Intelligence" (Turing), 72
concept mining, 88
conditional probability, 163–164
conflict resolution, 63
connectionists, 21, 157, 160, 176. *See also* neural
networks
Convolutional Neural Networks (CNNs)
  discussion, 183, 185
  handwriting recognition and
    character recognition, 189–190
    functional process, 191
    image challenges, 191–193
    overview, 188
  memory deficiencies, 193

G

Galilei, Galileo, 274
game therapy tools, 111–113
Gardner, Howard, 11
Gated Recurrent Unit (GRU), 196–197
Gates, Bill, 211
generalization, 151–152
Generative Adversarial Networks (GANs)
  discussion, 75
  neural networks, 193, 198–201
  unsupervised learning, 175
generative-based models, 195
genetic programming, 21
genomics, 29, 124, 151
geo-fencing, 236
Giant Magellan Telescope, 275
Gini impurity measurement, 171
gizmos, 269–270
Global Vectors (GloVe) embedding, 197
global warming, 296–300
glucose monitors, 108–109
GNMT (Google Neural Machine Translation) system, 130–131
Go, 64–65, 204
Goddard, Robert H., 281
Goodfellow, Ian, 199, 202
Google
  algorithms, 31–32, 145
  BERT neural network, 198
  data analysis, 142
  ML investments, 19
  neural network playground, 180–181
  TensorFlow software, 160, 187
  TPU, 77–78
Google Assistant, 50, 193
Google Brain Project, 76, 183, 191
Google DeepMind, 56, 65, 154
Google Health product, 123
Google Neural Machine Translation (GNMT) system, 130–131
Google Smart Reply chatbot, 196
Google Translate, 130
GPT-3 neural network, 86, 198
Graham, Bette Nesmith, 306

grammar checkers, 18–19, 91–92
graph nodes, 53–54
Graphcore, 80
graphic processing units (GPUs)
  backpropagation, 183
  deep learning, 185–186
  discussion, 73
  purpose, 74–75
  success, 75–76
  von Neumann bottleneck, 73–74
graphs, 128–130, 134
greedy search, 55
Gremlin project, 225
GRU (Gated Recurrent Unit), 196–197

H

habitats, 290–293
hackers, 87
Hadoop software, 144
Hadsell, Raia, 154
Haffner, Patrick, 189
Halevy, Alon, 205
handwriting recognition
  CNNs and
    character recognition, 189–190
    functional process, 191
    image challenges, 191–193
    overview, 188
  discussion, 87
hardware
  augmenting, 116
  discussion, 2–3, 67–68
  increasing capabilities of, 79–80
  specialized
    DLPs, 76–78
    environmental interaction, 81–82
    GPUs, 73–76
    sensors, 80–81
    specialized processing environment, 78–79
  standard
    deficiencies, 69–70
    new computational techniques, 71–72
    overview, 68–69

medical systems (continued)
  for extending lifespan, 111–114
  for extending physical abilities, 114–117
  patient monitoring, 108–111
  robotics and, 125–126
  security issues, 110
  for surgical techniques, 120–122
  telepresence, 117–119
medically biased data, 45
medication administration, 124–125
MEG (magnetoencephalography), 15
memory speed, 74
meteorology, 29
microcontrollers, 70
Microsoft
  data analysis, 142
  FPGAs, 80
  Tay chatbot, 95–96, 152, 196
military drones, 224–228
military robots, 219
"Minds, Brains, and Programs" (Searle), 88–89
miniaturization, 27–28
Minimum Intelligent Signal Test, 14
min-max approximation, 56–57
Minsky, Marvin, 251, 267
mistruths
  AI limitations with, 262–263
  of bias, 42
  of commission, 40
  computers and, 11
  discussion, 39–40
  frame-of-reference, 43
  of omission, 41
  of perspective, 41–42
Mitsuku chatbot, 14, 196
ML. See machine learning
mobile manipulator robots, 213–214, 217
mobile Neural Processing Unit (NPU), 77–78
mobile robots, 213–214
Model Predictive Control (MPC), 250
monitoring devices, 108–111, 170
Moore, Gordon, 27
Moore's law, 27–28

Moov monitor, 109
moral issues, 211–213
Moravec, Hans, 251
Moravec paradox, 251
Mori, Masahiro, 215–216
movable monitors, 110–111
MPC (Model Predictive Control), 250
MRI (magnetic resonance imaging), 15
Mueller, John Paul, 144, 147, 182
Multiconjugate Adaptive Optics (MCAO), 275
multimedia, 12, 128, 134–135
multirotor drones, 227
multithreading, 74
multivariate correspondence analysis, 197
Musk, Elon, 201, 211, 234
mutations, 124
MuZero program, 205
MYCIN, 61–63

N

Naïve Bayes algorithm
  conditional probability and, 163–164
  discussion, 159
  false positive paradox, 165–166
  perceptrons and, 178
  Quinlan dataset, 166–170
National Aeronautics and Space Administration (NASA), 218, 236, 281–283
National Institutes of Health (NIH), 119
native sensory enhancements, 127, 135–136
Natural Language Processing (NLP) model, 14, 87, 130, 195
Naval Research Laboratory (NRL), 177
Neumann, John von, 68, 72
Neural Engine, 78
Neural Magic approach, 71
neural networks
  approaches influenced by, 186–188
  architecture, 179–182
  artificial neurons, 157, 160, 176–179
  as augmentation, 177
  backpropagation, 182
  CNNs

About the Authors

John Mueller is a freelance author and technical editor. He has writing in his blood, having produced 119 books and more than 600 articles to date. The topics range from networking to artificial intelligence and from database management to heads-down programming. Some of his current books include discussions of data science, machine learning, and algorithms. His technical editing skills have helped more than 70 authors refine the content of their manuscripts. John has provided technical editing services to various magazines, performed various kinds of consulting, and writes certification exams. Be sure to read John's blog at http://blog.johnmuellerbooks.com/. You can reach John on the Internet at John@JohnMuellerBooks.com. John also has a website at http://www.johnmueller books.com/.

Luca Massaron is a data scientist and marketing research director who specializes in multivariate statistical analysis, machine learning, and customer insight, with more than a decade of experience in solving real-world problems and generating value for stakeholders by applying reasoning, statistics, data mining, and algorithms. From being a pioneer of web audience analysis in Italy to achieving the rank of top ten Kaggler on kaggle.com, he has always been passionate about everything regarding data and analysis and about demonstrating the potentiality of data-driven knowledge discovery to both experts and nonexperts. Favoring simplicity over unnecessary sophistication, he believes that a lot can be achieved in data science by understanding and practicing the essentials of it. Luca is also a Google Developer Expert (GDE) in machine learning.

John's Dedication

This book is dedicated to all of the people who have supported me through the various transitions in my life.

Luca's Dedication

This book is dedicated to the Suda family living in Tokyo: Yoshiki, Takayo, Makiko, and Mikiko.

John's Acknowledgments

Thanks to my wife, Rebecca. Even though she is gone now, her spirit is in every book I write and in every word that appears on the page. She believed in me when no one else would.

Rod Stephens deserves thanks for his technical edit of this book. He greatly added to the accuracy and depth of the material you see here. Rod's critical thinking skills force me to truly think through all of the book elements. He's also the sanity check for my work.

Matt Wagner, my agent, deserves credit for helping me get the contract in the first place and taking care of all the details that most authors don't really consider. I always appreciate his assistance. It's good to know that someone wants to help.

A number of people read all or part of this book to help me refine the approach, test the coding examples, and generally provide input that all readers wish they could have. These unpaid volunteers helped in ways too numerous to mention here. I especially appreciate the efforts of Eva Beattie, Suhas Shivalkar, and Osvaldo Téllez Almirall, who provided general input, read the entire book, and selflessly devoted themselves to this project.

Finally, I would like to thank Kelsey Baird, Susan Christophersen, Michelle Hacker, and the rest of the editorial and production staff.

Luca's Acknowledgments

My first greatest thanks to my family, Yukiko and Amelia, for their support, sacrifices, and loving patience during the long days/nights, weeks, and months I've been involved in working on this book.

I thank all the editorial and production staff at Wiley, in particular Kelsey Baird and Susan Christophersen, for their great professionalism and support in all the phases of writing this book of the *For Dummies* series.

Publisher's Acknowledgments

Senior Acquisitions Editor: Kelsey Baird

Project and Copy Editor: Susan Christophersen

Technical Editor: Rod Stephens

Editorial Assistant: Matthew Lowe

Sr. Editorial Assistant: Cherie Case

Production Editor: Mohammed Zafar Ali

Cover Image: © metamorworks/iStock/ Getty Images

Leverage the power

Dummies is the global leader in the reference category and one of the most trusted and highly regarded brands in the world. No longer just focused on books, customers now have access to the dummies content they need in the format they want. Together we'll craft a solution that engages your customers, stands out from the competition, and helps you meet your goals.

Advertising & Sponsorships

Connect with an engaged audience on a powerful multimedia site, and position your message alongside expert how-to content. Dummies.com is a one-stop shop for free, online information and know-how curated by a team of experts.

- Targeted ads
- Video
- Email Marketing
- Microsites
- Sweepstakes sponsorship

20 MILLION
PAGE VIEWS
EVERY SINGLE MONTH

15 MILLION UNIQUE
VISITORS PER MONTH

43%
OF ALL VISITORS
ACCESS THE SITE
VIA THEIR MOBILE DEVICES

700,000 NEWSLETTER
SUBSCRIPTIONS
TO THE INBOXES OF
300,000 UNIQUE INDIVIDUALS EVERY WEEK

# of dummies

Custom Publishing

Reach a global audience in any language by creating a solution that will differentiate you from competitors, amplify your message, and encourage customers to make a buying decision.

- Apps
- Books
- eBooks
- Video
- Audio
- Webinars

Brand Licensing & Content

Leverage the strength of the world's most popular reference brand to reach new audiences and channels of distribution.

For more information, visit **dummies.com/biz**

PERSONAL ENRICHMENT

Staying Sharp	**Facebook**	**Guitar**	**Investing**	**Beekeeping**	**Digital Photography**
9781119187790	9781119179030	9781119293354	9781119293347	9781119310068	9781119235606
USA $26.00	USA $21.99	USA $24.99	USA $22.99	USA $22.99	USA $24.99
CAN $31.99	CAN $25.99	CAN $29.99	CAN $27.99	CAN $27.99	CAN $29.99
UK £19.99	UK £16.99	UK £17.99	UK £16.99	UK £16.99	UK £17.99

Meditation	**Pregnancy**	**Samsung Galaxy S7**	**iPhone**	**Crocheting**	**Nutrition**
9781119251163	9781119235491	9781119279952	9781119283133	9781119287117	9781119130246
USA $24.99	USA $26.99	USA $24.99	USA $24.99	USA $24.99	USA $22.99
CAN $29.99	CAN $31.99	CAN $29.99	CAN $29.99	CAN $29.99	CAN $27.99
UK £17.99	UK £19.99	UK £17.99	UK £17.99	UK £16.99	UK £16.99

PROFESSIONAL DEVELOPMENT

Windows 10	**AutoCAD**	**Excel 2016**	**QuickBooks 2017**	**macOS Sierra**	**LinkedIn**	**Windows 10**
9781119311041	9781119255796	9781119293439	9781119281467	9781119280651	9781119251132	9781119310563
USA $24.99	USA $39.99	USA $26.99	USA $26.99	USA $29.99	USA $24.99	USA $34.00
CAN $29.99	CAN $47.99	CAN $31.99	CAN $31.99	CAN $35.99	CAN $29.99	CAN $41.99
UK £17.99	UK £27.99	UK £19.99	UK £19.99	UK £21.99	UK £17.99	UK £24.99

SharePoint 2016	**Fundamental Analysis**	**Networking**	**Office 2016**	**Office 365**	**Salesforce.com**	**Coding**
9781119181705	9781119263593	9781119257769	9781119293477	9781119265313	9781119239314	9781119293323
USA $29.99	USA $26.99	USA $29.99	USA $26.99	USA $24.99	USA $29.99	USA $29.99
CAN $35.99	CAN $31.99	CAN $35.99	CAN $31.99	CAN $29.99	CAN $35.99	CAN $35.99
UK £21.99	UK £19.99	UK £21.99	UK £19.99	UK £17.99	UK £21.99	UK £21.99

dummies.com

dummies
A Wiley Brand

Learning Made Easy

ACADEMIC

9781119293576
USA $19.99
CAN $23.99
UK £15.99

9781119293637
USA $19.99
CAN $23.99
UK £15.99

9781119293491
USA $19.99
CAN $23.99
UK £15.99

9781119293460
USA $19.99
CAN $23.99
UK £15.99

9781119293590
USA $19.99
CAN $23.99
UK £15.99

9781119215844
USA $26.99
CAN $31.99
UK £19.99

9781119293378
USA $22.99
CAN $27.99
UK £16.99

9781119293521
USA $19.99
CAN $23.99
UK £15.99

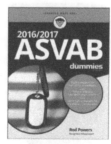

9781119239178
USA $18.99
CAN $22.99
UK £14.99

9781119263883
USA $26.99
CAN $31.99
UK £19.99

Available Everywhere Books Are Sold

dummies.com

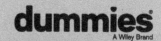

Small books for big imaginations

GETTING STARTED WITH Coding
Get Creative with Code!
Camille McCue, PhD

9781119177173
USA $9.99
CAN $9.99
UK £8.99

MODDING Minecraft™
Build Your Own Minecraft Mods!
Sarah Guthals, PhD
Stephen Foster, PhD
Lindsey Handley, PhD

9781119177272
USA $9.99
CAN $9.99
UK £8.99

MAKING YouTube® VIDEOS
Star in Your Own Video!
Nick Willoughby

9781119177241
USA $9.99
CAN $9.99
UK £8.99

DESIGNING Digital Games
Create Games with Scratch™!
Derek Breen

9781119177210
USA $9.99
CAN $9.99
UK £8.99

GETTING STARTED WITH Raspberry Pi™
Program Your Raspberry Pi!
Richard Wentk

9781119262657
USA $9.99
CAN $9.99
UK £6.99

EXPERIMENTING WITH Science
Think, Test, and Learn!

9781119291336
USA $9.99
CAN $9.99
UK £6.99

CREATING Digital Animations
Animate Stories with Scratch™!
Derek Breen

9781119233527
USA $9.99
CAN $9.99
UK £6.99

GETTING STARTED WITH Engineering
Think Like an Engineer!
Camille McCue, PhD

9781119291220
USA $9.99
CAN $9.99
UK £6.99

WRITING Computer Code
Learn the Language of Computers!
Chris Minnick and Eva Holland

9781119177302
USA $9.99
CAN $9.99
UK £8.99

Unleash Their Creativity

dummies.com

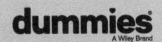